SAINT TIKHON OF ZADONSK

SAINT TIKHON OF ZADONSK

Inspirer of Dostoevsky

By
NADEJDA GORODETZKY
Lecturer in Russian in Oxford University

ST. VLADIMIR'S SEMINARY PRESS
Crestwood, NY 10707
1976

© 1951, 1976 N. GORODETZKY

First published in Great Britain in 1951 by S.P.C.K., London, under the title *Saint Tikhon Zadonsky: Inspirer of Dostoevsky*. This revised edition first published in the United States in 1976 by St. Vladimir's Seminary Press, Crestwood, NY 10707.

By the same author

THE HUMILIATED CHRIST IN MODERN RUSSIAN THOUGHT

TO MARJORY SCOTT

Library of Congress Cataloging in Publication Data

Gorodetzky, Nadejda, 1904-
    Saint Tikhon of Zadonsk, inspirer of Dostoevsky.

    Bibliography: p.
    Includes index.
    1. Tikhon Zadonskii, Saint, Bp. of Voronezh, 1724-1783. 2. Christian saints—Russia—Biography. I. Title.
BX597.T53G67   1976   281.9'092'4 [B]   76-49919
ISBN 0-913836-32-X

ISBN 0-913836-32-X

PRINTED IN THE UNITED STATES OF AMERICA
BY
ATHENS PRINTING COMPANY

Table of Contents

	INTRODUCTION	7
CHAP.		
1.	HISTORICAL BACKGROUND	15
2.	TRAINING	25
3.	ACTIVE LIFE	39
4.	RETIREMENT	63
5.	THE INWARD MAN	91
6.	WORKS	
	Sources	117
	Social Teaching	124
	Pastoralia	140
	Doctrinal Background	163
	Ascetic and Mystical Teaching	177
7.	GROWTH OF VENERATION	203
8.	ST. TIKHON IN RUSSIAN LITERATURE	215
9.	HISTORICAL SIGNIFICANCE OF ST. TIKHON	231
	APPENDIX	239
	BIOGRAPHICAL NOTES	245
	BIBLIOGRAPHY	275
	NOTES	297
	INDEX	315

Introduction

"TO YOU ALONE I make this confession. . . . I am going to portray the real Tikhon of Zadonsk, whom I long ago received into my heart with deep delight." Thus wrote Dostoevsky to his friend, the poet A. Maikov. And the first drafts of both *The Life of a Great Sinner* and *The Brothers Karamazov* contain the name "Tikhon," subsequently replaced by "the Hermit" and "Elder Zossima."

The purpose of the present work is not to study the resemblance between St. Tikhon and Dostoevsky's half-imaginary or composite characters, but to show the historical person who inspired the novelist.

The first five chapters cover the life of Bishop Tikhon. In order to help the non-Russian reader, I give a number of historical references both about Russia of the eighteenth century and about the position of the Church. Information of this kind becomes more scarce towards the end of Bishop Tikhon's life, because he spent his last fifteen years in retirement and was less affected by historical events.

Chapter 6 deals with his *Works*. Tikhon is one of the very few Russian saints who left abundant writings which are regarded as standard works on moral and ascetico-mystical theology. They cannot be ignored by students of Russian religious thought. The important question of his sources arises as soon as one begins to study these *Works*; it would require a research of its own. The problem has not been touched upon so far, but the scope of this book would not justify a digression into a highly specialized study of the philology and authenticity of some works and of the Byzantino-Slavonic or western influences in Russia. It would be presumptuous to attempt an accurate work at a time when the most indispensable materials are often unavailable. The study of the patristic writings also lies outside the field of my investigation and competence. I have nevertheless included a section on Tikhon's sources, in order to outline, however sketchily, his main spiritual and intellectual ancestry.

Chapter 7 treats of the growth of veneration for Tikhon of Zadonsk after his death and, eventually, of his canonization. This, too, could easily have been a subject for independent research.

I have looked through the works of prominent Russian ecclesiastics, so as to gather an authoritative and typical body of opinion on St. Tikhon, but I cannot claim to have exhausted all the sources. Research, in general, was made more difficult by the fact that much of the work was done during World War II, at a time when some libraries had to be closed and in others books and periodicals precious for our purpose had been lost through enemy action. Many of the notes were taken in haste—not always with a study of St. Tikhon in view—and thus remain unverified. It was obviously not possible to obtain books from the Continent or from the U.S.S.R. Some works became available only when printing was already in progress.

Was Dostoevsky the only secular writer who had read Tikhon? I made a cursory survey of the familiar authors. It seemed to me important to point out the contact between Russian religious and artistic thought, as only too often, and often justifiably enough, it has been said that between these two worlds there was an unbridgeable gulf.

A great many unfamiliar names will appear in these pages. In order to preserve the continuity of the story of Tikhon's life, information about these persons will be confined to notes. The period covered is 1724-83, and no notes are given on well-known historical or literary personages such as Tsars or famous authors. In the notes the names of monasteries remain untranslated.

Certain technical details require some explanation. I have adopted the spelling of names as found in the catalogues of the British Museum, in order to facilitate reference to the catalogues. In the bibliography and footnotes all references, unless otherwise specified, are from Russian books, though some of them have been published in Western Europe. Moscow is abbreviated to M., St. Petersburg to SPB., Leningrad to L. This work was actually finished in the summer of 1944; but it first went to press in 1951; several books of later dates were added on re-reading for publication. Titles are translated so as to enable the Western reader to understand the subjects of the different works. Only names of periodicals are given in Russian. There is also an alphabetical bibliography, with Russian titles. Dates are given according to the Russian Calendar—*e.g.*, 22 December, 1761, which according to the Western Calendar is 2 January, 1762. In order not to over burden the bibliography, I omit the works of history, the list of the early grammars and other text-books, and the secular writers of the eighteenth and the nineteenth centuries whom I have consulted, and limit myself to those directly mentioned in the text. The same principle applies to the early period of literature and history studied as a background to the sources of St. Tikhon. Biblical references are taken throughout from the Authorized Version, and the chapter or verse may thus differ, particularly in the Psalms, from the Slavonic or Russian Bible.

Russian ecclesiastics, especially monks, are known only by their Christian names. Sometimes it is possible to disentangle a story only by referring to their respective ranks or dioceses. It often happened that certain names were popular at particular periods: to take the example of St. Tikhon, in his own life-time two other bishops of Voronezh bore the same name. A monastic Christian name was different from the monk's or nun's original name. And if a monk made renewed and stricter vows, known as the ascetic "great profession," this, too, was an occasion for receiving a new Christian name. To help the reader, I give a monk's monastic Christian name, followed, where it occurs for the first time, by his family name in brackets. The same order will be adopted in the index.

I have tried to make sure of each name by checking up and comparing *The Dictionary of Russian Biographies* with P. Stroev's *Registers of the Hierarchs and the Heads of the*

Monastic Communities of the Russian Church (1877), Filaret's (Gumilevsky) *Survey of Russian Ecclesiastical Literature* (1859-61), with Evgeny's (Bolkhovitinov) *Dictionary of Russian Religious Writers* and Amvrossy's (Ornatsky) *History of the Russian Hierarchy* as well as other sources which will be indicated in the course of this work. Even so, some dates may be subject to correction, and some people, particularly minor personages, remain hardly more than names. I indicate the names of all persons mentioned in any of the materials on St. Tikhon to which I have had access. It has been of great help to discover these names and to be able to corroborate different parts of this study by finding out more details about this or that personage. I mention them in the hope that someone may in the future discover details which present conditions put out of reach.

St. Tikhon was baptized Timofey (Timothy). Russian custom demands that an adult be called by his Christian name together with the patronym: thus Tikhon while he was a lay teacher was called Timofey Savelich. His family name was spelt both Sokolovsky and Sokolov. At his monastic profession he took the name of Tikhon; thenceforward he was known as Hierodeacon Tikhon, then as Hieromonk Tikhon, finally as Bishop Tikhon. His name was known either as Tikhon *Voronezhsky*—of the diocese of Voronezh— or Tikhon *Zadonsky*, or *of Zadonsk*, from the geographical name of the community "beyond the Don" where he lived in retirement. This latter name became the more popular after his canonization.

Much difficulty results from the vagueness of the records. The early biographers were content with such definitions as "after that," "soon," etc. To arrive at facts has often necessitated something approaching detective work, though in some instances Stroev or some eighteenth-century biographer helped to establish a date in Tikhon's life. Yet the lack, at some points, of final documentary proof does not always allow one to make conclusive assertions, and I am prepared to revise certain views if more conclusive evidence should be discovered.

Our sources of information about St. Tikhon consist mainly of his own *Works*. I have been able to compare only in part the editions of 1825 and 1830 with the second edition of 1860, from which I take all quotations (indicating separate volumes by t). The *Works* passed through the Synodal censorship, and were published by the Synod in 1836, in five volumes. There is no way of being sure whether or not they were altered. It seems to me that they were not, or only very slightly, for at the time when St. Tikhon's works were submitted to the censorship the important men of the Synod were his friends and admirers.

St. Tikhon's life was briefly described by his friend, Bishop Tikhon III (Malinovsky). Metropolitan Evgeny (Bolkhovitinov), himself a native of Voronezh, a historian and a bibliographer, also compiled a short *Life,* first published in 1796, now in the Preface to the *Works* (edition of 1860 which was used by me). He claims to have verified the information given by previous records, and adds dates of official events in Tikhon's life and a few details about the appointment of teachers and clergy in the seminaries of Novgorod and Voronezh (which I have found very useful). Bishop Tikhon's two cell-attendants (monks acting as servants and private secretaries), F. Chebotarev and I. Efimov, left personal memoirs covering the period of his retirement. These were kept under Nos. 193, 194 in St. Sophia's Library and were added to St. Tikhon's *Works* in M. 1889 and later editions. (I quote Chebotarev from the periodical *Pravoslavnoe Obozrenie*, 1861, and Efimov from the Preface to the 10th edition of *Works*.) Chebotarev is factual in his *Notes* and likes to emphasize that, here and there, he uses his late Bishop's personal words. Efimov is inclined to stress the supernatural element. All the subsequent biographers repeat the details given by these two writers. Several booklets on the saint were published after the canonization. The most accurate seems to be the work of the priest A. Lebedev, 1865, from which I take many quotations. Once more, I can only deplore the fact that some works on St. Tikhon which I indicate in the Bibliography were inaccessible to me.

All these are documents of value. Yet even for a Russian reader there is need for a fuller and more critical biography; none of those I consulted gives any historical background or deals with the *Works* of St. Tikhon otherwise than by mere enumeration of citation of extracts, mainly of a didactic and popular character.

Thus the life and work of Bishop Tikhon of Zadonsk repay study, whether we approach him as a historical figure or as a key to the understanding of Dostoevsky's religious sympathies and ideals.

The book in its present form is an abridgement of a thesis submitted for the degree of D. Phil., on which I worked while holding the Yates Scholarship and Lectureship at St. Hugh's College, Oxford. It is with much sincere pleasure that I thank Miss B. E. Gwyer, at that time Principal of the College, as well as the Fellows of the College for providing me with the opportunity of doing this research. I thank Professor L. W. Grensted for his advice and encouragement in supervising it. I should like to express my gratitude to the Staff of the British Museum with their tradition of helpful service. Special acknowledgement is due to the printers who had to deal with the difficult task of producing this volume. Many friends have helped me in various ways whilst I was working: I would like to thank them all, and particularly Mr. and Mrs. J. N. Duddington for their hospitality in war-time London. To Mira Benenson, unfailing friend, I express my deepest gratitude for checking my English, patiently retyping the changing versions of the work and for giving most generously of her time and hospitality.

CHIEF EVENTS

1724 Timofey Sokolov born.
1738 He enters the school at Novgorod (11 December).
1740 He enters the Novgorod Seminary (October).
1751 Appointed teacher of Greek.
1754 Finished the course of studies (15 July).
 " Continued as teacher of Greek and taught poetics.
1758 Professed monk with the name of Tikhon (10 April).
 " Ordained deacon (end of April).
 " Ordained priest (July?).
 " Lectured in philosophy (autumn).
1759 Appointed Vice-Rector (13 January).
 " Archimandrite of Zheltikov Monastery in the diocese of Tver (26 August).
1760 Rector of the Tver Seminary and head of the Otroch Monastery.
1761 Consecrated Bishop of Keksholm and Ladoga [Novgorod Suffragan] (13 May).
1762 Head of the Synodal Office (summer).
1763 Nominated Bishop of Voronezh (February).
1767 Resignation (17 December).
1768 Retired to Tolshevo Monastery.
1769 Moved to Zadonsk Monastery.
1783 Died (13 August).

1

Historical Background

THE LIFE OF Tikhon of Zadonsk (or Timofey Sokolov, as he was originally called) covers the years 1724-83. His chief importance does not lie in the historical field, yet it would be wrong to disregard his historical background, for not only can we trace in his character and outlook certain features of his times, but we can also see the direct impact of wider political and national issues on the unfolding of his life-story. As a churchman he was affected in particular by the ecclesiastical changes of the eighteenth century, and the subject-matter of his teaching and writings was undoubtedly influenced by the problems and needs of his age.

His life spanned a turbulent period. During that period nine sovereigns succeeded one another or claimed the succession to the Russian throne. In addition, there were various adventurers who put forward claims in the name of Tsars previously dethroned or deprived of their rights. Wars, internal struggles and drastic reforms shook the land. The period began with the accession of Peter I (1672, r. 1682-1725), who left no stone unturned in his drive for reform: the State, the army, the newly established fleet, policies in home and foreign affairs, changes in the class system of Russia (the Table of Ranks, 1722), the Church, education, printing, even the very alphabet, simplified from the old Church Slavonic script to modern Russian (1709)—all were

15

ruthlessly accelerated into renewed life or became the expression of a new outlook. Tempestuous and brutal, this crowned revolutionary trampled ancient customs underfoot and, deriding convention, with a total disregard for life and wealth, established his new capital on the marshes of the River Neva (1703), thereby forcing Russia to turn westwards. Peter fought the Turks on the Azov (1695-1700) and unsuccessfully on the Pruth (1711); he defended his land against the Swedes in a war which, with interruptions and changing fortunes, continued from 1700 to 1721. The Battle of Poltava (1709) made him a national hero; the conquest of Finland (1713-14) opened up new vistas for Russia; the acquisition of territories on the Baltic, cleverly consolidated by royal marriages, established Russia on the Baltic Sea. Russia, hitherto unknown to Europe and deemed by the West to be a fantastic and barbarous country, was becoming a part of the western world. From this time onwards, throughout the whole of the eighteenth century, she was involved in the complexities of western politics and was continually being drawn into wars by virtue of new alliances. Peter mercilessly crushed all who stood in the way of his gigantic plans. To succeed to his father's throne he had had to depose his elder sister, Princess Sophie (Regent 1682-94), and to put down a revolt of her supporters, the *streltsy* (1698). He quelled, with equal energy, the revolts of the Cossacks on the Don (1707-8), of the nomadic peoples of the East (1705, 1706, 1711), and of the Ukrainian leader Mazepa, and would brook no opposition of his own kin. He forced his first wife to enter a convent, and when his son Alexis (1962-1718) sided with the opposition, he had him put to death. Peter then married an uneducated woman and, to secure her position and that of his children by her, he abolished the old right of succession (1722), thus opening the door to palace revolutions.

Peter I died in 1725. His second wife, Catherine I, reigned for little over a year. In 1727 the adolescent son of the late Alexis, Peter II (1715-30), succeeded her. The land was ruled by the rival parties at Court. The Supreme Council next offered the crown to Peter I's niece (a daughter of his half-brother, Ivan V), Anna Ioanovna, now the widowed Duchess of Courland (1698, r. 1730-40). Anna was to introduce constitutional liberties; having promised this, once in power she tore up the compromising documents and ruled as an autocrat. Everybody groaned under the regime of "the Germans" and Anna's favorite, Biron (Bűhren). The German political influences and Protestant pressure of Anna's reign left grim memories:

> Russia was oppressed by her secret enemies, the favorites. The simple-hearted patriots, so needed by the land, were brought to ruin and rooted up, whereas favors and salaries were poured upon unscrupulous pillagers who lived with us, as it were, only in their shadow, their souls and bodies belonging to foreign lands whither they sent the riches gained here by cunning devices.... Russia fell into such a state that it pierces one's heart to think of it. The powerful favorites infringed upon the very dogmas. . . . Bishops and clergy were unfrocked, banished, tortured; the oppressors succeeded in frightening everyone to such an extent that the very preachers of God became silent.[1]

The country was involved in the War of Polish Succession (1735-39), which, we shall see, had repercussions in Tikhon's early life. The Empress's sister Catherine, married to Charles-Leopold, Duke of Mecklenburg, had a daughter, Anna Leopoldovna (1714-76), who was betrothed to Antony Ulrich of Brunswick-Bevern (1714-74). In order to secure the position of Biron as regent, the Empress proclaimed that, should a son be born of the marriage of her niece, he should become her successor to the throne of Russia. A male child was born in 1740, and was proclaimed the future Tsar Ivan VI, who was to rule under the regency of Biron. The Empress Anna died on 17 October 1740. In November the mother of the royal baby, supported by the officers of the guard, overthrew Biron and declared herself Regent. Hardly had the coins bearing the effigy of Ivan VI began to circulate when another plot by the "Russian party" brought to power Elisabeth

(1709, r. 1741-71), the daughter of Peter I by Catherine. After twenty years of comparative quiet in internal affairs, though with depleted funds and continuous war (with Sweden, 1741-43, and the Seven Years War, 1756-63), Russia witnessed once more the accession of another German princeling. Elisabeth (secretly married to the commoner Razumovsky) chose as her successor the son of her sister Anna Petrovna by the Duke of Holstein, Prince Anton, renamed in Russia Peter III Theodorovich (1728, r. December 1761-28 June 1762). The Princess of Anhalt-Zerbst, Sophie-Augusta, was invited to Russia, taught the language and religion, received into the Orthodox Church and married to Peter under the name of Catherine. Peter Theodorovich was notorious for his pro-German sympathies, and unpopular with the nobility and the Church. He came to power when, on the 22 December 1761, Elisabeth passed away. Then, on the night of 22 June 1762, he was dethroned and murdered by the supporters of his wife. In 1764 a plot was conceived to liberate young Ivan VI from prison where he spent years in ignorance of his origin; he was shot during the attempt to rescue him, and the matter was hushed up. Catherine II began her long and brilliant reign (1762-96), following in many ways the ideas of Peter the Great. She worked on a new legislation, fostering western ideas, developing trade, cleverly managing foreign politics, pushing westwards at the expense of Poland (first partition, 1772; second, 1793; third, 1795), gradually subjugating the Ukraine (1782-87) and the Cossacks (1775), and at last bringing Russia to the sea in the south through the wars with Turkey (1768-74), and finally incorporating the Crimea (1783). Rationalism and Enlightenment became major slogans in the eighteenth century; the more superficial were content to parade as "Voltairians," and, not understanding deism, they counted theselves atheists. Profound social changes contributed to the estrangement between the ecclesiastical class and the rest of society. The Government, in need of officers, technicians, diplomats, prevented gentry from going to ecclesiastical schools, but it also barred the ecclesiastics from the specialized training required for various practical forms of public service. In point of practice, a great many leading figures in politics, law and education were still supplied by this rejected class, but they seemed to be accepted on sufferance. Confined, as a class, to the service of religion and—the more fortunate of them—to the study of theology, they were becoming a group apart. Even their studies were carried on in the Latin tongue, unconnected with their Slavonic—Platon Levshin's *Catechism*, 1765, was the first book on the subject in Russian. The uneducated sons of the poorer country clergy who were regarded for generations as part of the lower strata of society were supposed to devote themselves to the Church. Moreover, as a result of the Petrine reforms and of the secularization, the clergy became dependent on the Government for their appointments and for financial support. This dangerous situation led the clergy to adopt a subservient attitude to the civil authorities: whereas the priest would appear to a peasant as a man more affluent and idle and enjoying rather more liberty than he did himself, to a wealthy and better-educated Russian he would appear as an uncouth, ignorant and frightened servant of the Government. It was an age of luxury, of new palaces and gardens, of rapid rise to fortune and sudden loss of favor; an age of budding life in schools, theatre and literature; an age of despotism penetrated by the air of the French and American revolutions; an age of humanitarian laws and of bribery, of an enlightened, Voltairian gentry and of a starved peasantry; an epoch marked by one of the greatest peasant revolts (1773-75), under Pugachev.

There would be no need to mention these dynastic changes had not the personalities of the autocrats influenced the national life and the individual life of Tikhon, which was affected still more by the problems and fortunes of the Russian Church.

To understand the ecclesiastical world into which Tikhon, son of a village verger, was born, we have to go back and briefly review the main events directly affecting the Church since the middle of the seventeenth century, for the origin of many of the conflicts of his time was to be found in the years 1655-67.

It was then that the Russian Church was split by the

schism (*Raskol*), which was the outcome of the much-needed revision of the books used in church services. Mistakes had crept in through centuries of copying. An attempt to carry out some correction in the early sixteenth century ended in a conflict, the revisers being accused of heresy. Now the authoritarian, unbending Russian Patriarch Nikon (d. 1681) carried through the revision of some rubrics, introducing a new spelling of the name Jesus, a threefold singing of the alleluia, and a different way of making the sign of the cross—with three instead of two fingers. As each of the ancient customs had acquired sanctity for the mass of the people, and for many a priest a symbolical meaning, the opposition was violent. The growing sense of national and ecclesiastical independence seemed outraged by the fact that Nikon was supported by the Greek and other Eastern high clergy. Under the dispute about the wording of a prayer or a letter in the name of Jesus were hidden more complex religious differences. Some adherents of the "old books" and the "old belief" (nicknamed "Old Believers" or "Raskolniki," "schismatics") questioned the right of the official Church to make any changes or to control their beliefs by force; they opposed likewise the interference of the secular authorities in matters of faith. The justification of the Government, however, lay in the fact that Russia was felt to be Holy Russia, the bearer of true Christian tradition, the "Third Rome" which had succeeded the heretical Rome of the Popes and the faulty Rome of Byzantium, overrun by the Turks. Moreover, the gentle and devout Tsar Alexis Mikhailovich (1645-76) was sincerely concerned with matters of belief and of the sacred beauty and order of the Church. One of her zealots, he had to do violence to his own feelings in the condemnation of the Old Believers, among whom were some of his personal friends and some prominent churchmen greatly respected by him.[2] The mystical unrest of the Old Believers, their readiness to die for their faith and their conviction that the last days were near followed them into the "deserts" of the remote regions of Russia. There were cases of mass-suicides for the Old Faith. This atmosphere of strife and martyrdom subsided towards the beginning of the eighteenth century, but the blasphemous interference with the Church by Peter the Great, and his deriding of it, only confirmed the Old Believers in their conviction that Antichrist had appeared. The social, political and religious opposition took refuge in the Old Belief, and the latter remained for ever suspect to the Government and to the official Orthodox Church. Withdrawing beyond the Volga, to Siberia, into the North, or into the steppes and the Cossack regions, the Old Belief grew in strength, gaining the support of the masses. Its further destinies were complex: some groups—"the priestly ones"—although at conflict with the Church, sought to preserve the apostolic succession; the others, convinced of the corruption of the Church, became a "non-priestly" sect. The strictest adherence to old ritual was typical of both, and the oldest traditions of icon-painting were followed by them. Horrified at any novelty, the Old Believers presented in the country a paradox of opposition and revolt on the most conservative basis.

The Church meanwhile, eager to overcome superstition within, turned to the ecclesiastical scholars of the Kiev Academy. These Ukrainians, educated in close contact with Polish Catholicism, helped the Church schools of Russia readily, but came into ideological conflict with the Greeks, then teaching in Moscow. In the late seventeenth century there followed a controversy concerning the eucharistic bread and the moment of consecration.[3]

If, on the one hand, the Church fought the Old Belief, it had, on the other hand, to withstand both the Protestant ideas which began to penetrate Russia with the accession of Peter, and the State itself, which became the exponent of those ideas.

Peter I wished to subdue the old Russia, for the benefit of the new Russia to come. The Old Believers were his open foes, but the Orthodox Church also bred the germs of opposition. In order to control her, Peter, in 1700, when the head of the Russian Church, the Patriarch, died, delayed the election of a new one. This was a turning-point in Russian Church history; throughout its history, with greater or lesser energy and from varied motives, the secular powers had tried to control the Church. Now it became an acknowledged fact. The locum tenens of the patriarchal see, Archbishop Stephen Yavorsky, produced in 1713 a book which became the symbol of the controversy that was to rend the Church for nearly twenty years. The *Rock of Faith* claimed the predominance of the Church over the State. An ardent supporter of the Tsar, a man of undisguised Lutheran tendencies, Archbishop Theophan Prokopovich (1681-1736) retorted with his *Hammer against the Rock of Faith*. Long polemics, oral and written, ensued, aggravated by personal jealousies, by the championship of the "Ukrainians" (of whom Yavorsky was one) and by opposition to them. It was typical of the period that the western world, in the persons of a Protestant and a Catholic divine, should follow the Russian dispute in their writings. It seemed that the religious war of the west was now to be waged on Russian soil.

The Tsar instituted in 1721 an ecclesiastical administrative body of his nominees, the Holy Synod, though he abstained from touching upon either dogma or worship. The Patriarchate was abolished. The Synod could do nothing without the consent of the Emperor's representative, its Ober-Procurator, who was a layman. The ancient Eastern Patriarchates recognized the Synod as canonical (September 1723).

A significant document, the *Spiritual Regulation* (1721), reflected the lines of the Petrine reform. Compiled by Theophan Prokopovich, it reads more like polemics than ecclesiastical legislation. Its sharp criticism of the ignorant clergy, its distrust not only of the Russian monks but also of monasticism itself, its whole tone, justify the opinion that "it was the programme of the Russian Reformation."[4] It did not pass without protest. The Church was not silent, but it was silenced. The rapid removals from office and the banishment of bishops and clergy became habitual features of the reign, and almost a tradition in the subsequent decades. The religious controversies were stifled in the walls of remote monasteries or prisons. The secular State asserted its rights against the old theocracy. This controversy between Church and State went deeper underground about the time when Tikhon grew to manhood, though its aftermath shaped his destiny. He was to live under the sway of Erastianism, amidst wars and revolts. The encroachments upon the property of the Church not only affected the rich and powerful bishops of the past, but also reduced the mass of poverty-stricken lower ecclesiastics, sextons, subdeacons, bell-ringers, acolytes to further misery and defencelessness.

The Tsar, who in drunken company parodied Church ritual, had nevertheless to reckon with devout feelings and official decorum. Having founded his new capital on the Neva and fought the Swedes, he turned to Alexander, a canonized Prince, who had defended the land against a similar onslaught in 1240. This Prince was proclaimed the patron saint of the Neva region (1710). In 1723 the body of Alexander, who was buried in the city of Vladimir, was carried in procession through the land on its way to the new capital.

In September 1723 the body was brought in a boat along the River Volkhov and ceremonially received by all the clergy and people of Novgorod (which was Alexander's birthplace and seat). The relics were given a great reception. The coffin remained a day and night in the cathedral of St. Sophia. A famous preacher spoke on the true meaning of the veneration of the saints. Then the chest with the relics, transferred again to the boat, drifted slowly along the river alive with tilt-boats and canoes: the Bishop, all the officials and clergy accompanied the saint. The procession paused at the monastery of St. Antony the Roman, and the Gospel was read from the boat. Then they all stopped again by the monastery Khutyn', and after solemn leave-taking the procession rowed northwards, to where the new capital of the realm, St. Petersburg, stood.

The places visited by the relics were those where Tikhon would have to live.

The Feast of St. Alexander Nevsky was now fixed for 30 August, the date of Peter's peace treaty with Sweden. The saintly Prince, who had been professed a monk on his deathbed, and was thus represented on the icons as a monk, was from now on, by order of the Synod, to be portrayed only in the garments and posture of a princely warrior.[5] This religious ceremony, with its hardly disguised patriotic and secular meaning, was a significant opening to the year which saw the birth of Timofey Sokolov.

2

Training

HE WAS BORN IN 1724, in the village of Korotzk, which was in the Valday district of the Novgorod diocese.

Little is known about his childhood and youth. Some precious details taken from personal conversations with him have been passed on to us by V. Chebotarev, who became, in the 'seventies, his cell-attendant (a mixture of a servant, spiritual son and, if literate, private secretary). There are also the official dates given for his education and career. With the help of corroborating records, biographies of his contemporaries, historical and archæological documents, we can reconstruct to a certain extent his background and immediate surroundings, and elucidate some of his movements.

When Timofey, the sixth and youngest of the family, was a small child, his father, a village sexton, died. Peter was working his way towards a subdiaconate in Novgorod. Another son was conscripted for life-long military service. The third, Efimy, stayed in the village. The family lived in extreme poverty—"not even bread enough to eat." Such was their condition that a somewhat more affluent peasant, a coachman, offered to adopt the youngest boy. After much hesitation, the mother, in despair, consented. Efimy, returning home and asking for his mother, was informed that she had just taken the child to the coachman. He rushed after her, overtook her and, falling on his knees in the village street, asked: "Where are you taking this boy? What else but a coachman will he become if brought up by this man?

I cannot allow it, I would rather beg. We shall try to teach him letters; who knows, perhaps one day he will become a verger or subdeacon somewhere." Timofey was taken safely home. "And such were indeed his own episcopal words," emphasized the narrator of this story.[1]

The hopes of Efimy must have seemed too ambitious. A hard childhood awaited his brother. From his earliest days he tilled and harrowed the whole day long, in return for only a little bread. These years gave him a familiarity with nature, a peasant's love and esteem for a horse, a habit of hard work and a taste for solitude. But he hardly learned to read or write.

In 1737 the Government, short of men owing to the war with Turkey, issued a decree making liable to military service every youth of the ecclesiastical class who had no education and was not in a school at the time the decree was issued. Escape under a form or novitiate was also barred, for only widowed priests or retired soldiers were allowed to join a community. The Synod was made responsible for the control of the ecclesiastical schools; the pupils of leaving age and the incapable ones were to be sent into the army "to avoid unprofitable expenditure."[2] The decree created a real panic. Everybody rushed their sons to the schools. In Novgorod alone nearly a thousand candidates assembled.

Novgorod was one of the oldest cities of the land. In the Middle Ages as a member of the Hanseatic League, it thrived and had a strong tradition of self-government, till, in the sixteenth century, it was broken and obscured by Moscow. Built on the two banks of the River Volkhov, which were connected by a large bridge, it was famous for its eleventh-century cathedral, St. Sophia, and its old monasteries. It had also a school, founded in 1708 by the Metropolitan Job "for training men of all conditions and, among other things, for preparing a worthy priesthood," where Greek was taught whilst it fell into oblivion elsewhere.[3] In 1723 the Government amalgamated it with its newly created secular Arithmetic School; then Prokopovich, as Archbishop of Novgorod with residence in St. Petersburg, transferred this school to his private house, Karpovka; after his death in 1736 it was closed.

Both Novgorod and St. Petersburg had to start anew.

The Sokolovs made an effort to bring Timofey to the city. The mother could not afford any fees for him. She entrusted him, therefore, to the civil authorities, who found him rather illiterate, and decided to strike his name from the list of the ecclesiastics and to direct him to the military Arithmetic School.

This time his brother Peter came to the rescue. He besought the Church authorities to admit Timofey into their school and promised to pay for his keep. On the 11 December 1738 the boy entered the school, under the name of Sokolovsky (later to be abbreviated to Sokolov). It was his last chance; a youth over fifteen was automatically rejected as one shirking conscription. Peter's brotherly care far exceeded his income; he was married and a father. Timofey had to take odd jobs to relieve his brother: mostly, he dug other people's vegetable plots. But at least he was now at a school.

We may conjecture that the boys were studying some *Primary Reader*. The first known of these was printed in 1586 in Vilna. Another was issued in 1596, by the brothers Zizany; and still another by the famous Melety Smotritzky, in 1619. V. Th. Burtzev (Moscow, 1634) published a *Primer* with a *Eulogy of the Rod*, and Th. Polikarpov a *Primer for those desiring to Study Slav, Greek, and Latin Letters and for those striving for the wisdom which profits the soul*. In 1704 and 1708 there appeared *A Primer of the Slav Tongue, which is the beginning of learning for children eager to learn reading and writing*, with a harsh preface against episcopal ignorance. In Novgorod, in 1720, appeared *The first teaching of Youth, with letters and syllables; also a brief interpretation of the Decalogue, of the Lord's Prayer, the Creed and the Nine Beatitudes*. Written in the "vulgar tongue"—Russian vernacular instead of Church Slavonic—it was polemical in tone and voiced a warning against the darkness and quarrels of pseudo-theology and schism. It was published anonymously, but was known to be the work of Prokopovich. It might be worth pondering upon the influence which such a work would produce on a boy's mind.

The study of grammar played an unusually important role in Russia, for not only had the vernacular to be reconciled with the Slavonic grammar, but also the struggle that arose from the correction of the Church service-books and led to the schism in the previous century was recalled. The standard work was still that by Melety Smotritzky, often reprinted or revised in Moscow and used by subsequent writers. In 1706 Kopijewitz made an attempt at classifying the "living moscowite language"; so did Theodore Polikarpov in 1723, as well as Theodore Maksimov in his *Slavonic Grammar*, published in Novgorod, 1723. After 1755 all these works were superseded by the works of M. Lomonosov (1708 or 1711-65).

The crying need for education and the scarcity of schools prompted the activities of Amvrossy (Yushkevich, *c.* 1609-1745), a former pupil and teacher of the Kiev Academy, who in 1740 was nominated Archbishop of Novgorod. On 24 May he laid the foundation of a seminary for two hundred boarders to be transferred from the lower school. Among them was Timofey Sokolov.

> It is meet—the statutes ran—to take the greatest care in providing the Church with a teaching priesthood for the better establishment of Christian Law and devotion through the preaching of the Divine Word out of the Holy Scriptures.... The Synod and the Diocesan Bishops must strive to promote learning.... For it is useful and a necessity to a State; it is the enlightenment of human reason and the perfection of the knowledge and worship of the Almighty Creator; it is the affirmation of Orthodoxy, it is a guide to the fulfilling of the Divine Commandments and to true Christian life and salvation. Briefly: learning is the seed of wisdom and divine grace sown in human hearts by the Holy Ghost from whom all virtues blossom. It is therefore of the utmost importance that the ranks of the clergy in the Realm should be illumined by Divine study, in order that they may preach the Word of God and eradicate

evil passions, and in order that they may convert and baptize the infidel peoples who dwell within this Realm—Mordva, Chuvash, Cheremiss and others. All these could be given the light of the holy Christian faith by learned clergy and Bishops, diligent as befits their calling.

For the above mentioned grave reasons, a Seminary is being founded this day in the Bishop's House for study in Latin, Helleno-Greek and, if possible, in the Hebrew language, from Grammar to Rhetoric, Philosophy and Theology.

The Statutes were approved and signed by the Empress Anna.

There followed a detailed instruction on the administration of the Seminary, the provision of ample space, clothes and food, "a mattress for each boy and one pillow, two sheets and a blanket of coarse wool lined with a home spun sheet." The episcopal kitchen-garden, fisheries and farm-yards were to provide for meals. Common dormitories housed ten to twelve boys. Their morals and manners were to be strictly supervised, the gate kept under a watchful eye, lest they "waste their time in wandering in the streets of their own will, or in pranks and unworthy amusements." They had to proceed in couples, whether to church, to the classroom, to the dormitory or to a meal; during the latter they were to read aloud, in turn, "such works as pertain to their studies." The teachers and the bursar ("Commissar") were responsible to the Archbishop. Provision was made for an infirmary.[4] Unsatisfactory pupils were emphatically warned that they would be expelled and sent into the army.

The Seminary was opened in October 1740. The Archbishop's house was not large enough to contain it. The Empress suggested Khutyn' monastery, but finally that of St. Antony the Roman was chosen, a site some two miles away from the episcopal house. Founded in 1160, it was situated on the right bank of the Volkhov, in the vicinity of Khutyn' (of 1192) and of Yuriev (St. George's, founded in 1030). A large garden was thrown open to the pupils, and they were allowed to bathe and row on the river. Amvrossy embarked upon the enlargement of the premises and the erection of a stone building for the library. He rescued from St. Petersburg the rich library of his predecessor, Prokopovich, and endowed the Seminary with his own collection of books. He also left the old books and manuscripts of the cathedral for use by the students.

The needs of the pupils were not always as well met as the official statements had suggested. Timofey confessed that he lived in dire want. Such was the experience of most seminarists.[5] Timofey found it necessary to sell half of his bread ration in order to buy some candles, as he could not get through his work during the day, and had to sit up at nights, hidden in the dormitory behind a big Russian stove. These late hours, overwork and insufficient food undermined his health; though well proportioned and good looking, he was never strong.

The studious and quiet boy was often the victim of jokes. "Boys of well-to-do parents used to tease me," he said later in life: "they used to find my peasant bast-shoe, tie it to a string like a censer and swing it round me saying: we magnify thee." Timofey's holidays were spent at home. His mother died when he was fifteen.[6] He stayed with his brothers and contributed to his upkeep by taking odd jobs. In later days a legend grew that once he nearly froze on the road in his shabby clothes, but was found and saved by some traveller who on a future occasion met him as a bishop.[7]

The Archbishop could not enter into all the details of the school's life. Official functions took not a little of his time. From the abolition of the Patriarchate till 1743 Moscow was deprived of the ministration of the diocesan Metropolitan, whilst Petersburg became a diocese only in 1742. Novgorod was the prominent diocese: its bishop presided in the Synod. Amvrossy had the joy of welcoming the coming to power of Elisabeth, "that spark, the daughter of Peter," as he called her. He made an oration summing up the evils of the previous regime under Anna. Elisabeth was fond of the clergy, and patronized the Ukrainians, the countrymen of her favorite, Alexis Razumovsky. Nevertheless, being not only pious, but also frivolous and ignorant in matters of government, she was always short of funds, and in her reign the struggle for financial control of the Church was carried on by the Ober-Procurator Shakhovskoy, who, Amvrossy urged, should be replaced by an ecclesiastic.[8] Elisabeth was to be crowned in Moscow by the hand of Archbishop Amvrossy, on 28 April 1742. Later, in 1744, it was he who confirmed in Orthodoxy the future Catherine II.[9]

On her way to the ancient capital, Elisabeth passed through Novgorod, stayed at the Archbishop's house[10] and paid a visit to the Seminary. Mindful of a theatrical procession organized in the past by Prokopovich for the boy-Emperor Peter II, the staff was rehearsing congratulatory orations, choruses and a drama composed by the teacher Joasath Mitkevich (d. 1763).[11]

Did Timofey take part in that solemn reception? He was a good pupil and had a nice voice and handsome features. There is no direct indication that he was there, but he is mentioned in later life as personally known to the Empress. He himself seems never to have referred to things which might exalt him in the eyes of other people.

His life entered now into a quiet and externally uneventful course. The Seminary was modelled on the pattern of the Kiev Academy (founded in 1633 as Kiev Collegium by Peter Moghila, 1596-1646).[12] The teachers were trained there, as Amvrossy himself had been. The Novgorod Seminary was to be traditionally subdivided into four forms. That a certain elementary preparation had been acquired by the boys, was taken for granted, and instead of beginning with the "Analogy" and proceeding through the "Infirma" and "The Grammar" (where a boy would receive some introduction to Slavonic, Latin and Greek grammar, reading, unseen and composition), a boy began with "Syntarima," which was to cover catechism, arithmetic, music-reading for church choirs and a little instrumental music (Timofey's delight). Studies were therefore secular in content at this first stage. In 1742-44 Timofey worked on poetics and mythology, and later mastered these subjects sufficiently to teach them. He did not himself fall into the temptation of versifying, very prevalent among learned monks.[13] Of the period in "Rhetoric," although he had no particular taste for scholastic subtleties, he seems to have acquired the method, the system of question and answer, the clarification of his argument point by point, which were to become typical of his early writings. Much time was devoted to Latin: the pupils were supposed to know it, and even to use it in mutual conversation outside working hours. Greek, although taught in this Seminary, never became equally familiar to most students. The teachers, coming from the South-West, often spoke a jargon full of Slavonic and Polish phrases; the pupils spoke naturally a vernacular Russian, and said their prayers in old Church Slavonic. The effect of this training on their minds must have been curious. It is remarkable that Timofey preserved and developed amidst it all his beautiful, colorful language. He was a good student, but his personal spiritual leanings are revealed to us by the small booklet in his own handwriting, some fifteen pages in quarto, calligraphically written, signed by him and dated 1745. They were scriptural *Excerpts for the Good of every true Christian Soul*.[14]

A devout Russian holds in reverence his patron saint. It must have been a moving experience for the young man to read and to copy out the verses in the epistles addressed to the "Child Timothy."

The death, in May 1745, of the Archbishop Amvrossy did not change the quiet course of the scholastic occupations. Only in August 1747 was a successor to him appointed—also a former scholar from Kiev and latterly Bishop of Pskov, Stephen Kalinovsky. He, too, was to die soon—in 1754—leaving the diocese for the next four years without a bishop or even a suffragan.

Among the teachers of the Seminary, one Yamnitzky, should be noted, under whom, in 1746, Timofey began to study philosophy and the rudiments of theology: the Greek fathers, homiletics and Thomas Aquinas. Greek was taught by Parfeny Sopkovsky (1716-95). In December 1748 Yamnitzky died, and the students returned to the philosophy form, and only in 1750, with the Rector Mitkevich, did they again reach theology. He was an excellent teacher, a man of faith, intelligence and critical sense. He became one of the revisers of the texts dealing with early Russian saints, the *Kiev Paterik*.¹⁵ The wandering philosopher and poet, Grigory Skovoroda (1722-94), described him as "an image of Christ, quiet, meek and merciful, a pure mirror of virtue."¹⁶

Work must have suffered from scarcity of text-books. Tremendous riches were collected in some monasteries—in the St. Sophia's library in Novgorod (judging from the catalogues of 1775, when many volumes had been removed to St. Petersburg and several dispersed privately) there were some 1247 books of old print and 1189 manuscripts.¹⁷ Chronicles, liturgical and canonical books, lives of the saints, works of the early Christian fathers nevertheless did not supplant the need for comprehensive compilations and manuals. History was taken by the students from western sources: Stratteman, *Theatrum Historicum*, Buddeus, *Historia Ecclesiastica*, and the works of Baronius and a Polish Jesuit, Peter Scarga. There was also a Puffendorf translated by Gabriel (Buzhinsky). Both Protestant and Catholic books began to penetrate the seminaries, including even the doctrinal works of Hollatius and Breithaupt. The Russians wrote theology in Latin, sometimes with Russian sub-titles. The most widely used manual of the period was ascribed to Theophilact Lopatinsky and was said to be based on his *Scientia sacra* lectures in Moscow, 1706-17, and *Theologia theoretica* of 1717-19. Cyril Florinsky brought out a *Theologia positiva et polemica*.

Lectures were often copied, and the scarcity of text-books increased night-reading. In Moscow the students were allowed by the Synodal Press to work on its premises thrice a week and "sit one whole night reading and taking notes."¹⁸

The year 1751 was marked by the appearance of a new edition of the Slavonic Bible (third edition, conforming to that of 1580, published in Ostrog). There also came out a *Parallelism of various places of the Holy Writ, a Concordance carried out with the aim of revealing in certainty that which appears doubtful*.¹⁹

In the personal life of Timofey this year was important as marking the beginning of his educational activities. Though still a student, he was entrusted with the Greek class. No fees were given to him till in June he wrote to the Archbishop (who resided in Petersburg) asking for "whatever remuneration should be found fitting by His Grace." Like his colleague, a pupil-teacher of Latin, he was assigned fifty roubles and some bushels of rye a year.[20] Some details of this period are supplied by his school-mate, son of a monastic serf liberated by the late Amvrossy, Stephen Lagov (d. 1804 as Archbishop of Riazan), who was to write the history of the Novgorod Seminary.[21]

Occasionally the world broke into the secluded life of the Seminary. Its Rectors were usually nominated Archimandrites of St. Antony's, and enjoyed many privileges and almost episcopal prerogatives. They had to manage big estates, and there occurred clashes both with the Government when it infringed on their grounds and with monastic serfs.[22]

In July 1754 the first full course of studies was at last brought to its end. Timofey, aged thirty, was asked to stay in the Seminary and to continue as teacher of Greek and poetics. After more correspondence with the Synod, small fees enabled him to help his family, particularly his elder sister, who earned her living by scrubbing floors in well-to-do houses.[23] This position of a lay teacher was merely provisional. His family advised him to marry and to get ordained deacon. There was also a possibility of a secular career as teacher or official. Seminarists were rather in demand, as the best-trained men, and when, in 1755, the Moscow University was founded, quite a few were transferred to it. Timofey's own leanings were monastic. Had he not lived all these years practically as a monk, though less harassed than were the poverty-stricken parochial clergy, over-burdened with families, and not oppressed with manual or field work like "simple" monks, who hardly disguised their animosity against the "learned ones" from whom all the bishops were chosen?

These small colonies of monastic and scholarly life were surrounded by a forest, mostly of pine-trees. It was a somewhat mournful landscape, with a grandeur of its own, and very changeable, according to the season. The river froze in winter, but in spring, swollen by the masses of melting snow, it grew large and rapid and overflowed into the fields and villages to such an extent that one had to travel from house to house in a small boat. In summer, despite the marshy and dangerous spaces in the wood, it was hot and dry and the air was scented by the resinous trees.

Two small events of this period remained in Timofey's memory as providential. Once, as he rode through the wood, his horse began to rear and to struggle. The saddle came loose and he was thrown to the ground, and one foot caught in the stirrup. Once rid of the man, the horse stopped quietly.

Again, during vacation, on a visit to the Archimandrite of the Alexander Monastery, with other teachers, Timofey went up into the belfry to look at the view. He leaned on the railings, which suddenly collapsed. As though pushed by someone, he fell backwards against the bells; his head struck something hard, and he almost fainted. When, later, he succeeded in climbing down from the belfry, everybody commented on his white shaken appearance. He said: "Give me a cup of tea; I will tell you presently what has happened," and after tea he took the others to see the smashed railings and the scene of his escape.

His school years, when he used to read at night by the light of a candle, accustomed him to late hours. On a May night—which, in this northern land, does not grow dark, but covers everything with a white veil of light—he came out and stood on the flight of steps which looked towards the north. Many years later he spoke to his cell-attendant of that night. "I came out, and was standing there, thinking about eternal bliss. All of a sudden the heavens seemed to open and there was such a shining, such a brilliance of light, as mortal tongue cannot describe nor reason understand. This gleam was brief, scarcely a minute, and again the sky appeared in its usual form. From this marvellous sight I conceived a more burning desire for solitary life, and long after this wonderful phenomenon I felt a rapture of mind, and even now, as I recall it, my heart is filled with gladness and joy."[24]

Love of nature and beauty; retirement; the thought of eternity; and joy—these gave a clear premonition of the spiritual path which was opening before St. Tikhon.

Minor changes were taking place round him: Parfeny

(Sopkovsky) was nominated Rector and Archimandrite of St. Antony (February 1756). Mitkevich was transferred to Khutyn' community, soon to leave them and to become a bishop (1758). In October 1757 Dimitry (Sechenov, d. 1767) was promoted from the bishopric of Riazan to the see of Novgorod. This Russian, unlike his Southern predecessors, was a rude and grasping man, uninterested in learning. He spent all his time in St. Petersburg, and dominated the Synod. When the written declaration of two teachers, Timofey Sokolov and Stephen Lagov, who desired to be professed monks, was forwarded to him by the Rector of the Novgorod Seminary, the Archbishop delegated to him the performance of the ceremony. No novitiate was enforced on them, and the profession took place quietly in St. Antony.

The Orthodox rite of monastic profession stresses the idea of the death of the old man, rebirth and regeneration: as in baptism, a new name is given to the monk. The day before Palm Sunday, on Saturday 10 April 1758, before the liturgy, Timofey was professed under the name of Tikhon. His patron saint was the fifth-century Bishop of Amaphynt, a liturgical saint who, according to legend, caused a barren soil to bear a vineyard which produced fruit for his eucharistic wine.[25] Stephen Lagov became Simon. A fortnight later both travelled to St. Petersburg; Simon was ordained deacon and priest at once. Tikhon became a deacon ("hierodeacon"), and had to return to the capital in the summer to be ordained priest ("hieromonk"). During this summer, possibly even at the time of his ordination, he made the acquaintance of a man who soon became a leading figure in the Russian ecclesiastical world: Gabriel Petrov (1730-1801).[26] He also met Platon Levshin (1713-1812), who had paid a visit to the Novgorod Seminary.[27] Platon developed the educational work of the Moscow Ecclesiastical Academy, and was soon noticed by the Empress. At first sight Tikhon did not care for this man of somewhat opportunist tendencies, but later distinguished behind the "mellow voice and winning appearance" (as Platon naïvely described himself in his *Notes*) intelligence, a merry and sincere spirit and a touching love of learning.

That same autumn Simon Lagov became the Rector, and in a few months' time the Archimandrite of St. Antony. Tikhon lectured on philosophy, and on 13 January 1759 was appointed Vice-Rector ("Prefect"). Once a monk, he seemed not in the least nearer his ideal of solitude and spiritual concentration.

Soon the Synod was approached by the newly appointed Bishop of Tver, Athanassy (Vol'khovsky, d. 1766), who came from the Kiev Academy and intended to carry on its tradition of learning. He begged personally for the transfer of Tikhon Sokolov to his diocese. The Synod, "after due consideration, released and put the Vice-Prefect, hieromonk Tikhon, at the disposal and direction of the Bishop of Tver, for a post senior to that which he occupies at present." The word "post" or "job" was expressed by the monastic term "obedience." On 25 August 1759, Tikhon was instituted Archimandrite of the fifteenth-century Zheltikov Monastery of the Assumption, near the town of Tver. No details are known of his activities during this period. He became a member of the consistory, and in 1760, as Rector of the Tver Seminary, he gave a course of lectures on dogmatic and moral theology: they are supposed to be the foundation of his later book, *The True Christianity*. The same year he became the Archimandrite of the Otroch Monastery. This thirteenth-century community had poignant memories. Here lived in enforced seclusion the fiery apologist Maxim the Greek (1475-1556), corrector of the ecclesiastical books and victim of the superstitious ignorance of the Russians. Another sufferer was the Metropolitan Philip of Moscow, who, having protested against the cruelties of Ivan the Terrible, was banished here and strangled in 1569 by one of the notorious hangmen of the Tsar. There was still visible near the entrance to the Superior's room the frame of the door which led to the cell where the martyr's body reposed.[28] Although no biographer paid attention to this link with either Maxim or St. Philip, we find in Tikhon's writings similarities with those of Maxim, and no strong powers of imagination are needed to understand the effect of such surroundings and memories upon a sincere Christian.

The early biographers hinted, without any further detail,

that Tikhon met with some opposition in this community, particularly on the part of the bursar. However, before he could develop his full powers as head of a community, the ecclesiastical authorities made another claim upon him.

One of those small coincidences, which later events bring to light, and in which a hagiographer delights, happened, according to Chebotarev, during the liturgy celebrated by the Bishop of Tver at Eastertide, 1761. By mistake, instead of naming Tikhon "Archimandrite," he greeted him with "may the Lord God remember thy episcopacy." Apparently that same day, in St. Petersburg, Archbishop Dimitry, together with Parfeny Sopkovsky, now Bishop of Smolensk, was choosing a candidate for suffragan to the Novgorod diocese. Parfeny suggested Tikhon Sokolov.[29] The Archbishop considered Tikhon to be too young at thirty-seven. Moreover, he planned to bring him either to the Moscow Trinity Lavra or to the Alexander-Nevsky Lavra and eventually into the Synod (there was a recent vacancy due to the death of Silvester Kuliabko).[30] Seven candidates were considered. Parfeny insisted on adding Tikhon's name to the slips of paper which, according to the custom, were placed on the altar. Three times the ballot was headed by Tikhon. The Empress willingly signed her approval (it is at this point that early biographers hint that Tikhon was personally known to her). The Synod, by the Act No. 93, nominated Tikhon as suffragan to the Archbishop of Novgorod, with the title of Bishop of Keksholm and Ladoga.

Many years later Tikhon told his cell-attendant how the news was broken to him. This important detail shows how little he himself thought of advancement and how he still hoped for a life of solitary asceticism. He was away that day; having borrowed the monastery's coach, he asked to be driven into the wood, where he looked about for some lonely site suitable for a hermit's hut. He returned and attended vespers. Then a servant came telling him to call at once on his bishop, and as Tikhon proposed to wait till the end of the service before going to Athanassy, the messenger came again to fetch him. He was told of his nomination. His bishop wept when they had to part.

3

Active Life

THE CONSECRATION TOOK place on 13 May, 1761, in the cathedral of Saints Peter and Paul in St. Petersburg.

Tikhon now entered public life. Since Archbishop Dimitry resided in the capital, the Novgorod suffragan was left to deal with practically the whole diocesan administration.

As a local man, Tikhon had a great welcome. Bells rang, people and clergy gathered to meet their pastor, who was riding in the old-fashioned coach with small windows which was to become his usual conveyance: it was not thought right that a bishop should walk in the street. Some of his fellow-seminarists were there, some as priests, some in the office of deacon which they were to occupy all their lives. They had to present him with a censer; he reminded them of the bast-shoe with which they used to "magnify" and cense him when he was a boy. They were alarmed lest he should prove resentful—but he was merely amused at these memories (so he himself later told Chebotarev). Another person whom his new dignity overawed was his elder sister. She did not dare to come to his house. Tikhon sought her out; she began to address him with the ceremonious "you" instead of the familiar "thou." "You must visit me often and there will be a horse and carriage to fetch you," said he. Later, when she died, Tikhon personally read over her body the appointed prayers for the three nights preceding the burial. At one moment it seemed to him that his sister smiled at him. "You never know," he said: "she was a good woman." Tikhon kept in touch with his relatives, but was free from nepotism, that traditional evil of ecclesiastical life. Nobody from his family was promoted to the priesthood; one of his nephews was ordained deacon in his diocese.

An order concerning the discipline of the Seminary is almost the only official document left to us from this period. Once again political events had repercussions on Tikhon's life. The palace revolution of June 1762 brought to power Catherine II,[1] who assumed the role of the protector of all the wronged classes of the population, and the medals coined for the day of her coronation bore the inscription: "Orthodoxy and the Russian Homeland are saved."

In August the Court, statesmen and senior clergy proceeded to the ancient capital to take part in the coronation. Someone had to be left to assume responsibility for the current work of the Church. The post of Head of the Synodal office was given to the Novgorod suffragan. Tikhon must have arrived in St. Petersburg by the end of the summer, to stay till the return of the Synod. Possibly he did not even leave till February 1763. He resided at the Karpovka house, often used by members of the Synod.[2]

As soon as the coronation was over Catherine II set various commissions to investigate the conditions of the land. One of them was to study the position of serfs on monastic lands and the question of ecclesiastical property. Catherine was consolidating the secularization contemplated by Peter the Great. She had a gift for choosing the ablest men as her fellow-workers, and patronized the submissive and adaptable ones. Now that power was in her hands, she made a crushing speech on the contradiction between monastic vows and monastic possessions, and took a ruthless step when met with opposition. The Bishop of Rostov, Arseny Matzeevich, who dared to raise his voice against her, was arrested and tried.

Tikhon, as far as one can ascertain, had nothing to do with this affair, and no previous biographer has ever connected him with it. On the surface, he seemed to be honored by Catherine. When in 1763 the Bishop of Voronezh died and the Synod suggested three possible candidates, the Empress, "with her own hand," wrote on the report: "The

Suffragan of Novgorod to become the Bishop of Voronezh." At the same time she expressed a wish, enacted in a special order by the Ober-Procurator, that Tikhon should stop in Moscow on his way to the new diocese and attend the final stage of the trial of Arseny Matzeevich.[3]

In April Tikhon was already in Moscow.[4] A shattering ceremony of unfrocking took place in the presence of several churchmen and members of the Synod. Metropolitan Arseny was forced to divest himself of his episcopal robes and, under the name of Monk Andrew, was sent to a remote monastery in Karelia, and eventually to the fortress of Reval. With this object lesson as a warning to the ecclesiastics, Catherine allowed the Commission on Property to proceed with its investigations. She herself paid a call to the Trinity-St. Sergius Lavra, where, in July 1763, she chose, as religious instructor to her son Paul, the eloquent Platon Levshin, who addressed her as "the mother of my lord."

Tikhon left Moscow a sick man. Ever afterwards he was subject to a kind of nervous disease: shaking hands, giddiness and fainting spells.

His new diocese was regarded as one of the most difficult to administer in the country. The complexity of its regional problems required a close and careful study and much administrative skill.[5] This region had been for centuries "a field," a free border-land with a moving population—soldiers, hunters, run-away serfs, political opponents of the Tsars—who formed a body of independent men, the Cossacks. Defending the borders, the host of Don Cossacks was an autonomous body, with a freely elected head, vaguely connected with the central Russian Government. In the early eighteenth century, unable to resist Turkish invasions, they had to ask for assistance from the regular Army. Peter I used this opportunity to encroach upon their liberties. He made Voronezh a big city, the see of the diocesan bishop, and an important ship-building centre for the service against the Turks. Previously the Cossacks had nominated their own clergy, who were directly confirmed by the Patriarch of Moscow; since the abolition of the Patriarchate they had been controlled by the Synod. Now, any Bishop of Voronezh coming from the North represented the Crown, and was therefore regarded with disfavor by the local population. Moreover, the sudden changes of power throughout the century and the contradictory laws had made the position of bishops unstable; in the course of fifty years some ten of them had held office in the Voronezh diocese and had been banished, arrested or tried in court. At the same time, the region stood in support of the Old Belief, since many people had settled on the Don because of religious persecution in the seventeenth century. Catherine II, eager in her turn to colonize the South, had promised freedom and various facilities there to religious dissenters scattered over the Ukraine, Poland and even Austria (December 1762). When these people came to settle on the Don and Kuban', clergy were instructed to use the necessary pressure and to bring back these Old Believers into the true fold. Thus the causes not only of political and national independence but also of religious freedom were at stake. The Tsars, wishing to gain the support of the leading Cossacks, granted some of them land or privileges and ranks enjoyed by the Russian gentry. This introduced among the host a new element of class difference, which had not previously existed, and led to discontent and unrest. When, in 1771-73, Pugachev assumed the name of Peter III, serfs, nomads from beyond the Volga and many Cossacks joined in the rebellion.

Such was the land into which Tikhon was to arrive on 14 May 1763. He found the episcopal house outside the town in a state of dilapidation. The town had suffered from fires (1748 and 1761), which had caused great damage. The Cathedral had been burnt down. There was no seminary in the diocese, even the bells that chimed to announce his arrival had been damaged, and their tone differed sadly from the deep, musical voices of the Northern bells. A number of monks, clerks and servants were attached to the house, and custom demanded that they should receive their subsistence from the Bishop's revenue. It was like inheriting an estate which was more of a liability than an asset, and there was also the additional responsibility of fisheries, fields and stables with their famous Voronezh horses.

The late Bishop Ioanniky (Pavlutzky) left a considerable

sum, but the right to dispose of it was to be confirmed by the Economic College re-established in 1762. This sum would have helped Tikhon to repair the Cathedral and his house and to start a school; but correspondence on this subject dragged on till February 1766, when a Commission dealing with his application gave him the advice in a letter—dated 15 September 1765—that he should approach the Economic College directly.

More far-reaching measures were taken meanwhile by the Crown. On 29 February 1764 the *Ecclesiastical Statutes* were published.[6] These reduced Church lands, subdivided the dioceses and monastic communities into three classes and cut episcopal revenues, whilst imposing on the bishops the duty of establishing schools and of supporting a staff up to forty-nine in number and consisting of servants, bakers, coachmen, stokers, to be attached to their establishments. The Tsarina had gilded the pill by presenting gifts to several of the clergy and religious communities. Voronezh fell into the third category. The Bishop's fee (though impressive at first sight) was less than that of the Novgorod suffragan. And neither Tikhon nor any institution in his diocese was on the list of royal favors.

The period of Tikhon's life between May 1763 and December 1767 is the one about which there is most evidence.[7] It illustrates best his relations with his clergy, monks, seminarists and flock. It marks the beginning of his literary activities, which were brought to life by the necessities of the Church life around him.

His first contacts—and they were very disheartening!— were with the local clergy. They appalled him by their lack of the sense of vocation, their ignorance, drunkenness, absenteeism, quarrels and neglect of rubrics. Some candidates for ordination were Cossacks. Tikhon did not object to the custom of presenting local nominees, but required credentials as to the candidate's literacy, morality and freedom from any financial entanglement. Some seemed to have been ordained just to fill a vacancy or to obtain a living. "This is not a means of getting your bread," Tikhon objected (30 March 1764), when he found an interdicted priest celebrating the liturgy as a means of livelihood; at the same time he gave work to the son of this man, so as not to throw the family into utter poverty.

Full of a sense of responsibility, Tikhon did not feel the call to an administrative post. He seemed overwhelmed by his difficulties. Why was he not allowed to live that simple monastic life for which he had taken his vows? Imaginative, highly strung, he felt ill, and often fainting fits overcame him even during the Divine Service.

Only a few months after his arrival, on 7 August 1763, he sent a letter of resignation to the Synod on grounds of illness. The Synod—never in a hurry—replied eventually by advising him to consult a physician and to trust that his comparative youth would help him to triumph over ill-health.

Whilst waiting for the answer, Tikhon attended to his duties. On 9 August 1763 he wrote:

> Some deacons and priests seem to be unable to read the Scripture properly. It is evident that they either do not possess Bibles, or are unfamiliar with them and do not read them, neglecting thus their own salvation and that of the people entrusted to them. The will of the Heavenly Father is revealed to us in the New Testament through his beloved Son . . . without knowing it one cannot fulfil it.

In the middle of his semi-official instruction he exclaimed with delight:

> When you read the Gospels, Christ speaks to you; when you pray, you are speaking to him. O sweet colloquy, joyous and amiable colloquy! God speaks to man, the King of Heaven converses with his corruptible servant!

It was vain to demand of these men, themselves in need of training, that they should instruct the people. Hoping for such times as might bring seminaries and produce educated, zealous priests, Tikhon devoted himself to the task of teaching his clergy, and in the course of the year 1763 he wrote a book *On the Duties of a Priest—On the seven Sacraments.* It was followed by a *Charte*, a graphic history of dogma intended as reference for his clergy. Its rubrics showed, synoptically, the Seven Œcumenical Councils, their date, purpose, their main participants, the problem of heresy discussed, and the conciliar decision. In February 1764 he published *A Register of what is required of a priest that he may behave in a seemly manner in church and that he may adequately fulfil his duties*; next came out *A Supplement to the book on the duty of a priest: on the Mystery of Confession.* Clergy were asked to make use themselves of sacramental confession, and not only to administer it to their flock. Worded simply and with warmth, this booklet taught the priest to be strict with sin and gentle with the sinner. It begged him to show the penitent that sin is not a transgression of some particular law, but an act of ingratitude against the living love of God. The priest was to awaken in a penitent the firm intention to mend his ways.

These measures were accompanied by administrative ones concerning public worship. He decreed that churches should be kept clean and fenced, in order to safeguard them from dirt and to prevent the intrusion of animals. He gave strict rules concerning the careful handling of sacred objects, and especially the reserved Sacrament, which he sometimes discovered in vessels of brass and tin; the civil authorities were approached and asked to make provision for the sufficient supply and preservation of church wine (September-October 1763, March 1765). Following the recommendations of the *Spiritual Regulations*, he forbade the accumulation of private icons in the churches. He treated places of worship with the greatest care and respect, but had no liking for the gilded frames, brocades, silks and jewellery which adorned so many Russian churches. "Every church building, provided it is clean, can be used for church worship," he would say, turning people's zeal from making altar-cloths and vestments to clothing the poor, a duty which they overlooked.[8]

Disciplinary steps were taken against bureaucracy and sloth in the Consistory. Its members deemed themselves far superior to the ordinary clergy, whom they disregarded and often addressed most offensively.

Tikhon upbraided officials for rudeness to lower clergy, just as he protested against the law which allowed corporal punishment to be inflicted on priests (3 September 1763).[9]

"If you have to punish, do it unwillingly and avoid scolding and reproaching, for this is to abuse your authority," became Tikhon's habitual remark (10 September 1765). He proposed to accelerate administrative procedure by adding to the Consistory a member elected by the clergy (20 December 1763 and 23 January 1766). When the Consistory made light of some man's offence on the ground that he had good testimonials from certain officers, Tikhon replied sternly: "The ecclesiastical administration has no business with the world" (8 March 1765). He forbade the unauthorized use of vehicles which were often taken from the peasants, and fixed the price for hiring such transport (3 January 1764).

On the other hand, he forbade the clergy to travel without leave of absence (9 August and 10 December 1766). If they wished to officiate outside their church or diocese, they were to present certificates of authorization. These measures aimed in part at bringing to an end scandalous irregularities in the celebration of marriages involving minors or bigamists—cases common enough in this region of fluctuating population. Yet, when peasants and gentry treated their parish clergy in careless fashion (there were even instances of beating), Tikhon stood up for them. He had the offended clergy transferred, and even advised them to stop visiting, provided that baptisms were continued. The clergy themselves were rough men: they drank and quarrelled. He forbade them to enter public-houses, and threatened them with heavy fines if they were found drunk. He criticized the customary overeating and drinking just before the fasting at Lent. "I speak not against wine. Why should one not have some bodily comfort on a festival when man is glad, so that rejoicing in soul and in body, he may give thanks to God? It is not drink I object to, but drunkenness." In another context he repeated again that "wine in itself is good like any other creation of God," and advised the abstinent not to fall into another sin—

that of excessive self-esteem—("for Satan too never drinks"). Drinking was often the cause of disorders and quarrels. Tikhon not only reprimanded a priest for quarrelling with his colleague (30 November 1764), but, somewhat naïvely, forbade those who felt at enmity with anyone to celebrate the Eucharist.

The Bishop soon realized that his regulations would remain merely theoretical unless they were accompanied by sanctions. He had no patience with slack clergy. He was too young, too inexperienced and too quick-tempered to wait for them to change. So he became a strict disciplinarian and decided to touch their pockets—in the hope, doubtless, that in this way at least he might bring home to them the gravity of their offences. This severity was his way of being just. He was invested with authority, and would have to answer for his flock at the Last Judgment. If he could not convert his clergy to sincere and loving service to their flock, he would at least make them carry out their duty and prevent a divine institution from being dishonored by an unworthy priest. He laid down few regulations, but he demanded that they should be obeyed. There was nothing arbitrary in his actions. In practical affairs his zeal was often the zeal of a novice, but it was a very different thing from the personal passion of so many of his contemporaries and predecessors, who thought nothing of scolding, beating and terrifying their clergy. On the contrary, he strove constantly to enhance man's sense of dignity, and especially to raise the clergy in their own eyes and in those of other people.

The thirteen monasteries of the diocese were no consolation to Tikhon. Discipline and morals were slack. The monks would not be likely to understand complicated spiritual teaching. Tikhon insisted that at least the rite of profession be read aloud every now and again during meals as a sadly needed reminder to the monks of the promises and vows which they had made (1763). Superiors were told to report cases of absence to the Bishop, and monks were forbidden to wander about without the permission of their superior (15 December 1765). Drunkenness in monasteries was particularly hateful to Tikhon. He would say that he would rather see a monk eating meat in Lent than see him drunk. He warned the monks against visiting bereaved families where the mourners ended a vigil by excessive libations. Only a superior, accompanied by a deacon, was allowed to join in such ceremonies (17 May 1765). Over and over again Tikhon protested against drunkenness (22 August 1767). He ordered that a monk guilty of this offence be kept for three days on a reduced diet, but that he be given as much water or kvass[10] as he desired. This modification showed that Tikhon did not ignore bodily needs. Strict diet was to be enforced in cases of recurrent fault, in which case the man might eventually be deprived of all ready cash and provided with his necessities by the monastic bursar according to the instructions of the superior (22 August 1767).

Later he came in closer contact with certain monks, but even then his correspondence with them did not differ much from the letters addressed to some of his friends in the world.

Tikhon discouraged hasty monastic professions. When (Kornily) the Archimandrite of Zadonsk monastery informed him of a tradesman who desired to adopt a life devoted to God, Tikhon replied: "Let him simply stay for a while among the brethren; the black habit will not work salvation. A man in lay garb yet clothed with obedience, humility and charity, is in any case an untonsured monk" (21 November 1763).

In the community at Zadonsk he met a monk who became his closest friend—Father Matvey, later known as Mitrophan.[11] He trusted this man in matters of charity and in the distribution of alms, and was glad to entrust a postulant to him. On 25 April 1767, he wrote:

> Father Matvey, receive this new sheep of Christ. Instruct and edify one another spiritually, and pray for me a sinner. As for yourself, strive in the Lord, do not give in. Remember the passion of Christ and His Judgment. Read books, and you will better understand the way of the Lord, by which you will reach life eternal.[12]

In his work in the diocese Tikhon showed himself to be a real educationalist and evangelist. He had to begin with the clergy, but there was no place for training them. The seminary, founded in 1721 by Bishop Lev Yurlov, at which a Slavo-Latin school was started, had come to naught. Only two Slav schools existed in the diocese, both for beginners. Owing to the lack of means, Tikhon felt it more practical to concentrate all the pupils in the existing school at the town of Ostrogozhsk and in Yeletz, which was supported by small contributions from clergy and lower ecclesiastics. Deacon Maxim Efimov from Lebediansk was attached to this school as a teacher. Parents did not see the point of education. Tikhon had to decree that the clergy must send their sons (27 February 1765) and that families must send at least one boy. The best pupils were to be kept for further training.

Arrangements were made at a desperately slow pace. Tikhon provided timber for repairs and accommodated the boys provisionally in a monastery. Some regulations were laid down as to annual reports. The temporary teachers were priest Nikita of the Nativity in the lower forms and the Latinist Ivan Solntzev (31 March and 24 October 1765). Abuses began to creep in. A clerk, Kushansky, and a deacon, Ivan Korniliev, accepted bribes in cash and kind for letting the boys go home before the end of their training.[13] The Cossacks objected to education and did not desire a seminary to be established. "Lack of funds" was the pretext for not restoring the school which had previously existed in Cherkassy. Tikhon, losing patience, had the school opened by forceful methods (September 1766) and Cossack boys were sent there under the threat of a fine if they failed to attend.

In January 1766 the question of funds and accommodation was settled. The Economic College at last granted an annual income of 665 roubles, which was sufficient to support pupils and teachers. The best scholars from Ostrogozhsk and Yeletz were moved into the Bishop's house. Tikhon must have been reminded of his own school years at Novgorod. His nephew Philip, the son of his brother Efimy, was among the pupils. The Bishop managed to get five teachers from the Academy of Kiev and the College of Kharkov. Vassily

Lukianov was appointed Prefect, and the teacher of Rhetoric, Peter Liubinovsky of Kharkov, soon became the Vice-Prefect.[14]

In 1765 Tikhon compiled *Instructions for Seminarists*.[15]

Tikhon's daily life began to assume a more regular course. His mornings were dedicated to diocesan business. This involved frequent investigation into complaints and disputes. He could at times be impatient and even harsh with offenders, but he did everything he could to reconcile people.

"Sir I. L.," he wrote on 4 December 1764: "be reconciled, do not take vengeance upon the son of Captain Th. L. who is innocent of the offence done to you by his father.... This, my poor scrap of paper, will be an indictment against you and a testimony for me before the Judgement of Christ."[16]

Tikhon dined early and rested for about an hour. People came to see him. He spent the shortest possible time with visitors, unless they had genuine spiritual or physical needs. He took care to avoid worldly conversations. The poor were given precedence by him: to them he was as liberal with his time as with his alms; they could be admitted to him at any hour. He adopted reading as his recreation, continuing the study of the Fathers, and above all of his beloved St. John Chrysostom. He never went to bed before he had finished all his daily tasks or before he had prepared the next day's urgent business. He kept to his habit of late hours and night work. Indeed, without it he would not have been able to complete all his work and to produce all the written treatises of this period. We do not know what was his method of private prayer in that period, nor the time he allotted to it. He always carried the Psalter in his pocket—which in any case he knew by heart. He always read the Bible, and read it with devotion. Perhaps his most touching and sorrowful prayers were made during the night, when he wrote for his blind flock all those Instructions and Exhortations, with their careful enumeration of points—the words of prayer suddenly piercing through the somewhat scholastic form.

This was a period of intensive literary activity. The writings, mainly an answer to the specific needs of his flock, were somewhat schematic. Nevertheless, these writings were of importance, for in them he was able to give guidance to his clergy and to reach those people in his vast diocese whom he could not see personally. And in any case they were the first works of the kind to be written in Russia. The importance of such attempts to supplement the clergy's inadequate instruction and to supply a practical guide for their daily life was very considerable.

In 1765 he produced several works: *On the righteous judgment and keeping of the oath*—for the use of ecclesiastical administrators. Then, mainly for the seminaries and the cregy, *The Exhortation to the ministers of the Church*, a warning against drink, an exhortation to sobriety of speech, to brotherly love and to the forgiveness of offences; also to worthy preparation for the sacred ministry and to continuation therein, to attentive reading of the Gospels and Epistles, to the diligent absolving of sinners, to comforting the sick. This was "the booklet in ten points" that made him familiar to most of the clergy. The rest of his writings during this period can be described as moral and pastoral theology addressed to lay folk. For instance: *A brief Exhortation of what each Christian should be mindful of from infancy till death. Some notes chosen from the Holy Scripture which rouse a sinner from the slumber of sin and call him to repentance, with some examples thereof. An Exhortation to prompt conversion, for the benefit of every soul.* He wrote next *An Instruction on the duty of the Christian parents to their children and on the duty of the children to their parents.* Then, prompted by the excesses of Carnival week, he wrote *A word on the week preceding Lent.* In the spring, after he had witnessed a popular festival of pagan and immoral character, he wrote *The Exhortation to the inhabitants of Voronezh to abolish the annual festival named Yarilo.* Next he wrote four books of meditations and extracts from the Fathers, particularly from St. John Chrysostom—*The Flesh and the Spirit.*

Education of the popular masses went side by side with the training of the seminarists and of the clergy. Priests were instructed to preach and to interpret the Scriptures. On the Sundays of 1765 Tikhon himself delivered a regular course of instruction to his flock. Next he obtained from the Moscow Slavo-Greco-Latin Academy—possibly by consultation with

Platon Levshin—a lay preacher, Ivan Trubin. Later, Bishop Tikhon ordained him deacon.[17]

Every Sunday, about an hour before the celebration of Divine Service, the bells rang to call the people that they might listen to an exhortation. Trubin was advised "to speak clearly and briefly on things pertaining to salvation." He gave an explanation of the Lesson of the day, supporting it by references to the Gospel and to the Fathers, by examples from sacred and secular history and by an appeal "to natural reason." His Bishop advised him not to enter into complex points of theology, but rather to appeal to the people's moral sense, to call them to repentance and to the proper love and fear of God as opposed to superstition. The preacher was also taught to speak of the social evils, though in a tone of love and humility rather than in one of indictment. To safeguard him against the criticism of conservative people who would regard such series of talks in the church as an unprecedented innovation, Bishop Tikhon reminded everybody of the *Spiritual Regulation*, which stressed preaching and instruction as one of the first duties of the Church.

On Saturday the subject of the next day's talk was announced to the people. The clergy were expected to attend, unless they had themselves been celebrating the early service or lived too far away, and the Bishop kept check on these attendances. He cherished the scheme of sending out catechists throughout the whole diocese. His own pamphlets on various subjects were distributed and posted up in many churches.

The Sunday opening of public-houses was one of his concerns at this time. He begged the authorities to forbid the selling of drink, if only in the early hours of Sunday, especially since there were Government regulations to this effect (27 October 1722) which few observed (16 June 1765).

On 25 May 1765 he saw the inhabitants of the whole town and neighboring villages assembled in the market-place and wandering through the streets singing, dancing, kissing, and liberally indulging in drink. A man, embodying the mythical Yarilo—spring, blossoming, fertility—was adorned with ribbons and little bells on his clothes, and wore a cap of bright paper. This procession was an annual event after Pentecost unknown in many other parts of Russia.[18] Bishop Tikhon's coach stopped in the square, and he begged the riotous crowd to desist from pagan customs. He nearly wept with shame and sorrow, calling them from the deity of lust to the God of love. He invited people to his house, sought to show them the coarseness and wickedness of these amusements and preached about them in the cathedral. He asked clergy to warn their flock against superstition; he even expressed the somewhat naïve hope that those in power would protect the people from themselves by forbidding this occasion of sin. His sermon became widely known and was often reprinted. The Yarilo festival was eventually abolished.

Preaching was a natural outlet for Tikhon's thoughts and anxieties. Many of his undated sermons were later included in his *Works*. To his listeners he must have sounded like the messenger of that Bible which few of them possessed and fewer still could read. His references to the Old and New Testaments enlarged their horizon and enriched their spiritual world, which was otherwise limited to what little they grasped of the fixed lessons of the liturgical year. Some of his sermons can be approximately dated. One was delivered at the consecration of the church of Saints Peter and Paul in Akatovo—probably 29 June 1765, on the Feast of the Apostles. Then he called people in the language of the liturgy, "to lay aside all the cares of this life. Farmers! do not let your thoughts wander away towards your hay-making. Merchants, do not calculate your gains and losses during the service!" The official is advised "not to compile the drafts of reports." The judge is reminded that in a holy place there are no criminals in the earthly sense, but that every mortal is confronted with the righteousness of God. Tikhon's sermon on the Feast of the Holy Cross is typical. In it he reminded his hearers of the burden of suffering of which every man has to bear a part, and stressed that control over one's body is not the duty of monks alone, but of every Christian. Again, speaking on the day on which the Orthodox Church commemorates the Presentation in the Temple of the Virgin Mary, he drew the attention of the faithful to the Word of God which is to be known to all. He also taught how one should listen to it, and apply its message to daily life. His sermon on the day of the Assumption, with its powerful illustrations of social evils, must be considered separately. And the teaching he gives on the official day of Catherine's patron saint (27 October) is strikingly unlike those congratulations—patriotic at their best—of which such sermons usually consisted at this time. He took this opportunity to stress that the duty of the Crown—"as the Empress herself has shown by her various laws and efforts"—is to bring about righteousness, and he proceeded to explain at length the threefold duty of those in power: to God, to their neighbor and to themselves. A very personal note can be heard when he says: "To a Christian, power and authority are nothing but crosses."

At one point in 1766, he spoke with sorrow about the cool response to the efforts of his catechist.

> It is about a year now since the instruction began. People were indifferent enough to the poor man who "sweated" in preparing his instruction and who "collected like a bee" every impression and every bit of knowledge that could edify them. "If it were a case of getting riches, parents would have hastened to bring their sons. But neither do they come nor bring their children to hear someone who teaches how to gather incorruptible treasure. . . . They deem it of utmost importance to hear how to achieve a profit in trade or how to please some man of rank, but least of all do they ponder on the salvation of their souls. . . . In vain does the poor preacher strain his voice for an hour on end."[19]

One is not surprised to find the sad, almost tormented expression on his face as he is depicted in a portrait painted during his life in Voronezh. He is represented in episcopal robes, with a fine hand lifted in blessing and the pastoral staff in his left hand. He looks young, his features are regular, his fair and slightly wavy hair falls on to his shoulders. There is a shade of bitterness if not haughtiness in the expression of his lips. His large and somewhat slanting eyes are downcast, almost half-closed. It is an intelligent face, but certainly not a happy one.

Tikhon made several personal visits to parts of his widespread diocese. He was not always welcome. There were instances of peasants refusing to supply him and his attendants with horses. "You are not our boss," he was told in one village; "it is only the clergy who are under you."[20] Tikhon in this period of his life was hot-tempered, exacting, unbending. Like so many people without practical experience, he was eager to enforce things which in themselves were indubitably right, and which in his eyes were even more important, since they led to the realm of eternal salvation. It was only several years after his retirement that the sincerity of his care for the people was generally appreciated.

The opposition which he encountered was mainly due to the local situation, to disputes concerning the Old Belief and to the political struggle of the Cossacks against the attempt by the hard hand of the North to centralize power. Similar difficulties were experienced by the Bishop of Kazan.[21] In the eyes of the Cossacks, Tikhon was an official; no matter how great the strength of his personality showed itself to be, they withstood all regulations originating from Voronezh. Their chief wrote to the Bishop, advising him not to interfere with the schools, for, according to local tradition, the children of the clergy on the Don did not come under ecclesiastical jurisdiction, but under that of the Don Host.[22] Tikhon complained to the Synod about the Cossacks' infringements upon his duties. They would appoint or dismiss the clergy as they wished, and would sometimes reduce them once more to the rank of laymen and Cossacks.

There is an episode in the life of Tikhon that requires some elucidation. It is his action against the Old Believers. The biographies mention briefly that he set up a Commission to investigate the problem of the schism in the Don region, "not in a spirit of aggression but rather as a measure of defence."[23] According to the *Spiritual Regulation*, a bishop was to be informed by his clergy whether the people under their care partook regularly of the sacraments. If they did not do so, it was often a sign that they belonged to the schism. Tikhon frequently expressed the conviction that the schism was mainly the result of gross ignorance and superstition. He warned simple folk not to enter into long discussions, of which the schismatics were rather fond, and to evade all confusion by a humorous device, saying that in all matters they believed "as the Church did" and, if asked how then did the Church believe, by answering "just as we do." Many of Tikhon's contemporaries wrote about the Old Believers. He left no such writings. He was obviously more concerned with the general evangelization of the masses; possibly he hoped that in a fuller and purer Church life any schism would vanish of itself. But it was the duty of the Orthodox clergy to combat the Old Belief. The shortage of educated clergy made this task still more difficult.[24]

The Bishop was unable to reach all parts of his vast diocese personally. The Commission set up in the fortress of St. Dimitry, which could not but remain unpopular, was placed under the direction of Vassily Mikhailov, a deacon of the Cossack village (staniza) Sirotinsk, who lived in the Ascension Kremensky monastery. The Bishop asked to be notified of those who were willing to return to the Church (23 October 1763). He advised that those who had lately joined the schism and had then returned to the fold should be closely observed and not received for full communion until their intentions became quite clear (13 January 1765). A priest, Ivan Vassiliev, was to give them instruction. They were to perform odd jobs for the church and were paid a couple of kopeks a day.[25]

The episode appears in a very different light when treated by a Cossack historian. "The advocates sent out by Bishop Tikhon routed the near-by villages (staniza) and tried to impress the true faith upon the Old Believers. They carried the men back with them to the fortress of St. Dimitry; fire and the rack were the means of persuasion. But the Cossacks thrust back the intruders and arrested one of their own leaders who tried to help them. Outposts on the river Sala were taken away under the pretext that there were not enough horses. The Cossacks proved obdurate to the point of fanaticism, in their sympathies to the Old Belief."

In 1767 the priest Alexis of the staniza Yarizhenskaya was sent for three years to a monastery, whilst a deacon, Vlas Fedotov, "an open blasphemer and odiously superstitious man," was deprived of his rank and sent to the Voronezh Governmental Chancellory. The "books of sorcery" found on him were burnt in his presence. The question of the Don schism was brought up by the Synod in 1769.

Considering the manners of the times, one is inclined to give some credence to this account. The question of Tikhon's personal responsibility for these cruelties is somewhat different. He had an over-simplified conviction that "those in power" could stop the popular masses from doing wrong—he had asserted this belief on the occasion of the festival of Yarilo. But nothing seems to prove that he was aware of the measures of coercion and torture that are spoken of now. In fact, the same narrative seems to indicate that little notice was taken of him. "There was an order to send the schismatic Cossacks to the Bishop of Voronezh, but this order was not carried out."[26]

A later incident in Tikhon's life seems to bear out the theory that he was not personally involved in the persecution. It took place possibly in 1768, but may be mentioned at this point. The "priestly" branch of the Old Believers who were anxious to maintain the apostolic succession had tried various means of securing valid ordination, and among other methods they had approached Tikhon, who declined this honor. Whatever the details, this incident shows that the Old Believers felt for him none of the animosity which one might have expected from them had he been regarded as the instigator of the persecution.[27]

Not all Tikhon's life was, however, struggle and stress. There were in it those compensating moments of joy which came from acts of charity. "The joy in love of a fellow-man is a forestate of life eternal."[28] Then, there were friendships.

Mitrophan (Matvey) was the nearest to him of the monks, and, among lay people, the Bekhteiev family, especially their son Nikander. Tikhon visited their estate, and seized the opportunity when they journeyed to St. Petersburg to send a donation to his people and village. There were also the Rostovtzevs of the town Yeletz, of which, Cheboratev relates, his Bishop often said, "It is not Yeletz, it should be called Sion." Rostovtzev (Gregory Fedorovich, whom the biographies mention as "probably a tradesman") must have been a man of character, if it is he whose name we discover on the list of the deputies whom Catherine called from all classes throughout the country to assist the Commission in the Project of the New Code of Laws.[29] Michail and Dimitry, Rostovtzev's sons, often helped Tikhon in distributing alms.

Another person very dear to Tikhon was a certain tradesman, Kosma Ignatievich Studenikin, warden of the Prokovsky Church. Tikhon also kept in touch with some of his old friends; no letters have been found or published, but it has been mentioned that he wrote to Simon Lagov, to Levshin and to Gabriel Petrov, who were pursuing their high ecclesiastical careers.

Tikhon's relations with the officials and the upper class do not seem to have been very friendly. Though most of the wealthy "were professed Orthodox, who loved erecting churches and casting church bells, who observed the seasons of fasting and distributed alms on a feast-day, they were headstrong and revengeful. . . . People were afraid of meeting some of the landowners, who used to go about accompanied by deserters or gipsies, thus turning a hunt into a marauding expedition and flogging poorer folk."[30]

The following letter makes clear Tikhon's attitude towards such ostentatious persons.

> Alexander Ivanovich, my benefactor. Thank you for your love. What I told you about the church, I explain again in this letter and give you the following advice: make a church not too high, so that it may be used summer and winter, that is, a warm one, with a stove. Take as an example, the newly built Voronezh cathedral church. As for reaching up too high, I do not advise it. Make it less of a loss to yourself and it will no longer be a burden to the peasants. The parishioners, the priest, the clergy and

yourselves will find it more restful and pleasant to stand in a warm building; you surely agree that this is true. As for the boastful people who want to fly up to the clouds and without any humanity, skin their peasants to the last of their possessions in the meantime, do not listen to them, do not imitate them.

One day they will see that by building churches in this fashion they minister not to Divine glory but to their own vanity; and the tall churches will not help them in the slightest when they see the tears of the peasants shed before the dreadful judge, Christ; then will they be perturbed and terrified. What is the use of building churches and of destroying living temples? What is the use of raising high walls and leaving the peasants half-naked, without food, salt and the primary necessities of life? This is tyranny and not devotion. Christ says in the Gospel, "I desire mercy and not sacrifice." Think over what I am writing to you. Take advice, and reflect, and build. Truly, I advise this for your benefit. May God give you understanding and help. Entrusting you and all your houschold to him, I remain your servant and well-wisher, Bishop Tikhon of Zadonsk.[31]

A sharp personal clash took place once, between the Bishop and a landowner. Tradition relates that Tikhon was discussing matters of faith with a "Voltairian." Having no further reply to Tikhon's argument, the flighty nobleman raised his voice, and suddenly struck Tikhon in the face. And Tikhon, himself such a hot-tempered person, fell on his knees and begged the man's forgiveness for having so exasperated him. If one is to believe the family tradition of the irritable nobleman, Tikhon disagreed with his architectural whims: he wished to have a church on the river bank with a belfry separated from the main building, facing it from the other side. Tikhon said that this was not the usual type of sacred architecture. Whichever tradition is correct, the slap on Tikhon's face and his prostration are indisputable facts.[32]

Muscovy was giving way to urban and westernized fashions. Elizabeth had introduced the Versailles "politesse," the word Russians used for social polish, and which, without finding its equivalent in Russian, became yet another foreign term meaning "manners." She introduced gambling as a means of passing time, and this was becoming a real passion throughout the country. The two capitals strove in pursuit of western graces, culture and art. New discoveries of mineral resources in the land, the development of quarries and mines in the Urals played their part in the growth of luxury, in the wearing of precious stones by both men and women and in the craze for building which affected all Russia.[33] The architectural monuments of the century had their counterpart in the provinces, where everyone tried his hand at original houses with intricate parks, ponds and greenhouses. Servants were dressed in colored jackets and court-shoes; a serf, whose ear was tweaked at one hour of the day, would appear at some other hour in a heavy wig. The magnificence of the royal favorites, although short-lived, encouraged the lower strata of society to imitate them and led many to a life of luxury, bribery and debts.

There were two ways of facing the problem of social injustice. One was individual charity, and if people did not always attend the catechism, they could not fail to recognize the boundless compassion of their Bishop. Almshouses and prisons received from his house regular donations in money and kind, particularly on the occasion of festivals. Dressed as a simple monk, and under cover of darkness, he would visit the houses of the poor; he would enter, and leave on a table a purse or some necessary object. Another remedy was the education of those in power. If they would not listen to him as a private person and a Christian, they were bound to attend the services on State occasions and on big festivals. This may explain why the sermons of Tikhon touch only lightly upon the actual events remembered by the Church, and turn instead to accusations and exhortations concerning the social evils of his time.

Such is the well-known Sermon on the Assumption of the Virgin Mary which he preached in Voronezh. It was obviously delivered to a large congregation. "I see," he began, "the clergy, the high officials and the military chiefs, the soldiers, our defenders, and those of the courts of justice who with their collaborators sit day and night working out justice, and I see the useful merchant class, and people of all conditions." This gave him an excellent opportunity of speaking to them on the true faith which finds its expression in life and in deeds of love. Avoiding generalities, he took illustrations from their daily life.[34]

Tikhon's plea to his clergy "to stand up, to speak up" against any manner of injustice was no mere theory. He did so himself. This attitude was far from making him popular with those at the top of the social scale.

Humanly speaking, alone, often in spiritual isolation, misunderstood by most of those who surrounded him, overworked, he felt no power in himself to carry on. His health was completely undermined. There were days when he felt incapable of meeting anyone. His active life and the urgency of his duties made no provision even for a short break. He needed some peace and solitude to restore the forces of resistance and love. His courage failed him. He wrote to the Synod again asking to be set free from the episcopal robe, which, he said, was "too heavy for him." As there was a delay in the reply, he wrote again, insisting that he was physically incapacitated either for administrative duties or for celebrations. If the Synod did not think it possible to relieve him, could he at least be allowed to retire to the Zadonsk monastery till his health was restored? (16 March 1766.) There was no reply at all. In April 1767 Tikhon fell seriously ill and sent a note to his friend Mitrophan. "I am now at the Trinity monastery. Come up here speedily if you want to see me before I die, for I feel exceedingly weak." It was then that he took the decision to address the Empress directly. He begged to be allowed to retire to some community of his diocese and to be granted some small pension.

Then at last the Synod presented a report to Catherine; the resignation was officially accepted by her on 17 December 1767, and the successor was nominated on the same date. It was Tikhon II (Yakubovsky, the suffragan of Moscow).[35]

One of Tikhon I's last acts as a bishop was to help the

people of the town of Livny, which had suffered from a fire. He never forgot those who "wander about homeless, with wives and small children" and sometimes suffer from "the most inhuman thieves who loot from a fire, and thus ruin poor people who are already being ruined."[36] He went about raising funds, and was eager that they should reach the sufferers at an early date. He followed up this case after his retirement.

> Father Mitrophan—he wrote in 1768—I am sending you one hundred and fifty roubles by this messenger. Two Voronezh citizens gave them to me for alms. I send them to you, to distribute, that is, to go personally to the town Livny and share the money among those whose houses have been burnt down, the poorest ones. Or entrust this distribution to some reliable man, that he may do it without fail. Do it, make an effort, please do not refuse, it will do your soul good. Tell no one the name of the sender; say simply that you have been instructed to give it all to those in Livny who have suffered from the fire. May the Lord have mercy upon you and preserve you in life everlasting. Your servant and brother, Bishop Tikhon.[37]

An almshouse was built in Livny thanks to his help and insistence. The local priest, who supervised the construction, reported that the autumn had made the roads impassable, and suggested that a pause be made. Tikhon answered: "For Christ's sake, do try, do what you can that the poor may have some decent place to live in during the winter."

Tikhon was left free to choose any monastery he wished to live in, and was given a liberal pension of five hundred roubles. He received the Synod's order on 3 January 1768. But by this time he had already wound up most of the diocesan business and left his house, asking a friend to settle a few practical matters. People sometimes considered that he committed an act of self-will or disobedience as, before even receiving the official document of resignation, he moved to the monastery of Tolshevo. His official career was ended.

4

Retirement

TIKHON RETIRED TO the monastery of the Transfiguration, situated north-west of Voronezh, on the River Usman. Founded about 1635, this monastery was known as Tolshevo, probably on account of the dense wood which surrounded it. "Just the right spot for monastic life," Tikhon would say; yet apart from its natural location, there was nothing in it to hold any particular attraction for him. Tolshevo, like so many of the less important monasteries, housed soldiers who were sent there for breach of discipline and monks who had committed some grave fault. Morals were therefore sadly slack. Besides, however much Tikhon desired quiet and freedom, his heart was still attached to those whom he had left behind.

He wrote to Mitrophan:

> Father Mitrophan, dear brother in Christ. I have settled down in Tolshevo; we have parted. So be it, don't be sorrowful. My spirit is always united with you all. May the merciful God allow us to be together in the mansions of the Heavenly Father. Greetings to my dear people of Yeletz, to Kosma, his brother and other friends; tell them all of my desire that they may advance in the grace of Christ. I beg you and all of them not to forget me, a sinner, in your prayers. Wherever one is one cannot elude the snares of Satan. The grace of Christ alone is saving. . . . Take money for the eiderdown and do as

as I have told you: sell everything and use the proceeds for alms. If it is possible, retrieve the money that was given to the villagers of Utkino for firewood and distribute it to the poor of Yeletz. But if those of Utkino will not give it back, let them keep it. . . . I have nothing of my own, all is God's and not ours. . . . Your unworthy Tikhon.

His friends obviously missed him. Another of his letters, dated Tolshevo 1768, bears witness to this:

Father Mitrophan, brother to me in Christ. Do not be sorrowful because I have departed from you all. My spirit is with you all constantly; indeed I tell the truth, I do not lie. Stand fast, stand fast. It is for this that you became a monk; it was this that you promised at your profession. Soon the end will come, it will come, it will not tarry, and all who have endured to the end will be saved. To all my friends at Yeletz, to Kosma and his brother, my greetings. I beg you and all of them to pray for me. Your servant Tikhon, U.B.[1]

Much as he tried to comfort his friends, he himself found no peace. The people who surrounded him were utterly uncongenial. The Superior[2] and the monks were ardent supporters of the Old Belief. Moreover, some monasteries resented the presence in their midst of a retired bishop. Though he no longer had any official jurisdiction over them, a retired bishop was still entitled to certain privileges, and he could investigate the life of the community. If he wished to take part in the services, his presence required additional rites; for instance, if he came to the liturgy, he had to be clothed in ceremonial vestments, and a special small carpet, embroidered with an eagle, had to be placed before his feet.

It was thought that Tikhon was in disgrace. His successor had no consideration for him. The cathedral of Voronezh, which had sprung to life owing to his energy, was consecrated on 30 December 1768, but he did not go; possibly he was not even invited. Tikhon II even wrote to the Synod questioning his predecessor's right to celebrate divine service if he should wish to do so. The Synod, it is true, answered (29 May 1769) that this question was beside the point—Tikhon did not celebrate owing to ill-health. Nevertheless there must have been puzzled rumors as to why the Bishop had resigned at such an early age.[3]

This atmosphere of suspicion, calumny and misunderstanding was unbearable. In vain Tikhon spent hours gardening or working in the fields. His health, which had begun to mend during the summer, grew worse again towards the autumn.

It is possible that the episode of the Old Believers asking Tikhon to become one of them did take place whilst he was in Tolshevo. But if, as the story runs, he answered that there was no validity in their sacraments, one can understand the anger of the Superior of Tolshevo, who was devoted to their cause.

The tension, his spiritual solitude, the absence of any one who could give him advice or direction, all contributed as much to his ill-health as local water and the damp close atmosphere emanating from the forests and marshes. Therefore Tikhon took a drastic step: he decided to change his residence.

The obscure sixteenth-century monastery of the Virgin Mary, on a tributary of the Don—Zadonsk by its geographical name—to which Tikhon now moved, was familiar to him. It was situated in the midst of the growing village of Teshevka. More than once it had been burned down; it was simple and poor. Its few stone buildings dated from 1740. Teshevka became State property in 1764, and the monastery had hardly any revenues.

Again, though he lived in a monastery, Tikhon had the right to possess private property, to live entirely on his own, to take part in the life of the community or to shut himself off from it. He chose to live in a separate small apartment above the porch. His two cell-attendants, a cook and a servant, were with him. They formed a little community apart—not an unusual occurrence in a Russian monastery. But it may also have been a subject of gossip, and the Superior showed no delight at this new arrival.[4]

This year 1769 was not an easy one for Tikhon. He came to Zadonsk in a troubled spirit. He avoided people, stayed locked in his cell, could be heard there pacing quickly up and down, sometimes sighing deeply as he chanted verses of the Psalms which speak of distress. Faced with the freedom and the solitude which he had so much desired (though both were far from complete), he suddenly found emptiness. His physical strength had returned, and there he was with nothing to do, with long, unoccupied hours, and with a pension of 500 roubles a year in return for his idleness. He was suddenly deprived of a sense of direction and peace, he was all nerves, he frequently lost his temper and caused discontent even among his servants by his exacting and brusque ways. (It was in 1770 that Chebotarev and Efimov, later his biographers, became his cell-attendants, and remained with him till his death.)

He had once advised a monk who desired to leave his monastery to exercise patience and to stay where he was. "For if we do not wish to follow Christ who humbled himself for our sake, what are our vows" of baptism and profession?[5] He had told a monk that misunderstanding could prove to be a way of union with Christ, who was scorned and dishonored by men. "A narrow way is at first terrifying and painful, but later it becomes pleasant, peaceful, quiet and gay."[6]

"Later" was a horizon full of promise, yet vague. In the meantime, he struggled with himself and gained a deeper knowledge of his limitations. On several occasions he returned to the thought of temptation. "It is like an emetic," he wrote very realistically, "*it* reveals what there is inside us."[7] He tried to see evil in its fullness.

> It sometimes happens that wicked people give a man poison; likewise the serpent of old, the devil, pours deadly poison into our nature. This poison tortures the soul and makes it ill. See what pride breeds in a man, how it torments him, what mani-

fold ways it invents in search of the world's honor and glory and praise! Having once grasped them, with what care it keeps this treasure! How indignant a man is if someone despises him! How he sickens, is troubled, grumbles and blasphemes when deprived of honors!

And after speaking of attachment to wealth, of the rebellion of the unsatisfied flesh and of envy, he adds:

> And see what anger can do in a man; how indignant and noisy he becomes, how he swears, how he beats his head, trembling as in a fever.... Man, learn the sickness of thy soul, for without acknowledgment of illness there is no healing.... Christ alone can heal us, who sigh and pray to him with faith.[8]

He was in doubt concerning the path he must now choose. He was much too young and active to accept the pious routine of a small, uninspiring monastery with no spiritual tradition. He wrote about it to Gabriel Petrov.

Gabriel, now Archbishop of St. Petersburg and principal member of the Synod, had become a central figure in ecclesiastical life. The Empress considered him to be a clever and a reasonable man, and had even dedicated to him some time previously her translation of Marmontel's *Belisaire*.[9] He was on most commissions and attended all official solemnities, studied projects for new legislation and prepared his own and various other synodal publications. Under cover of all these activities he concealed the firm intention of fostering contemplative monasticism in Russia. He kept in touch with the "deserts" of Sarov, for they were in direct contact with the monks who brought the ascetico-mystical tradition from Mount Athos, rediscovered there by the Russian monk Paissy Velichkovsky (1722-94).[10] Gabriel was responsible for the reconstruction of the Valaam monastery, and appointed as its superior the Elder Nazary, who, though unlearned, was steeped in the teachings of this spiritual school.

He suggested that Tikhon should assume the direction of

the Iversky Monastery at Valday in the Novgorod diocese.[11] Tikhon, with his biblical and patristic type of spirituality, would have made a valuable contribution to this community, which had begun to follow the ascetico-mystical teachings.

Tikhon's restlessness seems to have been the result of doubt and indecision. A small episode recalled by Cheboratev illustrates it rather well. It happened that he mentioned the possible departure of his Bishop to an elderly monk, Aaron, whom Tikhon held in esteem. The old man replied sharply: "What madness! The Mother of God does not wish him to go." Chebotarev reported these words to Tikhon, who, after he had made sure that such were really the old monk's words, tore to pieces the letter which he was about to send to Gabriel. Nevertheless, his hesitation had not yet come to an end. One day he suddenly rose from the divan on which he had been resting. He looked as though he had undergone a very great strain; sweat covered his face. He said to Chebotarev: "Well, even were I to die, I should not leave this place."[12]

This decision brought him clarity. He organized his life so as to have time for prayer, writing and solitude, as well as for active service to other people.

First, he had to dispose of his possessions. He had brought with him some furniture, several cassocks, fur coats and various episcopal vestments. As for his pension, he made it clear that he would use it in its entirety to meet the needs of others, while he himself would be content with whatever his friends gave him of their charity.

But as soon as he began to distribute his pension he realized that it was no more than a drop in the ocean of poverty around him. His silk cassocks, his fur-lined coat, his good blankets and his silver watch were soon sold. His little apartment began to look quite bare. An old carpet stuffed with straw replaced the mattress, whilst an old sheepskin covered with nankeen served as a blanket; he kept two feather pillows. A cuckoo-clock, a few icons and some pictures of religious character hung on the walls. One of these pictures was a traditional piece of home-made art showing an exhausted old man reposing in a coffin: Tikhon had it nailed at the foot of his bed to remind him of death. He also had a picture of the Passion, perhaps of western origin, and some others representing episodes in the life of Christ. Later he placed a coffin and vestments for his burial in a cupboard hollowed in the wall of his cell.

His crockery was reduced to wooden utensils, two brass kettles and a brass basin, a teapot and two glasses. "He possessed neither trunk nor chest, apart from an old leather bag in which, if on a journey, he would pack some books, a few shirts, a comb, and eight undershirts of white flannel which he liked to change often because of perspiration."[13] A few coarse towels and—perhaps a small concession to the world—handkerchiefs of fine linen completed this baggage.

His clothes consisted of one heavy woollen cassock and two undercassocks for the winter, and the cheapest of furs—hare and sheepskin. He wore woollen stockings fastened by leather thongs. For two winters his indoor shoes were the peasant bast-shoes. His rosary was of leather. Some years later, Tikhon III of Voronezh insisted on giving him a decent garment, which he occasionally wore in church so as not to offend the donor. He seemed always in a hurry to go back to his shabby clothes. "This is all rubbish," he would say to his cell-attendants taking it off: "better hurry on with dinner, I am hungry."

His books were few in number, and he relied much on his excellent memory. He had the Bible, St. John Chrysostom, a few patristic works and two Western authors: Joseph Hall's *Occasional Meditations*—we do not know in what language, probably in Latin—and *True Christianity* by Johann Arndt in a Russian translation.

Tikhon organized his daily life without rigidity. He often spoke of the danger of monotony, and he allowed himself the freedom of changing occupations. He cherished the early hours of quiet, and visitors were asked not to disturb him. Some, however, often tried to disturb his privacy. He begged his servants to dissuade such callers, but when he was unable to avoid a visit "the interview was brief and joyless."

He regularly attended services, and if there were few strangers at an early service he stood in the choir-stalls, sometimes read the lesson and often chanted, preferably the ancient state to the special prayers recited on the birthdays of the royal family, but as the years passed he stopped attending such solemnities. On Easter Monday and Christmas he recited Matins in his episcopal vestments. But since vesting meant that he was dependent on the other clergy and that he might trouble them, he gradually adopted an ordinary monastic cassock or the priest's chasuble for services, and only placed the episcopal omophor (pallium) on his shoulders at the actual moment of receiving Communion, as prescribed by the rubrics. He did not celebrate, but received communion every week. This was unusually frequent, even for an ecclesiastic. It always moved him to tears; sometimes he could be heard sobbing behind the iconostasis.

Between the morning offices, and when he did not attend the late service, he usually wrote, as he also did during long winter evenings. Sometimes he prepared a sermon for the monastery. At other times he insisted that the Superior should order the so-called Synodal Instructions to be read aloud.

If he went to the liturgy he would often stop to speak to simple folk and sometimes he brought friends or a group of children back with him. He never went to the community refectory, though he had his simple meals at the same time. Even so, he often remarked that his meal was much too good, and would remember with an unfeigned pang those who had nothing: "Here I am, eating, and some poor people sit in prison; some have not even enough salt..." Whilst he ate, one of his cell-attendants read to him, mainly from Isaiah, his best-loved prophet. He was often moved, and would put aside his spoon and listen with tears in his eyes. Occasionally a monk or some pilgrim peasant shared his meal, but he never prepared any special dishes for his wealthier visitors. He frequently sent food to sick monks, and he would give orders to his cook if a special diet were required. Though he himself drank no alcohol since his retirement, he kept some spirits for the sick and made liqueurs with herbs which he believed to have medicinal value.

After the midday meal he would lie down for an hour. Then he read the Fathers. The Zadonsk library was poor.

He walked in the garden or went to a grove on the hill. It was in this way that he liked to meditate. He never parted with his Psalter, and often read it while walking. Later in the day people would come to see him. He would go to vespers, then listen again at home to the Scriptures, which Efimov or Chebotarev read aloud to him. He had a habit of interrupting them to ask whether they followed the text, and often he would explain it. Before going to bed he recited the prayers prescribed by the Rule with all the bows, genuflexions and prostrations—this would last long into the night. He slept no more than about four hours at night and an hour after dinner. The loving indiscretion of his servants records for us that Tikhon often knelt for hours or lay prostrate on the floor, his arms outstretched—a gesture reminiscent of the cruciform position which monks assume during the rite of profession. "Lord have mercy. Be patient with our sins. Hear us, Lord!" he would murmur.

The simplicity of his appearance and manners produced a lasting impression upon those around him, though the same simplicity—"bigotry"—did not fail to arouse criticism and scorn in many others. Sometimes he saw people pointing or laughing at him, and he would say to Chebotarev: "Why, the very serfs scorn me; it must be right." Or when the mockeries went too far: "Foolish people, do they not realize how easy it would be for me to stop them?" He avoided troubling his servants, and not only forbade people to attend to his personal needs, but often carried out various domestic duties himself. He gardened, dug and chopped wood. "Come with me," he would call to Chebotarev, "there is a big trunk in the grove; it would make two cartfuls of firewood. Otherwise we should have to buy it." Taking off his cassock, in short sleeves and with Cheboratev's thick gloves on his hands, he was capable of working for hours, cutting down trees. His friends the Bekhteievs presented him with an old horse, which he kept for about three years. Tikhon was fond of "the old man" and liked mowing grass for him. Sitting on a stump, he would talk to Cheboratev, now of the gospels, now "using the leaves or grass for his parables," now telling him many stories of his childhood. Often he expressed his regret at having to comply with the ceremonies expected of a Russian bishop, even in retirement. "If it had been possible I should have resigned not only my rank but even the hood and cassock; I should have gone to some remote community, there to do menial jobs as a peasant: to bake, to chop wood, to fetch water."[14]

He spoke approvingly of the Greek monastic customs which allowed utter simplicity and enabled a man, once he had resigned his office, to return to a purely monastic, non-episcopal status.

It must have been the same group of men whom Gabriel Petrov had met who drew Tikhon's attention to the monasteries of Mount Athos. He was also in touch with the monks of Sarov: they exchanged letters, but unfortunately no trace of them remains.[15]

There were one or two sites in the neighboring woods which particularly appealed to Tikhon. Their solitude, the thick foliage, the sudden rays of sun which illumined the glades and the ripple of a stream would cause him to repeat: "Is this not like a paradise on earth!" He spent long hours, digging hard, in two such spots, similar in this respect to so many Russian hermits; he even made a well.

A natural enough association of ideas between the stream and the continuous flow of life caused him to compose a meditation entitled: *The Waters which flow by*. The imagery, reminiscent of some pages of the *Imitation of Christ*, was very characteristic of him. His thoughts seem to have turned to some great river—the Don or perhaps the Volkhov of his youth, with its yellowish spring floods and the sharp clash of colors at sunset.

> We see the water of a river flowing uninterruptedly and passing away, and all that floats on its surface, rubbish or beams of trees, all pass by. Christian! So does our life. . . . I was an infant, and that time has gone. I was an adolescent, and that too has passed. I was a young man, and that too is far behind me. The strong and mature man that I was is no more. My hair turns white, I succumb to

age, but that too passes; I approach the end and will go the way of all flesh. I was born in order to die. I die that I may live. Remember me, O Lord, in thy Kingdom! I have been in good and bad health, now strong and now sick, and that too has passed. . . . I knew many honors; they also have gone. . . . People used to show me respect, to bow down to me; time has passed; I see no more of this. I have known gladness and sorrow, I have rejoiced and I have wept; the same happens to me now but, as the days go by, sorrow and gladness, joy and tears go with them. I have been praised and exalted, I have been criticized and abused; and the same who praised me, have cursed; and those who abused have turned to praise me . . . such is human constancy! Poor is man from his mother's womb to his grave. Born with a cry, he lives, tossed up and down as a ship on the sea, and dies with tears. . . . I used to live in a house of plenty, then in a hut. . . . Now again I live in a poor place, and this too will pass. . . . I have sat down to a rich meal and to a scanty one. . . . I have tasted things sweet and bitter. . . . I have listened to sweet music; it grew silent, and with it went my pleasure. I was well clad, I drove in a coach, surrounded by servants and serfs. . . . I had friends— some have become enemies, some have become false brethren. Where are the times when I was driven in a coach and four? Where are the days of reproach and unhappiness? These too pass away. Such is our existence in this world. Not thus will be the life to come, of what the Word of God and our faith assure us. Once begun, that life will never end. No illness, age, decrepitude, death or corruption will assail our body; it will become a spiritual, incorruptible, immortal body, whole, light and healthy. There will be peace, joy, comfort and bliss without end. The elect will see God face to face and will reign with Christ as members with the Head. And endless too will be the fatal eternity where the con-

demned will die all over again and will long for
death, and suffer and see no comfort.

As was his wont, he enumerated a few points in conclusion:
(1) to adopt a detached attitude to life; (2) to take
no pride in passing honors; (3) not to fall into despondency
when in trouble; (4) to suffer generously reproach and calumny, which God can turn into a blessing (Ps. 109. 28);
(5) to realize that he who bears this life's vicissitudes with
equanimity and patience knows rest and peace, dwells in a
Christ-like life, experiencing here on earth celestial joy and
foretasting in this passing life the sweetness of life eternal.[16]

A great deal of Tikhon's time was given to people in
need of help. He liked to talk to the peasants, and as he
often wore a shabby cloak, and as his speech was natural
and his language simple, they told him more of their troubles
than they would have revealed to a bishop. His support was
appropriate and substantial; here he would give a cow, there
a harrow, or grain in season, or timber for repairs, or a dowry
for a girl who otherwise would have been unable to marry.
It did not take long for the tale of his generosity to spread.
Crowds of people in need came daily to his door. Zadonsk
began to be like a place of pilgrimage, but, unlike pilgrims,
these suppliants brought no profit to the community. When
there was a dearth of crops, many came to live in Zadonsk
at Tikhon's expense. His five hundred roubles were quickly
spent; then he appealed to the generosity of others. Peasants
who wandered about in small bands in search of winter occupation made a habit of calling at Zadonsk. If there were
any sick, they were left in Tikhon's care; he personally looked
after the invalids, brought them tea twice or three times a
day—a great treat for a poor Russian—sat by their bedside
comforting them with affectionate words. If any died, his
cell-attendant and cook dug a grave and Tikhon attended the
funeral. In this way he would avoid giving extra trouble to
the monks or serfs of the monastery.

It became customary for charitable people to supply him
with vegetables, corn, wine and money. On days when he

could not perform some act of help to those in need he looked disappointed; he was bright and satisfied when there was a chance of giving assistance.

Frequent fires caused disasters on a very great scale in the villages; this happened in 1768 in the town of Livny and Yeletz in 1765 and 1779. It was more expedient for Tikhon to collect donations personally. And though he felt ill at ease in the tumult of the world—"after a visit to the world a monk never returns the same as when he left his cell"—he nevertheless went, and was successful in his requests.

Charity on this scale did not go without abuse. It is said that once two men came to beg his support, alleging that they were victims of a fire. Tikhon seemed to doubt their word, but did not refuse the help. But the deceivers, returning home, found their roof in flames. Full of superstitious fear, they rushed back to beseech forgiveness of the clairvoyant donor, who, they thought, must have seen through their story and sent this punishment upon them. The idea that he should be responsible for such a calamity horrified Tikhon.[17]

There was a more painful case. A captain (whose name is not revealed) came to enjoy such a degree of Tikhon's confidence that he allowed him to stay in his little apartment for nearly three years. Then it suddenly appeared that this man had forged Tikhon's signature, and had sent out various appeals for charitable purposes. Tikhon's name had been dragged into a religious fraud, his friendship betrayed. He sent away the man, who was trying to approach him again. Then he wrote to him that confidence does not easily return once it has been lost; but he gave him his forgiveness. "Be at peace as far as I am concerned, only do not neglect your own self." And he urged the deceiver to break the web of lies in which he had become entangled, starting afresh.

> Why seek profit and perish like Pharaoh? I desire for no one what happened to Pharaoh, but rather that they should meet the fate of the prodigal son. . . . While one is alive it is never too late to repent—I am not speaking of the death-bed repentance of one who has spent his life in sin—God alone knows with what

hope such a one departs this life. Better therefore to repent in time and to start a new life. . . . It is not the starting, it is the carrying out to the end which is praised. . . . Mighty before God is true repentance joined with belief in Christ. Read also Rom. 2. 3.[18]

One or two trusted friends helped Tikhon by looking for cases of real distress. Occasionally his messenger would pretend to leave a deposit for grain or cattle and then disappear. The Rostovtzevs were of great assistance in this way. A widow with five children whom Tikhon met in their house became one of his regular pensioners. When short of funds, he even borrowed money for the poor which he used to repay out of his pension.

So many began to seek his help that he could not see them all and had to send his donations through his cell-attendants. This provoked grumbling and discontent. So he would have to appear personally, intervene and listen to reproaches. He grew much more patient than he had been a few years before; yet even now he occasionally lost his temper, scolded his servants or dismissed a beggar. Directly afterwards he would come to apologize for the outburst, he would make a deep monastic obeisance and would dispatch his servant with some additional gift to the offended poor. "His doors were always open to beggars and wanderers whom he provided with food, drink and shelter."

It was not financial assistance alone that was demanded of him. He was asked to lend the support of his authority, and he would write a note to some Government official or supply a testimonial. A striking instance of his championship of a just cause was provoked by a chance meeting. Once, as he was walking in a grove beyond the monastery, he overheard sobbing and voices. Two women were crying, surrounded by small children. Their husbands, both vergers, had unexpectedly been mobilized and sent into the Army. Tikhon gave the two families a subsidy; after a while he took a bold step and sent one of his cell-attendants to St. Petersburg with a letter to Archbishop Gabriel. The matter was re-examined.[19] The two vergers, already somewhere on the western front in separate regiments, were restored to their families. A commission was set up in Voronezh to investigate the complaint brought against Theodossy, Bishop of Tambov. The Synod had to recognize that his way of dealing with men of the ecclesiastical class and of sending them to do military service "was not compatible with the government decrees."[20]

It was on this occasion that Cheboratev was dispatched to St. Petersburg; Tikhon used this opportunity to send a donation to a priest in his native district. He wrote in an accompanying note:

> I beg you to distribute it in the following manner: 1. seek out, both in the village and in the neighborhood, the poorest widows and others who have to pay the poll-tax or quit-rent; 2. having found this out, calculate how much of this sum would go to each person, and write it down on a scrap of paper; 3. divide it according to people's need; 4. do not say that I have sent this money if people ask you, for it is not mine, and my relatives, if they hear about it, may be cross that I did not send any to them. Say simply that it was sent to the needy by some man or other. I beg you, do this for Christ's sake; 5. if someone is poor and a drunkard or lazy, give nothing to him; put aside some ten roubles for the beggars who wander about the streets or beg under one's window, and, having gathered them together, distribute to each according to his need; 7. put down in this note-book what you give away, and send it back to me by this same messenger when he leaves St. Petersburg; 8. take for the trouble, three roubles for yourself, or, if this seems too little, take five out of this money if you wish. I beg you to make the effort for Christ's sake, who will reward your trouble in his grace.[21]

He sent gifts to the north, imitating the practice of those early Christians who collected alms for other local churches in distress.

The memory of the hardships undergone by his mother and sister was possibly one of the reasons why he felt so keenly for widows. At the same time, he did not wish to use people's charity for his own kin. He did what was reasonable for two nephews, one a deacon in Novgorod, the other just out of the Voronezh Seminary and ordained deacon. He occasionally sent a few roubles to his brothers. But he always made it clear that these came as from a brother, and not out of money given to him for the poor. "One must not abandon one's kin, but true love has compassion on strangers no less than on one's own family."[22]

> Nikita Andreevich, my brother in Christ—he wrote in 1773 from Zadonsk to a priest of the Novgorod diocese—I send you this money, a hundred and fifty roubles, by His Excellency Alexis Dimitrievich, my faithful friend and benefactor. Receive him as befits his rank and as you would receive me were I to come. He wishes to stay with you; accompany him afterwards to Valday. I entrust us both to God.... Give nothing to my brother in Korotzk or to my other relatives, for this money is not mine.[23]

Every now and then, under the pretext of a visit to some poor person in the vicinity, Tikhon would return to Tolshevo, as if to seek a full reconciliation. There he would share fully in the life of the community, never missing a single service, chanting in the choir and having his meals with the brethren. At night he would walk up and down in the enclosure, and round the church, then he would enter and go round it, kneeling here and there, approaching the altar to kneel again in prolonged prayer. His cell-attendants afterwards declared that it was at Tolshevo that Tikhon once had a vision of divine light.[24]

He also paid long visits to a small place belonging to the Bekhteievs. Lipovka was about 15 versts from Zadonsk. On such visits he would camp, together with his cook and a cell-attendant, in an empty house, whilst the Bekhteievs lived in Ksizovo. Tikhon was devoted to this spot, "isolated, convenient for reading, prayer and all mental activity."[25] On week-days he recited vespers, hours and matins, with the help of Cheboratev. The village had only one celebration, on Sunday.[26] It seems clear enough that he went to Lipovka as one would go to a retreat. "I wish I could stay here for ever, so much do I like this place," he wrote to a friend: "but people, *potissinum inimici mei, arripiunt ansam calumniandi ibi viventem.*" This letter, devoted to the means of acquiring inward rest and quiet, closes with a touch of humor. Playing on the word "quiet," inherent in the Russian "Tikhon," he ends: "This is what I wish for yourself and for me, Your restless Tikhon."[27]

The Superior Samuel disapproved of his travels. Many strangers heard him remark that this retired Bishop lived worse than any monk. The words were reported to Tikhon. He obviously preferred to take them as meaning "worse off." Whether there was compassion or criticism in the words of the Superior, Tikhon dispatched a servant to him with a loaf of sugar or a barrel of wine, saying: "Carry it to the Superior, in case he is short of things."[28]

However, Tikhon restricted his absences, and remained "shut up in the monastery, not going anywhere except in a case of extreme urgency." It was people's distress which over and over again drew him out of his seclusion.

This was a troubled epoch. In 1770 pestilence broke out and rapidly spread throughout the country. The Archbishop of Moscow who, during the epidemic, forbade the crowd to kiss an icon believed to be miraculous, was assailed by the mob and killed.[29] The war against Turkey continued, whilst the growing tide of rebellion within the country culminated in 1773-5, when the masses rallied to the Cossack Pugachev, who assumed the name of the late Peter III.[30] The prisons were filled with those whom the authorities suspected of sympathizing with the rebels, or with people arrested for debt. The nearest prison was in Yeletz, about forty versts from Zadonsk. Dressed as a simple monk Tikhon frequently went there to visit the prisoners. He would leave his coach outside the town, so as not to be accosted by his acquaintances. At times, however, he would drop in to see one or other of them, and they were all convinced that he undertook to arrive just when he was most needed, especially if there was any strife in a family: he was a born conciliator. "The merciful will only receive mercy but the peacemakers will be called the sons of God," was one of his sayings. In later years (1779) Teshevka became officially the district town of Zadonsk. Several Government offices were moved there. For some time, however, no building was assigned as a prison; men under arrest were stationed in the monastery, and were thus brought even nearer to Tikhon's knowledge and care.

In his diocese Tikhon had appeared mainly as a preacher, administrator and reformer. In his retirement he revealed himself as a man of all-embracing love and as a spiritual director. Very many came to seek his advice. Still more were affected by his writings.

The bulk of his *Works* were written during those years at Zadonsk. Towards the autumn of 1770 he began to write, in his own hand, chapters which may best be defined as moral theology. *True Christianity* was finished within two years. Then there were the *Letters to Friends*, and especially the volume of *Private Letters* of a doctrinal character, compiled partly from his sermons and meditations and partly from his answers to questions on matters of belief. Efimov asserts that while he was working on these books he had nothing but the Bible and some writings of St. John Chrysostom on his table. Some of his notes were posthumously collated in a volume entitled *Interpretation of the Psalms*. He also made several attempts to translate the New Testament into the vernacular. He knew that the people had developed a language different from the Old Slavonic of the Bible, and were in need of a fresh translation; he proposed (Efimov tells us) that the text should be "given on one page in Church Slavonic, on the opposite page in simple Russian." He thought, moreover, that the Old Testament should be translated from the Hebrew, and not from the Septuagint. However, he desisted, for fear of scandal. Most of his works were written by Efimov, to whom he dictated them. His shorter meditations on certain verses or words of Scripture, as well as those inspired by his daily impressions or by some popular saying, were finally assembled in four volumes, *The Spiritual Treasure gathered from the World* (1777-9). Many extracts from this work were copied and circulated among monks and his acquaintances.

It was above all by direct conversation that he reached souls. Both the poor people and educated and wealthy men came to see him, some perhaps out of curiosity. Tikhon had no illusions in this respect, and often he would hide from intruders. As years went by he grew more strict with himself, and found contacts with other people more exacting. It was the instability and extreme attitude of those who came to consult him which seem to have troubled him most, and in all his works and letters he repeatedly insists that perseverance, endurance to the very end, is the mark of a Christian.

One enthusiast, a certain Ivan Mikhailovich, was prepared to leave wife and children and to retire from the world. Tikhon tried to temper his zeal, and advised him to build up a spiritual cell within his ordinary life by avoiding society, by withdrawing even from his family into prayer in solitude; but he firmly protested against a married man prematurely talking of becoming a monk. He next spoke to him of Lipovka as a pleasant resort where his whole family could stay for a while. His nephew lived there, he said, and might afford him company, each stimulating the other: "Quia quis docet, bis docetur."[31] He insisted that the first need was to steep oneself in Holy Scripture and other Christian books which lead to the true knowledge of one's self—a knowledge also achieved through "the emetic of temptation." But peace, he said, is the result neither of life in the world nor of that in solitude, where the mind is still assailed by turbulent thoughts. Peace is the fruit only of a pure conscience and of patience, those inseparable powers which one acquires through sorrow— till one reaches the true quiet of eternity.

It seems that later on, when Tikhon withdrew into stricter seclusion, the monastically inclined gentleman returned to the world with particular zest. Tikhon's insistence on the value of fidelity and of perseverance was again justified.

His real spiritual child was Nikander Bekhteiev, whose character he recognized at first sight. Nikander, who, like all his contemporaries of noble birth, was on a regimental list, eventually went to St. Petersburg. It seems more than certain that it was to him that Tikhon wrote the *Letter to a young nobleman who lived in the capital*. It is worth quoting in full.

> I have received your letter through your father. Thank you for remembering me. Remember what I have already written to you. I have noticed in your young heart the rapture of future bliss: I desire that it may act in your heart and bear fruit. The way to this bliss is not the one which is followed by Christians of the present age, but that which is described in the Holy Scripture which you possess. Read it with reverence, concentration and prayer. It will show you bliss and, taking you by hand, will lead you to it—listen to it alone. Nevertheless, I also offer you some advice; take heed of what I say. In St. Petersburg, as often as you leave your own apartments, so often will you witness things which will lead you away from the path of piety. Fear vile company. Remember God. Pray before going to bed and in the morning. Eat with blessing and thanksgiving, do not imitate those who gulp like beasts. Seek no honors, but if they are bestowed upon you in spite of yourself, accept and do not rejoice in them. . . . Be simple in honors, only do what your sense of honor and the oath prescribe. Be kindly to all, but also have a kind heart, for otherwise kindness is nothing but flattery and craftiness. Forgive offences. Keep the memory of death in your mind. Close your ears to rumors, and turn your eyes from the *well-known* as though from monsters. Speak about no one unless it is really necessary. Remember that we shall leave everything here behind us and shall go naked into the other world.[32]

Nikander returned from the capital and disappointed his family by taking no part in society life. He spoke to Tikhon of his wish to join the community. The family forbade the young Colonel to visit Tikhon or Mitrophan. Later even their letters to him were intercepted.[33] Tikhon, the friend of the whole family, must have suffered not a little. Then, one night when the others had gone out, Nikander made a dramatic escape. He rowed across the Don, nearly twelve versts wide at this point, and landed at Zadonsk, to find Tikhon and Mitrophan waiting for him on the shore in the darkness. Tikhon was not told of this plan, but felt that something was happening that night, and foresaw the arrival of his young friend. He hid Nikander in a cave which, unknown to anyone, Mitrophan had dug beneath his cell for ascetic purposes. A storm followed. The Bekhteievs came to search the whole monastery except Tikhon's apartments. They complained to the diocesan Bishop, who eventually calmed them by pointing out that a devout family like theirs should not deplore a son becoming a monk, especially as there were two more sons at home.

It was fortunate for Tikhon that in 1775 Yakubovsky was transferred to another diocese; the new Bishop was a friend, in a way a spiritual son. Tikhon went twice to Voronezh, and Malinovsky came on several occasions to seek his advice.[34]

Tikhon often used small events in daily life as parables. One day a friend from Yeletz, Kosma Studenikin, came to see Tikhon and Mitrophan. After they had parted Tikhon went to his little apartment, while Kosma dallied in Mitrophan's cell. He had caught a sturgeon, too good to be wasted, though it was a season of fasting. The two could not withstand the temptation, and boiled it in a soup. Tikhon called upon Mitrophan, found both men at table, quite perturbed, and saying, as would a father of old, that love was above fasting, he even made pretence of partaking of the meal. This story is almost the only direct reference to his strict asceticism. He was so full of simplicity and kindness that one may easily be tempted to overlook the purely monastic side of his life.

A certain Kamenev, a "fool for Christ's sake," dwelt at Zadonsk. Once while Tikhon was sitting in the yard he ran up to him, slapped him in his face and shouted: "Don't think highly of yourself!" Tikhon gave him a daily salary of a few kopeks.[35]

One day Nikander Bekhteiev kept looking at Tikhon with somewhat envious eyes: it seemed to him that everything had been given to the old man, including beauty, thick hair and beard, whereas Nikander himself had scarcely any. "Do not fret, man," Tikhon remarked, guessing his thoughts; "many a saint of God was saved though he was quite bald!"

His appearance and the fact that his moustache and beard were neatly cut were greeted with disapproval by an itinerant monk, Stephen Gavrilov, who, having left the Smolensk region, went from place to place in search of perfection. He was of the lower nobility, a man of strong ideas and proud of his ascetic disregard for worldly things and of his drooping moustache. He did not fail to find fault with a man of good repute who used scissors. After a short visit Gavrilov left to look for some better example of asceticism. In the course of his pilgrimage he became drunk, lost his passport, was arrested and shorn like a convict, half of his head and beard and one side of his moustache, and thus he was brought to Zadonsk. Tikhon heard of the incident, and sent his cell-attendant to bail him out and eventually obtained his release.

The gentlefolk who frequently came to see him, especially after 1779, when Zadonsk became a district town, were on the whole more of a trouble than an occasion for real spiritual contact. He even did not go to church at the time of the annual fair to avoid the crowds. Sometimes as he looked out of his window and saw the men and women of fashion driving in to honor a service by their presence, he would say: "I wish they would adorn their souls as they ornament their bodies." He was moderate in his views, and fully admitted that people in the world had to dress according to their social position. It was luxury ("that offence against the poor") which exasperated him.

The ladies soon learned that he would not receive them if they appeared in wigs and make-up, with low-cut dresses. If they wished to consult him they had to come with their natural faces and in modest apparel. Certain persistent "devotees" were told that he was not feeling well, and had commended them to the care of one of the monastic clergy.

Children were the only visitors of whom he never tired. On some days there were as many as a hundred of them in his house. Many came with their parents to attend a service in the monastery, or alone, as is customary for Russian children. Tikhon would invite them after the service to his reception room. He taught them to make a prostration and to say together: "Glory be to thee, O God, glory be to thee." "Where is our God?" he would ask. "In heaven and on earth," the children would answer. The smallest ones, aged three to five, noisily shouted: "Lord have mercy!" or "Hear me, Lord!" or "Blessed Mother of God and all the saints, pray for us!" To the most intelligent ones Tikhon taught the Prayer of Jesus (which may be regarded as yet another link between Tikhon and the disciples of Paissy). He treated them to slices of white bread or apples, and occasionally to a coin or two. His gifts varied. He liked to find out the characters of the children, and he soon knew those who were generous or envious, of an angry and unforgiving or of a mild disposition. If the boys—as sometimes happened—broke into a fight, he made them ask each other's forgiveness.

Even when Tikhon was not well and did not himself go to a service, he continued to inquire after the children. Chebotarev had to tell him that they came to church, but, seeing that the Bishop was away, they slipped out. Tikhon smiled: "Poor things! they came for the sake of bread and pennies. Why did you not bring them in?" This smile is the more precious as, true to the eastern monastic spirit, according to Chebotarev, "rarely did he smile at anything, and if he did so, he would say, 'Lord forgive me, a wretch, for I have sinned before Thee'."

More and more frequently he missed the services. His health was on the decline. Platon Levshin, who in 1775 became Archbishop of Moscow, sent at this period the artist Baskakov to paint Tikhon's portrait. He depicted him standing in a dark monastic robe over which hang two panagias (an emblem of episcopacy, a round icon of the Virgin with Child). He is thinner and paler, his eyes look still larger in his drawn and somewhat sad but very alive face. A straight staff with a light-colored knob is in his left hand, a rosary in his right.[36]

On Christmas Day, 1779, Tikhon attended the service. His cell-attendant was reading the lesson of the day, and when he approached the Bishop for the prescribed blessing, Tikhon made the sign of the cross over him and asked him to help him to leave the church. They pushed through the crowd, and remained for a quarter of an hour in the north porch. Then they came back, and Tikhon stood till the end of the service. When it was over, many came as usual asking for his blessing, and he moved out of the church surrounded by people, repeatedly making over them the sign of the cross. He returned to his cell utterly exhausted, and refused to receive any visitors.

This was his last public appearance. Convinced that his end was approaching, he withdrew into solitude. Only a very few people who did not bring worldly distraction were allowed to see him from time to time. He continued his works of charity to the end, but through other people.

He did not go out either to church or elsewhere, but would only take a breath of fresh air standing or sitting on his back porch. He spent several hours a day on his couch, supporting his head with his arm or leaning on the table. The picture of the Passion on the wall and his coffin seemed to absorb his attention. Someone still read aloud to him, but he no longer interrupted to explain the Scriptures; he listened in silence, then, with a brief word of thanks, dismissed the reader.

He collected his writings, revising some of them. But he no longer wrote, except a few letters to persons of whom he heard that since his retirement they had lapsed, or who asked for his spiritual advice. In these last letters he speaks of death, of repentance and of the endless forgiveness of God. Some remained unfinished "by reason of weakness."

Tikhon's seclusion was to last for nearly three years, though in the course of them he was more than once thought to be dying. These years, devoted to solitude and the life of prayer, remain hidden to us, but their importance cannot be over-emphasized.

In January 1782 he had a slight stroke, during which he had a dream which to him seemed significant. He saw one of the monastic priests coming from the altar of the side-chapel, carrying a baby. Tikhon asked what the baby's name was, and was told that it was Basil. He wanted to look at it, but it gave him a slap on the left cheek. Tikhon looked upon the slight paralysis of his left side as a form of stigmata and a warning that his end was near. The Bishop of Voronezh came in haste and spent a whole day and night at Zadonsk, where he made frequent visits to his sick friend. Tikhon could not sit, and was propped up in his bed. His mental faculties remained unaffected to the end.

When he felt slightly stronger, he took his writings and, expressing the hope that they might prove of some use to the people, he addressed them to the Synod, leaving it to their discretion to reject anything valueless. He also made his last will, which was to be read in the church after his death.

In the final years of Tikhon's life people realized more vividly than ever the value of his personality and the loss which his death would mean to them. Filled with reverence and affection, as well as with a naïve materialism, they treasured and spread abroad every rumor of his words or dreams. They whispered that a monk had been reminded in a strange way of a tradition handed down from some hermit of old to the effect that Zadonsk would one day be glorified by a saintly man. The rumor was reported to Tikhon, to his grief and indignation. Next it was said that Tikhon had had a wonderful dream. In it he had seen a lovely meadow with a palace of crystal and a table laid for a festive meal; but he was not allowed to enter till he had accomplished three years of labor. There would be nothing surprising in such a dream, for since his early days Tikhon had always turned his thoughts to meditation on the after-life. Kosma Studenikin, one of the few who still saw Tikhon, relates another dream which Tikhon had discussed with him. Tikhon had dreamt that there was a tall ladder in the midst of the monastery, surrounded by a crowd which pushed him and tried to make him climb it. He was afraid and felt weak, but could not resist them, and thus, followed and supported by the people, he reached the top—and woke up. Kosma gave it an obvious interpretation: the Kingdom of Heaven is inaccessible in itself, but the way is made easier through the prayers of the people who had been helped by Tikhon or had profited spiritually from his writings.

Tikhon's life was drawing to its close. He could no longer rise from his bed. Every Sunday and on feast-days he received communion in his cell with such fervor that he would weep aloud, recollected Efimov. But "having partaken of the Holy Eucharist he would be filled with gladness and joy. Sometimes when I entered his cell he would say to me, 'I am drunk, Ivan,' remembering, perhaps, the words 'Drink, and ye shall be drunk'." After three and a half years of complete retirement, on Thursday, 10 August 1783, he allowed in all who cared to take leave of him. A crowd of monks and weeping people assembled in his apartment, many kissed his hands, many lamented: "What will become of us? Who will guide us?" Tikhon lay with closed eyes, and when he opened them he gazed upon the picture of the Passion. He would point to it and repeat to his distressed flock almost inaudibly: "I entrust you to God."

On Saturday night the Superior of Zadonsk, Hegoumen Samuel, came in, and sat by Tikhon's bedside. The servant, accustomed to Tikhon's ways, interpreted his silence as concentration in prayer. Tikhon opened his eyes and whispered into the ear of his servant that he begged not to be disturbed and had no orders to give. The Superior kissed his hand and told the servant to let him know when the end drew near.

Towards midnight Tikhon begged that the liturgy might be celebrated as early as possible, so that he could receive the last Sacrament. At three o'clock, as dawn broke, one of the cell-attendants again ran down with the same petition to the hieromonk whose turn it was to celebrate. He sent someone to wake up the Superior, but nothing happened, either because the Superior thought the request premature, or because he had not in fact been woken up. The monks, who had heard all these comings and goings, gathered silently in

Tikhon's cell. Mitrophan stood beside him, but thinking that the end had not yet come, he sent them out to matins. Once more Tikhon asked about the liturgy. An unbearable thirst was burning him; his servant lifted him up and gave him half a cup of warm tea. Then Tikhon begged again for the last consolation of communion. No one seemed to be in haste to start the celebration.

At a quarter to seven on Sunday 13 August the motionless dying man opened his eyes. His servants and the cell-attendants were in the cell. Efimov took Tikhon's head in his hands. Tikhon's breath was hardly perceptible. He closed his eyes as if going to sleep.

The news of his death spread at once. Crowds began to gather in Zadonsk, keeping watch round their departed friend.

For the burial Tikhon had prepared a linen shirt, and old habit, a leather belt with brass clasps and simple episcopal robes consisting of an old cloak, an epitrachelion, an omophor, a panagia and his monastic headwear with its long veil. All these used to lie on a little table in his reception-room. The coffin which he had prepared for himself proved to be too short, and the tradesmen of Yeletz sent another one of better wood, covered with black velvet and silver frills. Those who laid out his body said that his limbs were not stiff. He had specified that he was to be buried close to the steps leading to the church, under a stone which he had prepared, so that all who passed that way might remember him and pray for him. This request was not fulfilled—because of the great fervor of Tikhon's admirers.

On 16 August Bishop Malinovsky sent solemn episcopal robes to replace Tikhon's simple garments. The body was brought into the main monastic church and the Gospel was read day and night. On 20 August Bishop Malinovsky celebrated the requiem liturgy. The church was full to overflowing. Tikhon III gave a moving oration. Its theme was Ps. 1: "Blessed the man . . . whose will is in the law of God." He laid stress on Tikhon's simplicity, his shrinking from honors and glory, his loving zeal towards people, his untiring help as a teacher, friend and benefactor. That is why, he said, the departed might indeed be counted among the blessed. He spoke of the loss experienced by all who, like himself, had sought his spiritual guidance, though at least they still had his written works; but those whom Tikhon used to help would indeed feel orphans, for no one could equal his boundless and affectionate care for the needy. Then, even though this might have been only an oratorical device, he pronounced words full of significance; he addressed the deceased as a saint: "Servant of God, pray for us!" In the presence of all, the Bishop opened and read aloud the testament of Tikhon signed by his own hand. Tikhon left hardly any earthly possessions. He himself gave away his icons to his friends. What remained of his belongings was sold for the sum of 14 roubles and 50 kopeks, which were to be distributed to the poor. One or two small objects were kept as souvenirs by his cell-attendants.

The body was buried in the community's main church under the altar. Bishop Malinovsky ordered a tombstone with the following inscription:

> Here, on 13 August 1783, ended the life of the Right Reverend Tikhon the First, of Keksholm, later of Voronezh. He was born in 1724; consecrated Bishop on 13 May 1761; lived in retirement from 1767 till his death; he appeared as the image of virtue by his word, life, love, spirit, faith and purity. Buried here in the year 1783 on 20 August.

5

The Inward Man

THE DEVELOPMENT OF the personality of Tikhon could not altogether have escaped those who knew him in his daily life. Cheboratev, using long words, described Tikhon as a man "of cholerical temperament, even of a certain melancholy." At that time a certain form of sensibility was deemed a sign of refinement: "Hypochondria, adornment of a sensitive soul!" But when Chebotarev or Efimov spoke naturally, they painted Tikhon as quick, vivacious, sensitive and highly-strung. "When in good health, his speech was rapid, easy, adjusted to the understanding of his listener." But his days of depression were also obvious. People learned to recognize his mournful and his bright days by his humming of different psalms.

He was without any malice or vindictiveness. His sharp words were followed rapidly by an apology. His life seemed based on certain fundamental motives: love of God in Christ, love of people as co-sufferers with Christ and objects of his redeeming love, and hope of eternity. It was one and the same man who gave alms, who dictated his works, who prayed at night and who distributed apples to the children.

The two cell-attendants who left us their memoirs, knew Tikhon intimately and loved him, but many others did not, and made no secret of their opinions. As if speaking generally Tikhon wrote:

> If these false brethren notice that a Christian

estranges himself from their wicked acts and luxury, then he is a *schismatic*; if he lives simply and humbly and detests fashions, he is a *hypocrite*; if he retires into solitude for repentance and abstinence from sin—for it is easier to repent and to avoid sin in solitude—then is he a *bigot*; if, repenting, he is sad and sighs because of his sins, he is a *melancholic*; if he distributes alms, he is a *hypocrite*. If they learn that a Christian prays often, then too they open their mouths to say: "Look at this *zealot*." When, in accordance with Christian law, he does not take vengeance against those who offend him, then too he is attacked: "Look at the *fool* who can't defend himself!" If according to the same rule he gives his possessions to the poor, they reproach him saying that he is a mad squanderer.[1]

Impatience and irritability, caused possibly by a physical discomfort or appetite, and his days of depression—such traits were more open to observation. But equally obvious were his contrary characteristics, his readiness to help everyone, his unreserved charity, his striving after perfection. "There are times when I feel like hugging and kissing everybody, but at times—such a temptation!—I feel a real repulsion."[2] Not merely among the lukewarm, but among the devout he stood out by reason of his fiery spirit and his habit of linking every event and thought with God.

When dictating his *Works* he gave the impression of one inspired. He walked up and down, and spoke rapidly, profiting by the flow of his thought and emotion. Then his speech would grow slower, and, retiring into his cell, he would prostrate himself; sometimes he could be heard weeping. He would come out again with an expression of confidence and, pacing swiftly, would resume the thread of the dictation.

Reading the Bible, and especially St. Paul, produced in him an irresistible emotion, visible even to his servants. Often he left the book, fell on his knees, and the spiritual delight remained with him throughout the day: he would talk much and radiate happiness. He suspected that his cell-attendants had noticed his rapture, and forbade them to gossip about it.

Nothing in his manner gave encouragement to the spread of legends. His clothes were inconspicuous, he had none of the visible rigidity of an ascetic, he chatted simply with simple folk, he was sometimes sad or hot-tempered—it was through such ordinary channels that his cell-attendants now and again caught a breath of eternity.

Some of his remarks on the struggle against hot temper have a very personal accent:

> If by nature or by habit you are inclined to get angry, take care to avoid anything which excites in you this passion. Calm yourself even though only for a short while, and count how many days you have passed without being cross. Supposing that you are in the habit of getting irritable every day; well, if for a whole day, or for two or for three, you have not been angry, it is a sign that your anger is diminishing. If you see that a whole week has passed thus, go to church, and fervently thank your Creator for such a mercy. . . . And what if I manage to do this for five, six weeks at a time?[3]

To his servants he appeared neither distant, perfect nor supernatural. They ascribed to him no miraculous action. His care for the sick did not carry with it any form of healing. Were it not for his preaching, and works of active love, which could be no longer kept secret, he might have passed as one among a number of simple and spiritually reserved monks. There was in him that hidden, silent fervor, so highly praised and cultivated among the Orthodox, which seems to have prevented him from keeping any spiritual diary or working out a spiritual method. To teach of God was his duty as a pastor. Of that which God meant to him or had shown to him he spoke only to his nearest friends, in strict privacy, "keleyno." Any words which he spoke in a personal strain were sparks of a hidden fire, small lyrical outbursts which, through the veil of prose and theology, reveal a poet and a saint.

People knew his failures, his struggles, perhaps some of his victories, but from outside only. What little they recorded has an eye-witness value: conclusions have been drawn only since his death. Utterly sincere, he spoke and lived spontaneously, humbly, exposed to criticisms and sneers which he was too intelligent not to see. He felt completely himself only in solitude, in fullness of recollection and in unity of purpose. In a person so sensitive, other people inevitably provoked some reaction, some spending of the soul, and at times a purely superficial irritation or a deep fatigue—all things belonging to "the mind of the flesh."

The flesh as such played an infinitely smaller part in Bishop Tikhon's life and teaching than did the spiritual combat. Nevertheless, he knew, and did not conceal the "boredom" of unsubdued nature. "What torment and burning of the heart and of the whole body there can be in us through the lust of the flesh! Everyone knows it, particularly those who remain celibate. Like an evil fever, it produces flame and movement in the human body."[4] He was aware that this struggle could survive youth and could reappear in a man of age and spirit: "Know that the flesh with its passions will always rise against you—but withstand it with the arms of the spirit."[5] Chebotarev, with a monastic lack of prudery, writes that once, during a celebration in Lipovka, Tikhon was assailed by temptation of the body. He thereupon took a burning taper and several times in succession removed the wick with his fingers. According to Chebotarev, who may be over-simplifying the motive, Tikhon adopted in his last years a new form of asceticism: he gave up going to the bath-house, and at home only washed his head. This was a severe mortification for a man who was used to cleanliness (as his possession of several sets of underclothes clearly showed), and especially to a Russian used to his hot, almost Turkish, bath. Whatever the motives, the ascetic reasserts himself in Tikhon, since this form of mortification was habitual enough for any monk, eastern or western.

Tikhon's attitude to women remained throughout his life one of caution. The general advice he gave on this subject was moderate and simple: abstinence from wine, bodily excercise, especially certain harder types of labor, moderation in food, scanty sleep. The main armor was "a tear from a contrite heart" and practice in the constant remembrance of the presence of God.[6]

"The mind of the flesh," with its capricious self-seeking and grossness of naturalistic reasoning, was a more subtle and dangerous foe. Such reasoning issued from the doubts of a mind unwilling to apprehend "how God, one in substance, is yet of three hypostases; or how the world was created out of nothing—for naught comes out of nothing, everything having some origin; or how a Virgin bears without a husband and remain a virgin; or that God can become incarnate and be a man; or that a dead body crumbling into dust can rise." Only complete sincerity of mind and honesty of belief could have enabled an ecclesiastic to formulate in detail all these "soul-destroying opinions" about dogma, all these hesitations and questionings, "like those of Nicodemus." In his own case, his confident love of Christ must have helped him "to bring reason to the obedience of faith."[7]

Technically speaking, Bishop Tikhon may appear more as an ascetic than a mystic (though a closer examination reveals in him a strong mystical element). In so far as one is prepared to accept this definition, one can speak of his method of solitude and prayer. Tikhon had an unreserved belief in the healing power of solitude, which liberates the mind from the tumult of the world and allows it to become itself, quiet and recollected. He spoke of the free flow of good thoughts begotten by solitude and silence. The soul, unburdened by human worries and stripped of its defences and prejudices, is confronted with God and enabled to see itself in the light of divine truth. Whenever a personal note is heard, his solitude is revealed as a loving impatience for a personal meeting.

> God, in whom is everything, let all abandon me; thou alone do not leave me. In thee is my all: my help, my protection, my strength and refuge, my counsel, my consolation.[8]

Having hushed the impressions of the world and allowed them to die, his soul turns towards God, and he sketches a draft of "Thoughts to Remember":

1. The presence of God.
2. Prayer is a conversation with God.
3. Communion in the Holy Sacrament.
4. God says to thee: do this and that, and he promises blessedness.
5. The Word of God is a word from the mouth of God.
6. You are redeemed by the blood of Christ, the Son of God; you are not your own but his.
7. Our fellowship with the Father and his Son.
8. Christians are the dwelling-place of the Holy Ghost.
9. They are spiritual members of Christ.
10. Christ is the Vine, they are the branches.
11. Christ is the Shepherd, they are the sheep.
12. Christ is the Bridegroom, a Christian soul is his betrothed bride.
13. Christ came into the world for souls.
14. Christ has loved me for nothing; and I must love him for nothing, sincerely.
15. Christ united to himself human nature (John 1). God became man. The Son of God—the son of the Virgin. This is a great mystery.
16. Christ says: You are my friends. . . . To whom does he say this? To his unworthy servants. The mercy of thy loving-kindness, Lord! Glory be to thee in all and for all!
17. A life of much suffering in this world, death, the judgement of Christ, hell and the Kingdom of Heaven. My soul, mark this well and meditate.⁹

His ecstasies—or what little is known of them—are all connected with his experience of solitude (though it is also important to remember the strain of sacramental mysticism in Tikhon). The solitary hour in the garden of the seminary, at St. Antony's, of which he spoke to Chebotarev, his thoughts of the future life, the silence and the iridescent sky remained for ever engraved in Tikhon's memory.

He loved to pray in the open, and asked not to be approached when he was walking alone in the garden; if he must be disturbed, he wished to be warned by some little noise or cough. Chebotarev found him once in the garden, kneeling, facing the east, his arms uplifted. The man coughed and, unable to attract Tikhon's attention, he approached him and called him. Tikhon was so violently startled that perspiration appeared on his forehead.[10]

A similar case of Tikhon's ecstatic prayer was witnessed one morning by a monk who was just about to ring the chimes in the belfry. Bishop Tikhon was walking in the little garden near his cell. Suddenly he stopped, looked up, and knelt, pressing his hands to his breast. He looked so radiant that the monk rushed down to tell the brethren, and several of them climbed up to belfry. Tikhon had already resumed his walk, but the monks thought they discerned in his features the glow of ecstasy.[11]

Chebotarev also mentions that one night whilst Tikhon was praying alone in the empty church of the Tolshevo monastery he again had a vision of divine light.

At Zadonsk some time in 1770, Efimov entered the Bishop's cell unawares; Tikhon, he knew, was sitting on his bed writing the *True Christianity*. He found him kneeling on his bed, his arms stretched out to the picture of the Passion which hung on the wall, almost embracing the feet of the Crucified, weeping and saying: "And thou, to come down to me!"

From Efimov, too, we hear of a vision—the only visual image that is ascribed to Tikhon. It happened in 1779 "in a fine dream." The devout meant by this term a semi-awakened state distinct from sleep or dream. The biographer relates that once, as Tikhon was praying, begging not to be separated from a friend even in after-life, the Virgin Mary appeared to him "floating in mid-air, with several figures standing nearby." She said: "It shall be done according to your prayer." Efimov, by 1779, was an intimate, and enough of a confidant to have been told of such a dream or vision; but Tikhon did not himself transmit this incident to posterity.[12]

Tikhon mentions two spiritual experiences which "happened to one of our community." Both seem to be undoubtedly his own. It was known that he daily prostrated himself thrice and asked: "Tell me, Lord, of my end." One day, at dawn, he received the answer: "It will be on a Sunday." (And he died indeed at daybreak on a Sunday.)

Again, in a letter to a friend he wrote these significant words:

> To support your faint heart I write to tell you that this week a man of our community, when at midnight he was just about to fall asleep, heard such a singing above his head that his heart melted like wax with joy, and as soon as this singing ceased, he woke up. And after that, a great sorrow overwhelmed him because that joy had departed.[13]

Such incidents, familiar to many believing souls and valuable as a landmark and a key to some stages of his inward experience, do not throw enough light on the development of St. Tikhon's personality. They were the feast-days of his soul; his *Works* are witness to his everyday struggle, to the ground which he gradually gained. By selecting the passages in which he uses the first person (or at times the first person plural) we can to some extent retrace the path of his thought and devotion, and grow more intimate with his spiritual life.

He wrote many short prayers for various states of mind or needs. They mostly consisted of no more than a verse of Scripture slightly expanded.

Very revealing are two *Breathings of the Sinful Soul to the Son of God:*[14]

> Lead my soul out of prison, and I shall confess thy name.
> Jesus Christ, Son of God, have mercy upon us.
> Attract me, that I may come to thee.
> I am in prison, Lord, and darkness surroundeth

me; I am bound with many iron chains, and there is no relaxation.

Break the chains, that I may be free; shine through the darkness that I may see thy light. Lead me out of prison, that I may come to thee.

Give me ears to hear thee, eyes to see thee, taste to partake of thee, sense of smell to inhale thee. Give me feet to walk unto thee, lips to speak of thee, heart to fear and love thee. Teach me thy ways, O Lord, and I shall walk in thy truth. For thou art the way, the truth and the life.

Take all that is mine from me, and give me the will to do thy gracious will.

Take away the old, and give me the new.

Take away the heart of stone, and grant me a heart of flesh, to love thee, honor thee, follow thee.

Give me eyes to see thy love.

Give me eyes to see thy humility and to imitate it.

Give me thy meakness and patience.

Say but the word, and all shall be.

For thy word is an act.

I believe, Lord; help thou mine unbelief.

The second "Breathing":

Jesus Christ, Son of God, have mercy upon me.
Be the food and drink of my soul.
Be a fountain of water to my thirsting soul.
Be the light of my darkened soul.
Be my consolation in affliction.
Be my mirth when I am sad.
Be my liberation from imprisonment.
Be the triumph of peace and rest over my evil con-
[science.
Be the triumph of wisdom over my folly.
Be my advocate against those who calumniate me.
Be my justification against my sins.
Be my sanctification against my sins.
Be my victory over my enemies.

By my shield against my persecutors.
Be the sacrifice for my sins.
Be my strength in my weakness.
Be my life against my death.
Be my counsel in my perplexity.
Be my power in my infirmity.
Be to me, an orphan, my eternal Father.
Be judge against those who insult me.
Be king against the realm of Satan.
Be my leader in my journey.
Be my mediator in the hour of my death.
Be my protector after my death.
Be the life eternal of my resurrection.
Jesus Christ, Son of God, have mercy upon me.
Give glory to thy name, and to me eternal salvation.
Not to us, Lord, not to us, but to thy own name give [glory.
Amen.

This cry to God was sometimes uttered in the form of a dialogue, often taken from the Scripture; we can only guess what particular circumstances or moods provoked, at one time, these cries of isolation and, at others, these exultant songs. Certain allusions in his letters constitute more definite evidence; for instance, when he writes of old age, the "teach us the number of our days" (Ps. 90), the *De Profundis*, Ps. 27, with its "thy face will I seek." Many of these he copied out in full for his friends. At the risk of giving too lengthy biblical annotations, we reproduce these dialogues, for the choice of the texts is significant.

"Because he hath set his love upon me, therefore will I deliver him; I will set him on high because he hath known my name" (Ps. 91. 14).

"Cast me not away from thy presence; and take not thy holy spirit from me" (Ps. 51. 11).

"All that the Father giveth me shall come to me; and him that cometh to me I will in no wise cast out" (John 6. 37).

"And enter not into judgement with thy servant; for in thy sight shall no man living be justified" (Ps. 145. 2).

"For God so loved the world that he gave his only begotten Son, that whosoever believeth in him should not perish but have everlasting life. For God sent not his Son into the world to condemn the world; but that the world through him might be saved. He that believeth on him is not condemned, but he that believeth not is condemned already, because he hath not believed in the name of the only begotten Son of God" (John 3. 16-18).

"Remember not the sins of my youth nor my transgressions; according to thy mercy remember thou me for thy goodness' sake" (Ps. 25. 7).

"I will be glorified in the midst of thee (O Zion): and they shall know that I am the Lord, and shall be sanctified in her" (Ezek. 28. 22).

"For mine iniquities are gone over mine head: as a heavy burden, they are too heavy for me" (Ps. 38. 4).

"But go ye and learn what that meaneth, I will have mercy and not sacrifice: for I am not come to call the righteous, but sinners to repentance" (Matt. 9. 13). "Where sin abounded, grace did much more abound" (Rom. 5. 20).

"I will say unto God, my rock, Why hast thou forgotten me? Why go I mourning because of the oppression of the enemy?" (Ps. 42. 9). "Arise, O Lord! O God, lift up thine hand: forget not the humble" (Ps. 10. 12).

"Can a woman forget her suckling child, that she should not have compassion on the son of her womb? Yea, they may forget, yet will I not forget thee" (Isa. 49. 15).

"Hide not thy face from thy servant; for I am in trouble: hear me speedily" (Ps. 69. 17).

"For the iniquity of his covetousness was I wroth, and smote him: I hid me and was wroth, and he went on frowardly in the way of his heart. I have seen his ways, and will heal him: I will lead him also, and restore comforts unto him and to his mourners" (Isa. 57. 17-18).

"Teach me thy way, O Lord; I will walk in thy truth; unite my heart to fear thy name" (Ps. 86. 11).

"I am the way, the truth, and the life: No man cometh unto the Father, but by me" (John 14. 69). "I am the resurrection, and the life: he that believeth in me, though he were dead, yet shall he live" (John 11. 25).

"As the hart panteth after the water brooks, so panteth my soul after thee, O God" (Ps. 42. 1).

How a faithful soul converses with God:

"Lord, thou art my refuge. Thou art my hiding place; thou shalt preserve me from trouble; thou shalt compass me about with songs of deliverance" (Ps. 32. 7).

And the Lord replieth:

"I will instruct thee and teach thee in the way which thou shalt go; I will guide thee with mine eyes" (Ps. 32. 8).

"Look thou upon me, and be merciful unto me, as thou usest to do unto those that love thy name" (Ps. 119. 132).

"For all those things hath mine hand made, and all those things have been, saith the Lord, but to this man will I look, even to him that is poor, and of a contrite spirit, and trembleth at my word" (Isa. 66, 2).

"O Lord, who shall abide in thy tabernacle? Who shall dwell in thy holy hill?" (Ps. 15. 1).

"He that walketh uprightly, and worketh righteousness, and speaketh the truth in his heart. He that backbiteth not with his tongue, nor doeth evil to his neighbor. In whose eyes a vile person is contemned; but he honoureth him that feareth the Lord. He that sweareth to his own hurt, and changeth not. He that putteth not out his money to usury, nor taketh reward against the innocent. He that doeth these things shall never be moved" (Ps. 15. 2-5).

"Create in me a clean heart, O God; and renew a right spirit within me" (Ps. 51. 10).

"And a new heart also will I give you, and a new spirit will I put within you: and I will take away the stony heart out of your flesh, and I will give you a heart of flesh" (Ezek. 36. 26).

"The troubles of my heart are enlarged: O bring thou me out of my distress" (Ps. 25. 17).

"And call upon me in the day of trouble: I will deliver thee and thou shalt glorify me" (Ps. 50. 15).

"Lord, remember me when thou comest into thy kingdom" (Luke 23. 42).

"Fear none of those things which thou shalt suffer: behold, the devil shalt cast some of you into prison, that ye may be tried: and ye shall have tribulation ten days: be thou faithful unto death, and I will give thee a crown of life" (Rev. 2. 10).

"Forsake me not, O Lord; O my God, be not far from me. Make haste to help me, O Lord my salvation" (Ps. 38. 21, 22).

"Observe all things whatsoever I have commanded you; and, lo, I am with you always, even unto the end of the world" (Matt. 28. 20).

"O Lord my God, in thee do I put my trust: save me from all them that persecute me, and deliver me" (Ps. 7. 1).

"Come unto me, all ye that labor and are heavy laden, and I will give you rest" (Matt. 11. 28).

"For I am in strait betwixt two, having a desire to depart, and to be with Christ, which is far better" (Phil. 1. 23).

"Verily I say unto thee, Today shalt thou be with me in paradise" (Luke 23. 43).

This dialogue is one of the most revealing indications of Tikhon's inward life. It develops from repentance, human misery, and even the desire to escape, to the discipleship of one who willingly gives himself to be taught and led, and finally experiences a process of illumination, of change of heart, of total abandonment.

Despondency and sadness were often to be noticed in him, and he himself did not conceal the fact that his main difficulty was to conquer these moods of despondency or despair. Sometimes the cause may have been merely bodily fatigue and nervous strain. More often it was the result of a spiritual conflict. Sadness at the sinfulness of the world, instead of becoming prayerful "godly sorrow," turned into despair. Was it possible, he asked himself, to persevere in the hope that a sinner would at long last respond to the true love of God?

At times his own failures brought him despondency: would he ever be able to attain the fullness of Christian life?

There was a certain practical way of fighting against this temptation.

> Mighty is this wicked power even against those who prosper in the world, and more so against those in retirement. I advise you to convince yourself and force yourself to prayer and every good action, even if you do not feel the wish for it ["as a lazy horse," he often said]. God seeing such labor and application will give good will and zeal. Such good will and a certain attraction to prayer is often a result of habit. Get into the habit of being used to it, for the very habit will draw you to prayer and good actions. A change also stimulates zeal: that is, when you alternately do one thing and then another. Do this: now pray, now work in some way with your hands, now read a book or ponder about your soul and eternal salvation and so on—that is, pray and read a book, and do some handiwork, and pray again, and again do something else. And if despondency overtakes you too strongly, go out of your room, take a little walk, and in walking think of Christ and other things, and meditating, lift up your mind to God and pray. So will despondency pass away. The thought of sudden death, of the judgement and of eternal pain or eternal bliss drives despondency away. Think about them. Pray and sigh to God, that he may himself give you zeal and willingness, for without him we are incapable of any work.[15]

He spoke also of the relief which the singing of religious songs can bring. "If you fail, greater despair will overcome you . . . but if you fight and are victorious, joy, consolation and considerable spiritual power will come of it."

Not in vain did he especially remind his clergy to be solicitous for those who are given to despair. The very titles of his shorter meditations and letters illustrate his constant preoccupation with this form of spiritual disease.¹⁶ He acquired the conviction that despair of this kind did not seem to trouble a worldly man but was rather a diabolical influence discernible by a soul which is zealous and engaged in spiritual combat.

> I myself often have this feeling, and have it just now, and I have noticed it with other Christians: for you are not the only one to whom such things happen. But I do not despair of salvation in Christ, and I believe in the resurrection of the dead and the life of the world to come as we read in the Creed—and this I counsel also for you and for others. In the Scriptures we see that Christ came for our sake, that he might "find" us too; he does not judge sinners but unrepentant sinners. When the thought overpowers us: how can we be with the apostles, prophets, martyrs and other great saints who shine with such virtues? Let us thus answer our doubt: we desire to be with the thief, who at the very end of his life uttered only one cry of repentance and was heard. Let his words become our words of prayer, our prayer before communion. This despair comes from the devil in revenge for the mercy of God; pray as Ps. 38. 21. "Forsake me not, O Lord"; or Ps. 3. There is profit in these thoughts for they distract our attention from worldly vanity. To be in such a state and to fight against it is a sign that one is in faith and the state of grace; let us sing: "The Lord is my light" (Ps. 27). Woe to those who do not repent; but those who seek repentance and salvation, in faith and prayer, may expect the mercy of God "in whom there is plenteous redemption" (Ps. 130. 7). "The Lord will perfect that which concerns thee" (Ps. 138). "Our soul waiteth for the Lord" (Ps. 33. 20-22). Read all these, reflect, grow strong. The Lord may help you. And *remember* me a sinner."¹⁷

It is easier for a man to endure every sort of exterior temptation than a twinge of conscience mixed with despair. More than ever is patience needed, silence and heart-felt sighs. What we need in such a case is, as St. Paul said in Rom. 4. 18: "against hope to believe in hope." We must listen not to what one's own thoughts say but to what God promises. Ezek. 18. 22, 23: "All his transgressions . . . shall not be mentioned unto him; in his righteousness that he hath done he shall live. Have I any pleasure that the wicked should die, and not that he should return from his ways and live?" and again, Rom. 5. 20: "Where sin abounded, grace did much more abound," and other such comforting words. To this effort and patient hope the prophet exhorts us in Ps. 27. 14. "Be of good courage, wait on the Lord, and he shall strengthen thine heart," and he emboldens us by reminding us of the mercy of God, Ps. 9. 12: "he remembereth them; he forgetteth not the cry of the humble"; and he gives us his own example in Ps. 40. 1: "I waited patiently for the Lord: and he inclined unto me and heard my cry," and also Ps. 27. 13: "I had fainted—unless I had believed to see the goodness of the Lord in the land of the living."[18]

These verses reflect the various stages and degrees of affliction which Tikhon suffered—lack of hope, personal grief produced by the injustices and lack of understanding which so often beset him, even purely human anger against these, and aridity of the spirit; they reflect, too, sadness because the divine love, which is offered to all, receives no response. Each verse was alive to him, became his own self-expression. The very omissions are revealing and so are his complaints and lamentations and his longing for God, the outpouring of his whole being in words of adoration.

Read slowly—as they must have been slowly chosen, copied out, meditated upon—these pages of spiritual texts introduce us into Tikhon's inward life. In sorrow and despondency he chooses these verses from the psalms, which he intersperses with a prayer from the litany.

"Hearken unto the voice of my cry, my King and my God; for unto thee will I pray. My voice shalt thou hear in the morning, O Lord; in the morning will I direct my prayer unto thee. Have mercy upon me, O Lord, have mercy" (Ps. 5. 2-4).

"Consider and hear me, O Lord my God: lighten my eyes lest I sleep the sleep of death. . . . How long wilt thou forget me? For ever? How long wilt thou hide they face from me? How long shall I take counsel in my soul, sorrow in my heart daily?" (Ps. 13. 3, 2).

"Hold up my goings in thy paths, that my footsteps slip not"—to the end of Ps. 17.

"Who can understand his errors? Cleanse thou me from secret faults" (Ps. 19. 12).

"But thou art holy, O thou that inhabitest the praises of Israel. Our fathers trusted in thee, they trusted and thou didst deliver them. . . . Be not far from me, for trouble is near; for there is none to help. Be not thou far from me, O Lord: O my strength, haste thee to help me" (Ps. 22. 3, 4, 19).

"The Lord will perfect that which concerns me: thy mercy, O Lord, endureth for ever: forsake not the works of thine own hands" (Ps. 138. 8).

"But the fruit of the Spirit is love, joy, peace, long-suffering, gentleness, goodness, faith, meekness, temperance: against such there is no law" (Gal. 5. 22, 23).

"Pray always for these."

In his days of peace, Tikhon would write down or sing: "O praise the Lord, all ye nations; praise him all ye people. For his merciful kindness is great towards us: and the truth of the Lord endureth for ever. Praise ye the Lord." And these would be interrupted by the "Glory be to thee, O God, glory be to thee." "Bless the Lord, O my soul; and all that is within me, bless his holy name. Glory . . ." (Ps. 103. 1).

"Praise ye the name of the Lord, praise him, O ye servants of the Lord" (Ps. 135. 1).
"O give thanks unto the Lord, for he is good: for his mercy endureth for ever" (Ps. 136. 1).
"I will extol thee, my God, O king: and I will bless thy name for ever and ever" (Ps. 145. 1).
"Praise God in his sanctuary; praise him in the firmament of his power" (Ps. 150. 1).
"Bless all the works of the Lord, sing to the Lord and exalt him for ever" (Song of Three Chil. 35).
"Glory to God in the highest, and on earth peace, good will towards men" (Luke 2. 14).
"Sing all the works of the Lord and exalt him for ever and ever. Bless the angels of the Lord, praise him all the heavens" (Song of Three Chil. 35, 36, 37).

Quotations like these fill pages of his *Works,* and give a singular impression of personal experience.

The thought of God was never separated for Tikhon from the person of Christ.

> To me Christ and his holy yoke is better than the whole world. Here do I wish to be with him, that there too I may be with him . . .[19]

When answering a question put by one of his correspondents as to why one should despise the world that has been created for us, Tikhon wrote:

> Let the voice calling to solitude resound in us. Nevertheless it is not because of people that we retire from the world, but because of sin. We must hate sin, not people; they are to be loved and prayed for. Love bids us and compels us to pray for others as for ourselves. . . . God is the bliss and gladness of the soul. The more it seeks him the more it desires him, and it will desire and seek till it can see face to face; and the more it drinks of this live and

overflowing source, the more it will thirst for him throughout all eternity. That is why souls which are spiritually sad cannot be comforted with anything except God and his holy word.[20]

An overwhelming sense of the presence of God did not abandon Tikhon amidst tribulations and in moments of despondency. In sorrow God was even nearer "not according to his omnipresence, but through his grace. All his martyrs and saints have understood this and they suffered and endured all. . . . The same is true of those who in our own times work for him with fear, faith and love and who cling to him. Therefore they despise every consolation and sweetness of this present world and are satisfied and comforted with this single inward treasure."[21]

Having first tasted of sorrow and having endured with Christ (2 Tim. 2. 1-13), men who in this life remain pilgrims and strangers are emboldened "to strive to be not only among those called but even among the elect—that we too may be worthy to eat and drink in his kingdom" (Luke 22. 30), "O Lord, grant this, Merciful One, hear us!"[22]

He seems to have absorbed the gospel story mystically. He contemplates every action of Christ not as a moralist but as an adoring disciple.

"One who loveth us!" he exclaims commenting upon Christ washing the disciples' feet: "Write in my heart this thine action, that always looking at it I may follow the same."[23]

Absorption in the actions of Christ leads to imitation of them, to a nearer and deeper penetration into their meaning and a growing desire for contemplation.

Simple folk often wish to see a Tsar.

> But you can say: "Whom have I in heaven but thee? and there is none upon earth that I desire beside thee" (Ps. 73. 25). "As the hart panteth..." (Ps. 42. 1). "Every one appeareth before God..." (Ps. 84. 7). "For now we see through a glass, darkly; but then face to face: now I know in part, but then shall I know even as also I am known" (1

Cor. 13. 12). "We know that, when he shall appear, we shall be like him; for we shall see him as he is" (John 3. 2). Have peace "looking unto Jesus the author and finisher of our faith; who for the joy that was set before him endured the cross, despising the shame, and is set down at the right hand of the throne of God" (Heb. 12. 2). "Blessed are the pure in heart: for they shall see God" (Matt. 5. 8).[24]

Tikhon often applied to the soul the Pauline metaphor of the looking-glass. By the power of the Spirit, the divine image blurred by sin is ready to shine through. Not only in the future life shall those who "have endured unto the end" see the saints, the new Jerusalem and Christ himself, but even before, in this terrestrial life, the soul experiences "the insatiable blessedness of contemplation." The psalms express for him once more the craving of the soul of God. Then in the words of the Lenten hymn, he calls: "I see thy bridal chamber, O my Saviour, all adorned; but I have no garment to enter therein. Illumine thou the raiment of my soul, Lightgiver, and save me."

He copied out the story of the Transfiguration (Matt. 17. 2)—linking it with the verses of Phil. 3. 20-31: "For our conversation is in heaven; from whence also we look for the Saviour, the Lord Jesus Christ; who shall change our vile body that it may be fashioned like unto his glorious body," and he concluded with a cry of hope and triumph: "It will be! It will be!"[25]

This hope of transfiguration filled him with awe of the divine grace, which made man's answer to this process of illumination account for "nothing." The humbler was his acceptance of grace, the stronger became his confidence in the power of the divine will not only to save, but to restore man to the state of bliss.

My spirit is willing but my flesh falls behind it. Carry me a weak one, thou who art mighty; and lead me as a giant leads a little child. Let us run! By what? By the beautiful and saving ways. "They

have seen thy goings, O God: Even the goings of my
God, my King, in the sanctuary" (Ps. 68. 25). Where
to? Into thine eternal and most glorious kingdom.
Let us hasten there: that I may be here and there like
unto thy image. Amen!²⁶

Overcome with adoration, he exclaims: "Who am I, Lord,
that thou givest me such, oh such graces?"²⁷

Union with God was for Tikhon more than a hope: it
was a certainty to which he referred over and over again.
Prayer, this real colloquy with God, was to him a token of
profound union—"a real greatness, not of great human, royal
origin, but sonship in God." A sweet impatience tormented
him:

> When shall I come and see the One who for the
> sake of me a sinner came into the world, bore hard-
> ships, suffered and died. . . . Whom have I in heaven
> but thee? . . . I desire nothing in heaven or on earth
> but thee alone, the Word of God and the Son of the
> Virgin, Jesus Christ, my God, God of the gods, my
> Lord.²⁸

Almost the same language is repeated in a letter dealing
with *The True Desire of God in a God-loving Soul:*

> Not only in things terrestrial, but in heaven too I
> seek or desire nothing except thee, my God and my
> Creator! Thou alone art everything to me. In thee
> alone I find what I cannot find in all thy creation. I
> shall only then be satisfied when I shall see thee; I
> shall cease desiring only when I have found thee;
> I shall be comforted only when I shall come to thee;
> I shall be filled only when I shall appear before thy
> face. . . . My soul, seek the only One. . . . My soul, you
> have no part with the earth; for you are from heaven.
> You are the image of God: seek your First Image.
> For like strives after like. Each object finds its centre
> and element—fish in water, fire in its upward move-
> ment—everything strives to its centre. My soul, you

are an immaterial spirit, immortal. . . . In him alone you will find your rest.[29]

Meditating upon the words of John 15. 18-19, Tikhon wrote:

> What is there more comforting to a soul than these words? Sweet is the love of God, comforting and joy giving. This I wish, this I choose. Let all the world hate me if it wishes; let them do to me what they want, so long as God alone loves me and keeps me in his mercy. His love and mercy are to me above all the love and favors of the world. The good is to me, Lord, thy mercy! I wish nothing in heaven or earth except thee alone and thy love.[30]

Turning to the example of the Teacher, Tikhon longed not only to imitate his humility, forgiveness and forbearance, but to unite his heart to the divine love.

> To love is easy and sweet. Oh! if we could only see the heart of a man who bears the evangelic yoke of Christ, you would see in it a paradise of joy and gladness, you would see there the Kingdom of God, even though on the surface he was worried and surrounded by grief and tribulations, as a rose is surrounded by thorns. There can be nought but comfort and true joy in a heart in which reigns the kingdom of God. My poor soul! Sigh, pray and strive to take upon you the blessed yoke of Christ, and you will live on earth in a heavenly manner. Lord, grant that I may carry thy light and goodly yoke, and I shall be always at rest, peaceful, glad and joyous; and I shall taste on earth of the crumbs which fall from the celestial feast, like a dog that feeds upon the crumbs which fall from the master's table.

The period of most importance in St. Tikhon's inward life—those last years when he listened in silence to the scriptures and spent whole hours in solitude—remains veiled from us.

His writings speak of the victory of the spirit, and the renewal of seasons in the image "of that blessed spring" to which he calls his readers: "Beloved Christian! strive by the grace of Christ to reach unto the resurrection of the righteous."[31]

The last chapters of *True Christianity* (some of which may have been added before the manuscript was sent to the Synod) deal repeatedly with eschatological themes: *The Second Coming and the triumph of the righteous. On the triumph and glory of God's elect.* . . . The book ends in ejaculations of ecstasy:

> Lord and Father, Only Begotten Son, Holy Ghost, God in Three Persons, Creator, Redeemer, Provider, Light inextinguishable, pure Truth, Love eternal, eternal Mercy, incomprehensible Might and Wisdom, Eternity for ever existing, Principle without beginning, Power acting in all, Life of all the living! Quicken me, illumine me, enlighten my mind that I may see thy love and thy grace which thou hast revealed to mankind! Amen.

Such lines lead one to think that the years of retirement were the most profound of his life—the risen life hid with Christ in God of which St. Paul speaks in Col. 3. 1, 3.

Lives of saints have often deliberately followed a certain pattern reflecting the outline of the gospel narrative. Without trying to fit a historical life-story into any religious or literary pattern, one is nevertheless aware of a possible comparison, for there is often a certain resemblance between the main lines of the life of Jesus and the outline of many a Christ-like life. So it was with Bishop Tikhon. Humbly, but with the deep conviction of one who is chosen, he consciously tried to follow Christ. Yet even in his life as shaped by circumstances one can trace the pattern of an obscure childhood, of the period of preaching and public ministry, of success and rejection, of loneliness amidst men and a growing triumphant experience and conviction of union with God. There was also the hour of abandonment when, dying, he in vain claimed and begged for the last communion.

Tikhon's voice was heard for the last time when his will was read at his funeral, which in its triumphant praise of God had pierced through all his earthly trials and conflicts.

Glory to God, for he has created me in his image and likeness! Glory to God, who redeemed me, the fallen one; Glory to God, for he was the providence of my unworthy self. Glory, for he called me, a sinner, to repentance! Glory, for he has handed to me his holy Word as a lamp shining in a dark place, and by it he taught me the true way. Glory to God, for he has illumined the eyes of my heart! He has granted me to know his holy name! Glory to God, for he has washed away my sins in the waters of baptism! Glory, for he has shown me the way to eternal bliss. And this way is Jesus Christ, the Son of God, who says of himself: "I am the way, the truth and the life." Glory to him, for he did not ruin me in my sin but in his mercy was patient to my transgressions! Glory to God, for he has shown to me the vain enticements and vanity of this world. Glory to God, for he has helped me in the multitude of temptations, griefs and tribulations! Glory, for he has preserved me in accidents and mortal dangers. Glory to God, for he has defended me from the enemy Satan. Glory, for he raised me when I fell. .Glory to God, for he has comforted me in my affliction. Glory to God, for when I erred he converted me: Glory to God, for, like a father, he punished me. Glory to God, for he showed me his dreadful judgement that I might be afraid and repent of my sins! Glory to God, for he revealed to me eternal pain and eternal bliss that I might flee the one and seek the other! Glory to him, for to me, the unworthy, he gave food to strengthen the weakness of the body. He gave me clothes to cover the nakedness of my body; gave me a house in which to rest! Glory to God, for all the other benefits which he gave to me for my sustenance and comfort. As many breaths I have taken, so many graces have I received of him. Glory to God for everything.

Today, my brethren, I address my words to you. I cannot talk to you as before with my lips and voice, for I am without breath and without voice; but I converse through this brief letter. First: The temple of my body is demolished and, as dust, is given to dust, according to the word of God: "dust thou art and unto dust thou shalt return." But with the Holy Church I believe in the resurrection of the dead and the life of the world to come. My hope sits at the right hand of God, Jesus Christ, my Lord and my God. He is my resurrection and my life; he tells me: "I am the resurrection and the life; whosoever believeth in me even if he be dead shall live again." He will wake me, who am asleep, with his all-powerful voice. Secondly: I have departed from you in the way of all flesh and have gone away, and already we do not see each other as before. But we shall see each other there where all nations that have lived from the beginning of the world till its end will gather. Lord, show us mercy that we may meet there where God is seen face to face, where those who see are made alive, comforted in joy, gladness and eternal bliss! There do men shine like the sun, there is true life; there, true honor and glory, there gladness and joy; there true blessedness and all that is eternal and endless. Lord, let thy mercy be upon us for we put our trust in thee. Thirdly: To my benefactors who have not abandoned me in need and sickness but in their charity and mercy have provided me with all sorts of goods, many thanks. May God reward them on the day when each will receive according to his deeds. Fourthly: All who in any way whatever have offended me I have forgiven and I do forgive; may God forgive them too, in his grace! I beg you also to forgive me if perchance I, being human, have offended someone. Forgive and it shall be forgiven you, says the Lord. Fifthly: As

I had no possession, I leave nothing behind. I beg
those who have lived with me and have served me
to exact nothing. Forgive, my beloved ones, and
remember Tikhon in your prayer.

This last message, his last personal greeting to all, bore
a signature in his handwriting: "your well-wisher Tikhon,
unworthy Bishop."

6

Works

SOURCES

BISHOP TIKHON'S doctrine and outlook were traditionally Orthodox. He was brought up in the atmosphere of a well-defined religious teaching. But what aspects of it, within the limits of this field of study, did he prefer? Had he been subject to any influences? Can one at least sketch an outline of his sources?

Holy scripture was for Tikhon the basic and final authority. The psalms were used by him devotionally, and played a very important role in his teaching of others. In this he followed the universal monastic tradition. Next to them in his Old Testament references come the prophets, particularly Isaiah. A cursory glance at his writings, whether at his *Instructions to the Clergy* or his *True Christianity*, reveals the predominant place given to the word of God. The Bible, more particularly the New Testament, is quoted so abundantly that it is hardly possible to distinguish any tendency or preference. One could say, perhaps, that he adopts Pauline argument, and is closer to the Epistles than were many other Russians of his times. He favored the pastoral epistles. Unlike many Russians who were fired by the imagery of the book of Revelation, Tikhon, although he so often turned to the thought of the future life, gave no predominance to the Apocalypse.

A true Orthodox, Tikhon relied to a great extent on the

patristic writings. One finds, scattered throughout his *Works*, quotations from the Fathers. Of the West, we find Saints Ambrose, Jerome, Augustine (references to the last are mainly from the *Soliloquium*).[1] Of the East, he mentions the historian Eusebius, some monastic events in the life of St. Antony, cites a few lines from the (pseudo) Macarius of Egypt and of St. Ignatius of Antioch, and points to the "soul-moving" sermon on the departure of the soul by St. Cyril of Alexandria and to the hymns of St. John Damascene. Much more space is devoted to St. Basil, that great light of Orthodox monasticism, though not so much on the subject of monasticism as on that of children and their upbringing, on virtues and, in many instances, on eucharistic teaching.[2]

The predominant patristic influence is that of St. John Chrysostom. Not only is he quoted with such frequence as to reveal that Tikhon had widely read the voluminous works of the Bishop of Constantinople, but a whole separate treatise, in two volumes, *The Flesh and the Spirit*, is entirely supported by references to Chrysostom. It is tempting to suggest a certain parallel between their lives and struggle, to compare Tikhon's departure from his see with the exile of Chrysostom, to note a similarity in the tone of their last epistles. They both shrank from honors and distrusted those who solicited the episcopal rank; once elected, however, they had the highest esteem for their calling and a strong sense of responsibility. Both were "evangelical" in the tradition of the school of Antioch, with its emphasis on the historicity of the gospels and their moral implications. In Chrysostom, the liturgical doctor of the Eastern Church, Tikhon found a teacher of the realistic mysticism which indissolubly links the person of Christ with the sacrament of the altar. Their attitude towards monasticism was similar. Above all, they were akin in their compassion, their deeply Christian type of humanism, and in their spontaneous love of the poor and the afflicted. Social evils provoked in them a similar uncompromising indignation.

Liturgical books are also occasionally mentioned by Tikhon, particularly when he wrote to the clergy who would have been familiar with "page so and so, readings for such and such feast."

A markedly restricted space is devoted in his works to the saints generally or to the Russian ones. This may be due in part to the fact that latterly St. Dimitry, Bishop of Rostov, had dedicated his life to the revision and editing of the lives of the saints.[3] Indeed, Tikhon recommended the reading of the *Chetyi-Minei*, the sixteenth-century compilation of the lives of the saints. His teacher, Joasath Mitkevich, was editing the records of the early Russian saints, the Kiev *Paterikon*. There was therefore no need for Tikhon to dwell upon this subject. Yet one cannot help feeling that restriction in this field of study was also governed by personal choice. Tikhon was so deeply gripped by the gospel story itself, so devoted to the Bible and to the person of Christ, that no man or men, however holy, could hold his attention for long. Above all, he wished to preach Christ.

It is not easy to point to definite borrowings from Russian religious writers. Tikhon gave patristic names in order to support his words by the authority of the acknowledged Doctors of the Church. There was less need to mention his countrymen: it was considered that they all lived within the boundaries of the same spiritual and intellectual world, and took subject-matter from the treasure store of the Church's wisdom. One can therefore speak of parallels, of coincidences or of likenesses between writers rather than trace the exact origin of their thought. In some instances, moreover, it would involve excursions into a highly specialized field of Byzantine-Slavonic influences, which lie outside the present survey. Much belongs also to a world-wide Christian tradition, particularly sermons with the examples of quarrelling clergy, of money-making priests seeking orders "not for Jesus but for the bite of bread," or with diatribes against drink, superstitions, deceit in trade, the oppression of the poor or false miracles. It is enough to mention here among those spiritual predecessors of Tikhon who voiced opinions similar to his a few prominent names: St. Theodossy of Pechersk in the eleventh century and to a lesser extent, Cyril, Bishop of Turov; Serapion, Bishop of Vladimir (thirteenth century); Ivan

Vishensky (or Vishnevsky, a Ukrainian monk and priest in the seventeeth century). One might note separately the idea of brotherhood through baptism and communion which is also to be found in Kliment (Constantin) Smoliatich (twelfth century) and the emphasis on Christ, "who walked in poverty and had nowhere to lay his head"—an emphasis so peculiar to the popular *Spiritual Songs*, and to Russian devotional ideas up to the end of the nineteenth century.[4] One might also compare St. Tikhon's criticism of misuses in the life of the Church with those raised at the councils in the fifteenth and sixteenth centuries, in particular the Stoglav Council (1551). One associates Tikhon with all the reforming movements within the Russian Church. Whatever particular patristic works or sermons of various eastern and western preachers of the middle Ages Tikhon might have read, a great many were in circulation, and there is no possibility of tracing them. A systematic collection of didactic Sunday sermons came out in Russia only in the seventeenth century.[5]

When we read the note which Tikhon sent to the Synod together with the collection of his works, we recognize the traditional attitude of an Orthodox writer. It was the business of the whole Church to judge which of his works were right and worthy of further publication. Many monks of old made similar dedications: "Ye who are spiritual, for God's sake correct my works in the spirit of meekness and do not curse me, a sinner."[6] Such words were repeatedly found in the epistles of Maxim the Greek.

Inasmuch as he lived in the times of secularization, he was not directly concerned with those who championed a monastic life unburdened by possessions. There are no direct statements on this subject in his *Works*; but his whole life and teaching leave no doubt that in this thorny question he was more likely to side with the supporters of "non-possession." Their champion, St. Nil of Sora (1435-1508), was defeated and accused of excessive tolerance to the unorthodox. His writings hardly circulated, and one is inclined to think that Tikhon was not personally acquainted with the *Rule* of St. Nil, with its strong biblical note, which is also an important document on contemplative monasticism in Russia.[7]

One influence strikes us as unmistakable. Though Maxim the Greek is not mentioned by name, either by Tikhon, or by any of his biographers, the Bishop was obviously well acquainted with his writings, both through having lived in the Otroch monastery and through having studied in the library of St. Sophia's cathedral of Novgorod, where the *Works* of Maxim were to be found. It was not the doctrinal polemics that struck a cord of sympathy in Tikhon, but that biblical and moral trend which made them both imitators of St. John Chrysostom. Actually, many passages found in both of them originated in the works of St. John Chrysostom, and we can only conjecture how many of these came to Tikhon directly or by way of Maxim.[8]

If the expository style of Tikhon's sermons links him with these latter writers, his imagery when he speaks of the beauty of nature connects him with the Cappadocians and with those numerous samples of both biblical and patristic literature which can be regarded as the first inspirer of poetry.

In Tikhon's catechetical definitions of the eucharist and of penance one discerns Catholic phraseology. Undoubtedly this can be traced back to the writings of Peter Moghila, considered as standard works by those Kievan scholars who had taught Tikhon.

Was Tikhon, a Russian of the eighteenth century, typical of his epoch? What was his connection with the ecclesiastical world of his day? It seems obvious that he could not sympathize with the Old Believers or with any who laid emphasis on the sacred ritual as a way to salvation. He was a non-ritualist; his concern was the living word of God rather than rubrics. Still less was he influenced by the controversy on the moment of eucharistic consecration. He avoided doctrinal disputes, and preferred a frank act of faith when reason was powerless.

A question of great interest in raised by an allusion in Lebedev to the correspondence of St. Tikhon with the elders and monks of the community of Sarov, where another saint was practising asceticism (Seraphim, 1759-1833). Sarov had also a link with the monastery of Valaam, supported by the Metropolitan of St. Petersburg, Gabriel, whom Tikhon knew.

Both these communities began to follow the spiritual methods rediscovered at Mount Athos by a Russian monk, Paissy (Velichkovsky). Some Greek monks, we know, had visited Tikhon at Zadonsk. Some of Paissy's disciples came to the Voronezh region in the early nineteenth century. Was Tikhon directly in contact with any of Paissy's disciples? How much did he know of this movement which led to the revival of Russian contemplative monasticism? It is important to point out this possible field of research, though at present we possess no documents on the subject. We see Tikhon at any rate connected with those who strove, like Gabriel, for the reform of monastic life and, like Platon, with those who were active in the field of theological education.

The period became notorious, on the other hand, for its official document, the *Spiritual Regulation*.[9] In spite of its polemical ardour and Protestant exaggerations, the *Regulation* bore upon some misuses in the Russian Church, and could in parts be acceptable to a zealous man eager to pour the cleansing spirit into Church life. Tikhon's criticism is due to his sincere concern for the Church's purity, and does not contain the elements of spite and rationalism found in the *Regulation*. In that respect Tikhon is at one with his generation and seems to join with them. It may be of interest to trace the close parallel between Tikhon, Platon Levshin and Georgy (Konissky, Bishop of Mogilev, 1717-95) in their ideas on the sacrament, especially on confession and in their expository sermons.[10] Konissky's book on *The Duty of Parish Priests* (1776) is strikingly similar to Tikhon's pastoralia. Whether there were borrowings, or who the first author was, we have no means of ascertaining, apart from those elements that belong to the general tradition. Konissky wrote this book in collaboration with Parfeny (Sopkovsky, who by then had become Bishop of Smolensk, but who had taught Tikhon in the Novgorod seminary). It may be that some scholastic tradition was handed down to both Georgy and Tikhon through their teacher.

All these men reacted against reliance upon external rites and veneration, and laid stress on personal, sincere and true

Christianity. This return to the gospels seemed to some suspect of a Protestant flavor.

Two western representatives of Protestantism were among Tikhon's chosen authors: Hall and Arndt. Joseph Hall, Bishop of Norwich and Exeter (1547-1656), suggested in his *Occasional Meditations* (written in 1601-5) an approach to events of daily life as to so many parables of the spiritual world.[11] Tikhon entitled his meditations *The Spiritual Treasure gathered from the World*. This was a novel form for a Russian religious writer, but on close comparison it becomes evident that the actual images and impressions which provoked the meditations are not those treated by Hall. *Vier Buecher vom wahren Christentum*, by Johann Arndt (first published in 1605, and in Russian translation by Simeon Todorsky in 1735) can be recognized in Tikhon's work on *True Christianity*. To speak of an influence would seem to us an exaggeration. There is some resemblance in a few headings, in chapters on faith and its fruits, on repentance, on the road to glory, on the Cross, on prayer as the food of faith, on the love of God and men. What united him with these pietist writers and, through them, with the evangelical western world, was a certain distrust of speculation, a concentration on the person of Christ as he is described in the gospels, the endeavor to live the divine love here on earth, a call for human and professional virtues as the expression and an outflow of this divine love, and a marked emphasis on the personal relationship between God or Christ and the soul.[12] In view of a tendency among some recent writers to connect Tikhon's work with Arndt's *True Christianity*, it may be worth remembering that as early as 1745 Tikhon collected scriptural *Excerpts for the Good of every true Christian Soul*.

Of the Catholic western tradition Tikhon may have known the *Imitation of Christ*. The book is not mentioned in his *Works* (neither are the preceding authors), but the likeness between some of Tikhon's meditations and those in the *Imitation* seems apparent.

His *Works* were thus the product of solid culture and manifold influences. He is outstanding, but he is not alone. With the Russian religious writers of his time and of old, with Maxim the Greek, that admirer of Savonarola, Bishop Tikhon goes back to the Christian fathers of the East and West and, as did St. Basil and St. John Chrysostom, joins the ranks of those preachers of the gospel who were so ardent in expressing the fullness of the good tidings. This lends to his pronouncements that wholeness, that simplicity and spontaneity which no learning can ever give.

For purposes of practical examination we shall consider his writings under a few subheadings: those addressed to his flock, as his *social teaching*; those to the clergy as *pastoralia*; then the works dealing with the *doctrinal background*, and with its application to the spiritual life, *ascetico-mystical* teaching.

Social Teaching

Bishop Tikhon had no theoretical views on society or politics. His ethical teaching flowed directly from his religious conviction. His whole outlook was imbued with the spirit of the gospels. Society was inseparable in his mind from the loving God and the individual man in his relation to both his creator and his fellow-creatures. The evils of "this world of sorrows" were dark, like black shadows in contrast to the light of divine love. Nevertheless, as a pastor in a concrete world, he had to speak of this supernatural love. The originality and the convincing power of his words lie precisely in the application of his doctrine to the realities of his age. The very repetition of examples, the somewhat lengthy argument, so typical of the eighteenth-century writer, both bear witness to his vigilance and immediate sense of social justice and responsibility. When he explained "why one must love one's neighbor," his language lost all formality; reminiscent of the epistles of St. James and of the writings of St. John Chrysostom, it was yet Tikhon's own voice:

> Every man is our brother, created in the image and likeness of God, redeemed by the Blood of Christ, a member of the one Church, called to eter-

nal salvation. To love is to dwell in God—union with God is a great thing. He who loves is Christ's disciple. All other gifts are nothing without love. One cannot love God without it. He who loves his brother remains in the light, he who hates him is a murderer. Love is the foretaste of eternal life, where there will be nothing but love of one another, consolation and joy in one another. Love of one's neighbor is assimilation to God and the approach to him. General welfare derives from mutual love. O how happy would all be if they could love one another! There would be no theft, robbery or extortion, no murder, violence, deceit, cunning, reproaches, malicious words, scolding, calumnies, scorn; neither keys nor locks nor watchers would be needed to guard one's belongings. There would not be so many weeping and shedding tears of blood, there would be no hearing of the plaintive voices of widows, orphans and so many poor and defenceless people crying out to Heaven. The courts of law would not be overburdened with complaints; starving brethren would not wander in the streets and markets; half-naked members of Christ would not shiver from cold and frost; dungeons would not be crowded with prisoners arrested for debts, poll-taxes and arrears; finally, there would be no beggars or paupers but everything would be dangerless, restful, peaceful; all would be equal. O love, bond of perfection, love!"[13]

Thus, equality lies at the root of his Christian conception of man. Every human being is a temple of God, his soul can be fed on holy communion; he is called to prayerful converse with God and is ministered to by the angels. To the "haughty rich" Tikhon opposes this paradox of humility and glory; a Christian's nobility comes from heaven, and though on earth "sorrow and the cross are his flag," side by side with them goes the adoption of the sons, the inheritance incorruptible: Phil. 2. 5; 1 Peter 1. 4; 1 John 3. 1.[14]

On the ground of all men's common origin and end, he

urged his flock to acts of material and spiritual mercy:

> Charity can be both spiritual and material. It is real when it extends even to the worthless and the lazy. The greater the need, the more splendid the charity. It should be perfectly voluntary, untinged with vanity or desire of praise. What we give must be the outcome of our own toil and must not come from riches gained through cupidity. Forget your previous acts of charity for fear of becoming vain. Choose those who are in the greatest need, yet do good to all, even to your enemies.[15]

True alms are those which cause the giver some discomfort or privation. Charity is the outcome of the love of God, and soon becomes natural, just as in a body "a hand tends an injured foot."

Tikhon's advice on spiritual mercy which he gave both to clergy and to the laity is interesting. He begged them to exhort the others or to warn them against moral danger, but "secretly and amicably." "Love will find the words—this does not require eloquence. Often a roughish word seasoned by divine love does what the most expressive orators cannot achieve." Compassion towards a soul appeared to him as natural as an act of practical help: "Surely, it is not too difficult to pay someone's debts to get him out of prison, or to pay for the liberation of some prisoner of war?" but, failing the means, people should at least have the desire to help: "for your heart-felt sorrow and compassion for the poor are of no less value than what you actually do for them." And "mercy and almsgiving pray to God better than men do, ceaselessly interceding before him for the giver."[16]

The education of society in that spirit of mutual assistance must needs begin with the training of the individual. One of Bishop Tikhon's first booklets was that on *The Duty of Christian parents to their children and of children to their parents* (1765).[17] Its biblical references were mainly Deut. 6. 4-8; 11. 19; Ps. 78; it owes also much to the teaching of St. Basil. It must be borne in mind that it was the first attempt in Russia to give some religious instruction on the family. The striking feature of this little work is the respect for the child's personality. It aims at stirring parents to the fullness of the love of God, so that by word and example they might teach it to their children and put it as the basis of family life and of society. Tikhon's love for children far exceeded his written admonitions. With what care he begged people to watch over their behavior and speech, so as not to wound the soul of a child who might accidentally see or hear them (the idea taken over by Dostoevsky). With a charming touch reminiscent of his own ways of treating the young, he said that God sometimes attracts us by promises of rewards "as one can attract a small child with an apple." Could his love be less? Was not its prototype the divine love of Father and children?

"As a sapling, if it is allowed to bend in any part, grows into a crooked tree, so is a child." To the upper classes he said sternly:

> God will not ask you whether you taught your children French, German or Italian or the politics of society life—but you will not escape divine reprobation for not having instilled goodness into them. I speak plainly but I tell the truth: if your children are bad, your grandchildren will be worse... and the evil will thus increase... and the root of all this is our thoroughly bad education.

(It is curious to compare this criticism with the similar protests heard from the representatives of the secular literature of his times: the satirists, Kantemir and Fon-Vizin, the well-known author of memoirs, A. Bolotov, and the famous publisher, N. I. Novikov.) Tikhon warned his listeners against the life of idleness and pleasures and against the unhealthy incitements to sex curiosity resulting from dances among adolescents—all new forms of society life begotten at the time of Peter and his successors. Tikhon wanted the young to be humane rather than polished. And we know from his life how he fought to give them education.

He advocated teaching children fundamental religious

truths: that God is one, that Christ was God incarnate; the purpose of redemption; the ten commandments. He advised parents to take children to services, particularly to the liturgy, and, at home, to bring them up in the habit of attending a morning and evening prayer of thanksgiving. He believed that a child would understand a reminder of the baptismal vows, of the brevity of life and the judgement to come, of the fate of the wicked and the eternity of joy. A parent, he stressed, ought to be a true friend and guide, "a father in the spirit as well." He should teach by word, and avoid any bad example, "even punishment of their serfs." Strictness may be a duty; it may be a mistake to spoil a child by "being soft and weak," but, if corporal punishment becomes unavoidable, it would be abhorrent "to display anger and rage." (The traditional authority on this point was Sirach, but how different seems the spirit.) The child was addressed earnestly by Tikhon as an understanding being. If he had suffered innocently, "he should meekly yet with firmness make it known," and then, "overlooking the weaknesses" of his parents, he should seek reconciliation.

Women, who in so many early Russian religious writings appear as the instruments of the devil, did not altogether escape Tikhon's criticism. Yet with regard to them, too, he brings a new note: consideration for their human personality and rights. Even when he upbraids them, it is for some concrete faults, and mostly for those which have repercussions on social life. This is very different indeed from the *Domostroy*, the famous sixteenth-century work on household manners which, true to medieval ideas, allots to the woman the place of her husband's most obedient friend—or slave—and housekeeper.

Tikhon lived at a time when women of the upper classes—a Petrine innovation—were just beginning to enter society. Enthusiastic about western fashions, they went about in wigs and used cosmetics—"spoiling the picture of a great master" (a patristic metaphor). "If only they remembered the pure face of Christ which was slapped and spat upon!" At home their clothes were unprepossessing; when they went out they wore finery. "What does this signify if not that they seek to attract" someone outside their family circle? Much worse, this thirst for fashion provokes "Eve, whose character is always the same, and who always tempts," not only to incite passions, but also to influence her lover or husband: a wife, wrote Tikhon, is often the cause of bribery, corruption and inhumanity to the debtor and the poor.

Among the masses a woman had no status. As a serf she was the plaything of her masters. Hard-working, beaten by the men of her own family, she had neither a defender nor a say in the choice of her bridegroom. In the light of these circumstances, Tikhon's words on marriage acquire a meaning which they are in danger of losing for a modern and educated person. He teaches that marriage is as an act of mutual love and respect, both of soul and of body (Eph. 5. 22-23). If, with St. Paul, he writes on the submission of woman, he also stresses the husband's duty to teach, love and elevate her. The custom of abandoning wedlock in favor of ascetical abstinence must have been common enough for the Bishop to refer to it. His disapproved of forms of abstinence likely to provoke the other party to a breach of fidelity. Mutual consent in love and in abstinence was the Church's and his own advice to them. He was seeking to place woman on a footing of equality in the sphere in which she was most deprived of rights and which was the most normal for her— marriage and the family. Above all, he taught husbands no less than wives, addressing human beings and strongly reminding them that "in Christ Jesus there is no male or female."

His fundamental theme is that of rich and poor. "Let no one think that I mean that, in itself, wealth is damnation or that poverty saves one." Money, like so many other objects of the natural world, is "neutral." It may either be considered as a gift of God or become dangerous when the heart attaches itself to it and when it begets self-esteem. Wealth should be stewardship. He took 1 Tim. 6. 17 as the basis for his teaching on riches. "How do you spend your money? You are its guardian, not its master and squanderer. It is not given you for your own fancies but for the sake of your neighbor in need." He was prepared to admit the existence of a righteous wealth; if spent soberly, without self-indulgence and in the active practice of good works, it could even become useful instead of harmful.[18]

Wealth is seldom accumulated, however, "without offence to the poor, without some cunning." Even if one cannot trace the actual guilt in the making of this or that fortune, the life of a rich man prevents him from sharing with others. Possessions mean inequality; they breed envy in the deprived classes, "for it is not a small grievance to live in penury with wife and children and to pay taxes." Thus wealth is a likely source of separation from the fullness of divine and neighborly love.

To help a man in need is "to understand that Christ is begging through the poor and to help Christ."[19] For Tikhon felt this mystical imputation to the poor of the incarnate life of Christ—typical of Russian thought—but knew its very different aspect in ordinary life. A soul can voluntarily enter upon the path of poverty as a condition of the mystical life, or at least can spiritually understand and accept it; but in the daily life of the majority, poverty degrades, fills one with longing for possessions—"this poison"—teaches one cunning and lies. It is a source of envy and false self-importance: "even a servant in a rich house would often forbid a poor man so much as to approach the door." A man who so untiringly helped the poor had the right to say that it was equally important for both rich and poor to have a detached and generous attitude towards property. "Not he who possesses much is rich, but he who is content with what he has."

Tikhon vigorously condemned usury, whether it came from the nobleman or merchant, or from the enriched, enterprising and close-fisted peasant. "Do not take more than you have lent; and if it is too hard for your debtor, forget about it altogether." Yet those who avoid paying their debts commit a theft, a lie and a breach of promise, "the consequences of which are later suffered by poor folk" who can gain no more confidence.[20]

Tradesmen were warned against their particular form of deceit or to speak simply, of theft. It is a sin to sell rotten wares as good ones, sick cattle as sound, marten as sable, a cheap object as an expensive one. It is theft to increase the weight of salt by adding water. It is a sin to demand exorbitant prices. Worst of all, not only do such people lie, but even swear, as they lie, that they are telling the truth. If only those who call out their wares and those who buy would, each in his own business relations, dwell in the simplicity and truth of Christ!

Nor did Tikhon spare the employer who "withheld wages" from the working man or who suddenly lowered the wage he had promised. But he also warned the employee against a perfunctory and negligent accomplishment of his duties—his "form of theft." Tikhon's sincerity consisted precisely in that, while showing clearly where his sympathies lay, and while strongly supporting and defending the oppressed against the powerful, he never flattered them. Instead of excusing and patronizing them, he spoke to them as to full equals in Christian dignity and therefore just as responsible for their lives and characters as any of their more fortunate brethren. He knew that among them there were deceivers, idlers, drunkards, people who were cruel to their children and wives.

The relationship between landlord and serfs was a constant source of sorrow and preoccupation for him. The peasants were for him "poor little sheep, beloved, patient sufferers," and he addressed to the gentry severe and uncompromising words when they, as members of the Church, also came to listen to him.

> You believe the gospels which teach us that Christ imputes to himself anything given in his holy name to a poor man or a beggar. Why then do you not feed the hungry? A buffoon who entertains you, a flatterer who shamelessly flatters you, departs from you well satisfied. Christ, the giver of the heavenly kingdom, you send away empty-handed.

Liberal is your hand to squander in banqueting; but you would not lose a penny to save a poor peasant from selling the last of his cattle to pay you his rent. The hounds, your pleasure, feed from your table, while your servant does not always have bread for his need. You lose hundreds a night in gambling. How thrifty you become over a rouble for the deliverance of a wretch thrown into a dungeon for debt! Such then is your faith, such its fruit!

How unlike is this sort of religion to that striving of a godly soul which, in its effort, is like "a laborer in the field dripping with sweat through the summer and scorched by the sun in the hope of gathering the longed-for fruit."[21]

To the masters he said that it was strange "to possess" souls and bodies of men "no worse than yourselves, and often indeed better."[22] That he profoundly disapproved of serfdom there is no doubt. Surrounded by serf-owners and landowners, he assured the slaves that Christ, who assumed the form of a servant, was their model and their pledge of higher dignity.

Though you are called slaves, you are freemen of Christ; in your body you work for men, but your souls are free from the works of sin; you have no freedom and nobility like your masters, but your souls are bejewelled with Christian freedom and nobility. Rejoice, for the inheritance of the sons of God awaits you also. . . . They will leave all they possess. Remember the poverty of Christ! Poor people, you beloved sufferers, do not faint in your hearts; here you suffer with Lazarus, but together with him you will dwell in the bosom of Abraham!

Such promises were far more than words of consolation. Eternal life held for Tikhon himself tremendous reality. Above all, he accompanied such exhortations with practical help and with remonstrations to the masters.

Will you escape judgement and condemnation, you who are false to your baptismal vows, who offend the dignity of another Christian by misusing your power, by burdening your peasants with hard work, rent and taxes? Such men live lawless lives, forgetting both divine and earthly justice. They say: "I am still young, let me buy some more villages and peasants. . . . I shall snatch this from such a widow or from that low-born fool. There is no one to protect them or to stop me. The Tsar is far away, the hands of the judges shall be filled from my purse, and everything will go smoothly. Then I shall build myself a rich house and shall ornament it, I shall get myself an English carriage and a team of lovely horses, I shall plant a pleasant garden with avenues and galleries. In it I shall construct lovely ponds, so as to have somewhere to go out with my friends, for walks and enjoyment. I shall store up good wine and good food. I shall try to have vocal and instrumental music for the better enjoyment of myself and of my guests."

In sorrow for the oppressed and anxious also for sinners, Tikhon said:

Will you escape judgement, you who enter another's wedding-bed, who shed the blood of brethren, offenders of widows and orphans, you who devour all the labors of your laborers and workmen; you blasphemers who seek to efface from the face of the earth any one who grieves you by ever so small a word?

If existing conditions could not be changed, at least Tikhon would teach masters their duties to their serfs. "Let orders be in conformity with the commandments of God"; let masters have care for the nourishment, life and health of their subjects; by a reasonable administration bring about the welfare of their families, houses and agriculture; let them observe fidelity and honesty in respect of their peasants' wedlock. They should listen with favor to any petition from the serfs, teach them, give them rest and release, not occupy their holidays with work, so that they may at least have time to say a prayer and to attend a service—and they should pray for their servants and slaves. (For—his mental conclusion is easily read—should they really do so, slavery itself would crumble away.)[23]

"It is a sin to offend a man of wealth, but it is inhuman to offend a poor man." To Tikhon's mind every injustice is a violation of the divine order: "in which the sun gives light to the moon, the moon turns its rays upon the earth and one star contributes to the shining of another." How often he repeated that "the palaces and theatres of the gentry are paid for by their serfs." When some objected to his exhortation to simplicity on the ground that they had taken no monastic vows, Tikhon replied: "My beloved, all these words of love, poverty and service were spoken before there were any monasteries at all."[24]

He was grieved and confused to see the growing pomp of festivities, and of daily life, where the debts of the gentry fell as a yoke upon their serfs. "Luxury and avarice are contrary sisters, but both mortally wound the human heart." He saw people sitting "at the feet of the world." "Beware of luxury as of the plague, it weakens the soul, it teaches the Christian to grab another's belongings and it restrains his hand from almsgiving," he wrote to a friend. "It is all luxury arising from sheer vanity, it is an offence against the poor."[25]

> In what land is there more theft, robbery, extortion and other lawless deeds than in one where the ruler is inspired with this pernicious love of the world? For expensive coaches with expensive horses, for ponds or gardens or theatre galleries—whence come the funds? The master must collect them from his serfs, he has to strike them with still heavier poll-taxes.
>
> This affects all classes: tradesmen, judges, officials, all

flatter the rich and powerful and resort to lying, extortion and bribes.

> We see this epidemic raging throughout our land. Everybody has become a magnate, all strut about in fox and sable coats, they refuse to ride in anything but an English coach, they cannot drink simple vodka, they must have foreign wines, and in their stables they keep no less than six horses furnished with the most expensive harness.

This is no merely puritanical exposure of luxury, but a reminder of One "who went barefoot from one land to the other." Are such manners compatible with the image left by the earthly life of Christ? Bishop Tikhon contrasts these offensive customs with the privations and sufferings of the poor and the voluntary endurance of Christ. Each sentence is interspersed with ejaculations from the Lenten litanies, so familiar to the Orthodox, yet with some addition of personal grief: "Glory to thy patience, glory to thy endurance, glory to thy love!" This meditation is one of the most vivid chapters on the humiliation of Christ.[26]

Bribery and cynical breaches of law, like ulcers, spring from luxury, "deceit and, in the courts of law, breaches of oath so terrible as to deserve tears." Corrupt officials were to Tikhon worse than thieves, for they possessed rank and income, and were considered as servants of the State. As a consequence of these abuses, he foretold the coming wrath of God: "famine, fires, earthquakes, invasion by the enemy, terrible bloodshed" . . . But even rebellions did not shake the conscience for long.

> You write that since the pretender was caught, people are carrying on as before. . . . Yet, when he was approaching our parts, and imprisoned and ruined people, many of the gentry left their houses and their peasants, many abandoned their dwellings and estates and wished to go away, some actually went,

he wrote to a friend from Zadonsk.[27]

Tikhon, opposed to all violence, disapproved of rebels who "lawlessly, shamelessly rise against legally established authorities; they are enemies of their own country and of the public welfare."[28] "We see such sons of perdition and troubles of the native land who assume the names of lofty persons and bring rebellion and ruin to their land."[29] Society, he believed, is founded and maintained "by moderation."

He had no sympathy with the rebellions, which could only lead to further repression. But he felt for those who were caught. He helped those thrown into dungeons for debt and addressed to them words of unfeigned affection.

> Beloved sufferers of Christ, be strong. Your body is in prison but your spirit is free; your hands and feet are bound but your sacred souls have been released through the grace of Christ; you see no light of day but heaven is open before you. . . . Remember that you are co-sufferers with the martyrs and confessors, and Christ our Lord was bound for our sins. After this prison you will reign with Christ with whom you suffer.[30]

To those who were in hardship or banished, he said:

> If you are exiled, think of the convicts, who in rags and half-naked, are estranged from their native places, who are beaten daily, whose days are spent in forced labor, whose nights are passed in dark, filthy and stinking dungeons, who remain without any comfort and who yet endure.[31]

The indifference of society to all these wounds of the nation particularly distressed Tikhon. When war broke out with Turkey, he wrote in a private letter:

> Our brethren fall by bullets and the sword; others live in continual sorrow and fear; but here we enjoy ourselves madly as though fighting against our own land, like foolish sailors who would dance

whilst their ship was wrecked. The country is groaning under calamities; the public purse is being depleted by war; the young men are no more, only boys and old men are left. But people seek pleasure as if, together with our enemies, they rejoiced over our disasters."[32]

What was Tikhon's attitude to those in power? One finds frequent reminders in his *Works* of the honor and obedience which are due to those in authority. To the victims of injustice or punishment he even counselled resignation. He exhorted people to pray for those at the head of society, and thus to pray for the welfare of the whole country. Must one conclude that he merely repeated those commonplaces of submission which were more or less expected of him? Still more, must one reckon him among those numerous ecclesiastics for whose submissiveness the Russian Church has so often been blamed?

A closer examination shows that the answer is in the negative. Tikhon had a somewhat compassionate attitude towards those in authority. He was sorry for the temptations inextricably bound up with power. "Many would have become saints were it not for their honorable position." He advised moderation in judgement of those "who stand high and lonely like a tall tree," and whose slightest defects spring to notice.

To those in authority he spoke of their lofty duties and of the evils which disfigured this epoch of Russian life. He abhorred calumny and denunciation no less than favoritism, flattery and bribery, and pointed out the brevity of fortunes gained in these ways. He vigorously exposed a style of life pertaining to high rank: "an offence against the poor, a betrayal of one's baptismal vows, a forgetfulness of Christ who had nowhere to lay his head."

Judges, governors, Tsars were there, he taught, to minister to truth and justice. Tikhon begged them not to listen to denunciations, to seek truth and to be afraid of punishing the innocent. If it did happen that they were obliged to inflict some form of punishment, Tikhon implored them to punish "unwillingly." He particularly begged them to beware of "offending words, for that is scolding, mocking and not a legal punishment. Punish, but do not torment. Do not act in anger. Let the time pass, cool down. If need be, show your authority, but remember that all Christians are equal, that you are no better than the person you deal with. Pray for help from above." On the whole, he considered that, to a Christian, a position of authority is nothing but a cross.

Any form of vengeance, injustice or violence, whether it came from those in power or from their subjects, was to him a breach of brotherly love—"a civil war."

Tikhon did not spare the Tsars. "Christian treasure is seldom found in the crowns, titles or great names of the world, in purple and fine linen, or within beautiful and rich walls, but mostly in rags and mangers." He spoke to the rulers of the example they should give: of legal justice, or impartiality, of mercy to their enemies. "Happy the crown adorned with charity and justice"—these jewels are indeed different from the jewels of this world.[33]

Of a ruler's personal conduct he spoke thus. "Whosoever wishes to rule others must strive to become the ruler of his own passions—this should be a Christian's desire. Those who are in Christ have crucified their flesh with its lusts—there you are, my lords the Tsars, may God have mercy upon us!"[34] It should be remembered that this was written under Catherine the Great, and that Tikhon insisted on power "legally established" and never mentioned the "divine right" of monarchy.

His conception of a ruler's duty far transcended that personal morality which a good bishop might be expected to urge. He warned those in authority not to throw the country into wars of aggression:

> Take heed not to involve her in an unjust war. Touch nothing that belongs to others, lest you lose even that which you already possess and lest you shed in vain the blood of your subjects; this is a frightening possibility, and to do so would be a grievous sin before God. It is terrible to shed the blood of one person, and how much more terrible to shed the

blood of many. Rulers will have to answer to God for every one killed in an unjust war.[35]

All misuses generate another evil. That is why outbursts of hatred and rebellion shake the land. Nature itself seems to be involved in the sin of men, and fires, earthquakes, plagues break out over Russia. The sins of untruthful judges, of oppressive landlords, of officials who steal from the public purse, all this "lawlessness and violence" provokes the wrath of God.[36]

Tikhon believed also that at the last day "all judges, all powers will appear at the Universal Judgement. Then will Tsars rise and render account before God the Judge. . . . Princes and magnates, landlords, pastors, all those in authority, from the highest to the lowest, all will have to stand before him and acknowledge all their unjust lawless and soulless dealings with the people who were entrusted to them." Again: "Authorities, landlords, judges, your wrongdoings cry to heaven and denounce you to God; God hears the cry of the oppressed and will call you before his Judgement seat; beloved, repent while there is still time."[37]

Social evil contaminates more than one man; it spreads throughout society. Divinely constituted relationships of equality, respect and brotherly love are forgotten. "The present times see the wickedness which comes when truth is downtrodden and injustice takes its place."[38] The whole of society is affected. The time has come to call out: "Make thy face to shine upon us." A personal sin is healed by repentance; but now Tikhon called to the whole land: "The time has come when we must say: we have sinned with our fathers, we have committed iniquity, we have all done wickedly!" Not individuals alone but the whole nation had offended against divine righteousness. For all the cruelties of Russian life, Tikhon exhorted all to unite in faith and action: "For the sins of all, we must propitiate God by corporate repentance."[39]

Pastoralia

Tikhon, as a bishop, had to be the leader and teacher of his clergy. His writings of a pastoral character often embrace both the priest and the layman, and in this often lies their novelty. His writings of a more specifically ecclesiastical type cover a period of nearly twenty years, and witness to the development of his inward life and thought and also of his literary expression. The early works are in formal style; he enumerates points in an argument or makes use of the question-and-answer form of catechisms. In his Voronezh period, he wrote works of a disciplinary character or brief instructions on doctrine and worship. The free and poetic imagery of his later works could hardly be foreseen in these first attempts, but the motive power—his ardent devotion and his care for people—are unmistakable throughout. His was an arduous task of training unwilling minds; he had to raise the ideals of a clergy content with their half-illiterate state and teach Christian love amidst the strife of a turbulent historical epoch, in the social framework of an absolute State paying lip-service to religion and served by an enslaved peasantry. Here, too, Tikhon's instructions throw a vivid light upon the conditions of the Russian Church of his day. It is useful to consider therefore his first *Instruction to Seminarists* (1765), which consists of twenty-eight points and, slightly abbreviated, runs as follows:

> Remember that you are called to this vocation by God for the benefit of others.
> Study carefully and ask God's help for your work.
> Let it be your intention to apply all that you learn to the service of men and to the glory of God. A learned priest will be more capable of weeding out evil manners and vices.
> Learning avails nothing without a good life. What is the use of teaching others what you do not practise?
> Diligence in study and a good life will bring you reward in heaven; but, even in this life, learning

brings honorable promotion. In order to grow deeper into your calling, you must:

1. Attend the divine services on Sundays.
2. Penetrate into the liturgical year, and seek by reading and singing to grow familiar with it.

Enter deeply into the sacred reading, prayers and singing; avoid conversations and laughter.

4. Carefully avoid vain repetition of the divine name and all forms of current and profane oaths; say, as Christ taught, only "yes" and "no."
5. Show respect to your parents, the authorities and the elders.
6. Have brotherly love towards your comrades; neither provoke nor reproach them.
7. Do not talk about the adults who are in authority over you, for such talk only results in the vice of judging.
8. Watch over yourself and be mindful of the task to which you are called; neither discuss other people nor sneer at them.

Take care not to quarrel, avoid calumny or fighting among yourselves.

10. Beware of bad language, jokes and blasphemies.
11. Do not apply any rude or frivolous nicknames to each other.
12. Take no amusement in indecent or rowdy games.
13. Keep chaste, lest you be excluded from the ranks of the Church.

Next come a few points on discipline and manners: warnings against fisticuffs, public-houses, women, indecent songs or verses copied for friends, and all forms of theft, deceit and drunkenness. Those in lodgings should behave quietly and be tidy; none should lounge about in the marketplace or eat in the streets, like the peasants. The *Instruction* ends with this unofficial note:

"If a boy be found incorrigible he will have to be barred

from the ecclesiastical rank—from which necessity may God in his mercy preserve us."

The Instruction to the monks (1765) comes also within this category of disciplinary advice. But in it he gives certain counsels specifically to monks, reminding them of their vows—"baptismal vows and especially the freely undertaken vows of your profession." He tells them to read the Rule often, to keep their promise of obedience, to respect and pray for their Superior and to avoid judging his ways, even if he is far from perfect. He particularly recommended stability—that is, a daily life of quiet, within the premises of the community; indeed, they must so much respect this enclosure that they could say: "Were I to die, I should not leave this place." He laid stress upon the danger and temptation to which a monk exposes himself by wandering through cities and villages. Words and impressions of the world waste the quiet which has been stored up in silence.

> Your very habit and vows will be brought against you or for you at the Last Judgement. Know that the world with all its allurements will pass away. Yet if we are found naked in virtue, shame will forever remain with us, the whole world will see it—the saints will not recognize us, the angels will be repelled. . . . Live as if you were continually condemned to death.

For a monk's daily life he recommended a method which he had noted down for his own use: "solitude: for the very word monk means a solitary. Avoid idleness. Work with your hands. Be always occupied; that is, pray, read, do some task, meditate." He advocated variety in daily occupations and shorter and more concentrated prayer; and in this he was original, as most monks were more used to monotonous occupations and to long hours of services or prayer in their cell.

The main points of his teaching are summarized in a letter which he wrote to a monk:

> Detach your thoughts from the world; remember

death and the Judgement. Think of it often, especially at night, for this is a peaceful, quiet time suitable for thinking. Remember often, especially during the night, the suffering of Christ. Pray, even compel yourself to pray, repeat that you will not go away. Reject at once all tempting thoughts, but know that they will come again. Be prepared to bear persecution. Between your different tasks read useful books, especially the gospels and the epistles—and meditate upon them."[40]

In none of Tikhon's known *Works* does he teach any method of spiritual life apart from that which emerges from all his exhortations to clergy and lay people in general.

Tikhon exposed the faults of the Church frankly and unsparingly. Not in vain did he recommend Ezekiel, Chapter 34, to the attention of the clergy.

He did not spare rapacious bishops: "Money-loving is always hideous."[41] To a priest who gave the excuse "that one had to live," he answered that the sacred ministry is not a livelihood. He condemned "the popes, the clerics and other people who read the gospel or church services so hastily and perfunctorily that instead of becoming any better it makes them worse."[42]

"The lazy popes"—he did not hesitate to use this disparaging term. He expostulated against "the blind leaders," "the dumb sign-posts" which are stumbling-blocks rather than indicators.

The vigor of his condemnation of the "false piety" of certain priests and monks who cover sloth and religious failure by their black habits finds a parallel only in his sermons to the gentry.

Not because such were the instructions of the *Spiritual Regulation*, nor because most enlightened clergy of the time held these views, but because it was in keeping with the whole of his outlook, Tikhon warned the clergy and monks against ministering to their own profit. He also condemned self-admiring preachers, avid of their own renown and eager for praise. This too seemed to Bishop Tikhon a form of deceit.

Above all, he raised his voice against certain forms of "deceit and robbery" which usually were not reckoned as such. "For robbery can be," he said, "secret and deceitful as well as open. Nor is the church exempt from such deceit. What is the use of fasting and prayers which hide vanity and hypocrisy? There are worse things. Money has been obtained from credulous and humble people under the pretext of religion." Like Platon Levshin in his *Orthodox Theology*, Tikhon wrote: "It is robbery for hypocrites to make money under a cloak of piety, or by lawlessly exposing false relics of saints, or icons which, they claim, work miracles, thus inducing simple folk to make donations."[43]

He protested against religious self-deception and false piety hidden behind formal acts of devotion:

> Many people erect high temples and decorate them, they build tall belfries and cast great bells, they sew rich vestments for the churches and frame the sacred books, the icons and the cross with gold and jewels. With these material gifts they wish to please the immaterial God; but they despise the poor men who have been thrown into prison for debt, they leave them to their fate; and thus they do what God has not ordained and do not what he has ordained. I do not condemn by this the building of churches, I only condemn neglect of the Word of God. Churches are necessary, but not the magnificence of churches. Public worship can be held in any temple, provided it is clean, but people—the living temples of God—cannot exist without food, clothes and rest.[44]

Tikhon's views on the calling and duty of the clergy were both simple and lofty. Much of them was based on the Scriptures (Acts 20. 28; Eph. 4. 11; Ezek. 34). The pastoral epistles, he said, are a measure of the virtue which must adorn a pastor. The apostle shows in his epistles to Titus and to Timothy how zealous and careful a pastor must be. By pastors we mean bishops and clergy. The very name indicates what they should be, for they are shepherds of the living, reasonable sheep ("sheep of the Logos") created in the divine image and redeemed by the blood of Christ. You must not seek after honor or rank and at the same time expect to be called by God. Reflect, if you are called, whether you are prepared to lift this sacred burden.

The teacher must be ready to learn; he who exhorts to goodness must be good, pure, prayerful, of careful conscience. A pastor must incite to true repentance—by warning the wicked, by encouraging the faint-hearted, by uprooting superstitions, heresies and schisms and by fighting social evils:

> If people, whoever they may be, act against a law, and you know about it, beware of keeping silence; reprove them, beloved, even if you have to suffer for it. Be not like a dumb dog that does not bark while the thieves are plundering the house. . . . Thunder with the word—but have pity upon the sinners.
>
> The church is the place for teaching. Yet whereever he is, a pastor can teach, following Christ's example. As the gospels show us, any matter can be the occasion for a word of instruction: sitting at a meal one can speak of the table of the Kingdom of Heaven, etc. . . .
>
> You must first think out and understand well what you have to say to people. Food is salted and cooked before it is served up. Likewise, a pastor must first inwardly digest the food of the Divine Word, season it with the salt of reasoning and only then propose it to those who hunger.
>
> Words of censure, when spoken generally and publicly, must be strict and sharp so as to stir sin-

ners. If, however, spoken to an individual sinner, they must be affectionate and full of compassion.

Expose unrighteousness, whoever be guilty, even to the point of suffering for it.

Do not flatter the rich instead of teaching them. Speak the word of God as a messenger of God.

Beware of preaching the word for the sake of human praise.

Teach by your whole life. Lead people to the true native land of heaven.

Pray—and learn from 1 Tim. 3. 2-4.

How often he insisted upon this metaphor of a messenger:

> Be the salt, be the guide to the heavenly fatherland and not a sign-post perched on the road, which indicates the way but itself moves nowhere. Call others to the great supper of eternal bliss but go yourself too before them.[45]

He warned the clergy of the account they would have to give for their flock. With a peasant's consciousness of the responsibility of a shepherd for his sheep, he spoke of the reasonable sheep.

> It is for the sake of the sheep that Christ-loving bishops wear a mitre and carry a staff. And how could a shepherd tell his master: "I do not know where the sheep is"?[46] See how amazing was the early Christian pastors' care and zeal for their flock. I do not speak of those of the present day; everyone knows about them! And I understand by pastors both bishops and clergy.[47]

Because he had such a strict and lofty idea of priesthood, he advised men not to undertake the burden of this honor unless they were fully aware of its weight.

> For if it is God's appointment, you will stand

in honor in the life of the apostolate, in readiness to bear the cross and persecution with a heart full of burning zeal.[48]

Theirs is a prophetic ministry:

> Of old, God sent prophets, in our day bishops and clergy. Therefore they are messengers, they are salt, they are the bowels of their flock which make their sustenance digestible. Beloved, you have stepped into the calling and duties of an apostle: imitate the apostles by teaching and by life that with them you may have part in the Last Supper of eternity and that you may bring many with you.[49]

Vigilant, valiant, full of loving art in dealing with people, pastors must "guard the house of Israel, the Church entrusted to them"; but also they must keep a watch over their own souls. "Read the Epistles to Timothy and to Titus." Think of Peter. Whom did Christ order to tend his sheep? He who professed to love him. For loving Christ goes together with tending his sheep. God will "know thy works" as the Book of Revelation says. "Prayer is your weapon." A pastor is the builder of his flock—it is dependent upon his integrity. Tikhon knew the hardships of this apostolate amidst an unrepentant or indifferent people and the temptation to give it up. "Nevertheless, you should never stop, but always thunder with the word, and meanwhile in your heart sympathize with and compassionately love the sinners who are perishing, and never despair of any one so long as he lives."

While he thus exhorted his clergy to a life worthy of their calling, Bishop Tikhon at the same time begged the lay-folk in their charge to adopt a special attitude towards them:

> Listen to the word of God handed down to you through the priest, and do as it teaches you; look upon the priest as the messenger of God; love him as your father; care for him as he cares for you; do not believe calumnies about him and do not spread

gossip; be not scandalized at his shortcomings, and pronounce no judgement; pray for him, for his duty is heavy and the forces of evil are raised against him; if he teaches without carrying out his teaching himself, remember the words of St. Matthew 23. 2, 3.

Whenever Tikhon expounded the duty of a priest or any Christian, he always began by confronting his listeners with the Bible. This was the real foundation of his teaching.

> God in his mercy gave us the Holy Scriptures, that we might read them, and reading might fulfil what is sent by God to man, revealing his holy will and teaching us how to live. Consider with what attention and willingness then we ought to read God's letter to us. If an earthly king—our Tsar—wrote you a letter would you not read it with great joy? Certainly, with great rejoicing and careful attention. The King of heaven has sent a letter to you, an earthly and mortal man: yet you almost despise such a gift, so priceless a treasure. Whenever you read the gospel Christ himself is speaking to you. And while you read, you are praying and talking with him. God speaks to man, the King of Heaven talks with the corruptible creature, the Lord holds converse with the servant. What can be more pleasant . . . more instructive?[50]

St. Tikhon continued to teach reverence towards the word of God: "Listen diligently, reflect on what is read, and endeavor to put these words into practice. The word of God was not given to us in order that it should repose in writing on paper, but that we might use it spiritually, that we might be illumined, led into the way of truth and salvation, correct our manners, and live according to its rules in this world and do things well-pleasing to God." It is a "seed, and its fruit is in us—heavenly and holy living. By this word we are called unto life everlasting. The word of God is a help against sin."[51]

One of the proofs of the divinity of Christ, declared Tikhon, is that in spite of all persecutions, "the sacred Bible, which contains the heavenly teaching, has remained intact. Those who read attentively feel within them a spiritual action. The Holy Scripture gives testimony to itself through its power and action, through the comfort, exhortation, detachment, repentance, etc., which it inspires. It is confirmed by signs and miracles and testified by the blood of the apostles and martyrs." A serious proof of its veracity is also the fact that "the apostles did not conceal their past faults but wrote them in the Scriptures and published them abroad."[52]

He wrote that all errors and vices came from ignorance of the Word of God which exposes them, that it is indispensable to anyone who desires to live according to the will of God.[53] The Bible reveals to us the divine will. Through it, our faith grows and increases, mankind reaches unity of faith and grows into the stature of Christ. It gives us the hope of sonship, of glory, of love.[54]

The word of God is the condition of truth in the whole Church and a corrective of our own faith, "for our feelings are much more liable to deceive us." It is literally as necessary as daily bread. This is particularly true for pastors. Yet the Word is to each and all. People of any rank or class, clerics and lay folk, the noble and the simple, men and women, can and must read it or listen to it. It would be a grave error to limit it to the clergy. Such an idea is "nothing else than the snare of the devil who fears the living faith and salvation."

How, then, should the Bible be read? "One must most specially read the Holy Scriptures and after them other Christian Orthodox books, little by little, with understanding; if you do not follow, put it aside—later on it will become clear of itself." One must apply in deed what has been read: "If you only sharpen your mind from the book without setting right your will, you will be worse for the reading than you were before: for learned and intelligent fools are often more wicked than simple ignoramuses."[55] He advised that reading of the Bible be supplemented by reading the Fathers, which would help in its interpretation.

The Bible should be read

like a King's letter, with devotion, keenness and zeal; not in order to show one's wit but for the sake of salvation. Hide it in your heart like a treasure and feed thereon. Think that for you and me and for each debased, miserable and sinful man the gospels are an appeal to repentance and a promise of mercy. Read without paying attention to the behavior of people around you. Pray for the enlightenment of our reason and will and apply the text to our need—for instance, to our need for blessedness—that God may plant in us the root of blessedness, true faith. And, having finished reading, give thanks.[56]

He said boldly that the slackening in the preaching of the Word was a sign of divine wrath; but that it was also a bad sign when the Holy Scripture was preached to a people who listened lazily, without any eagerness. For it is the word which, having entered a heart, makes of it the seat of spiritual wisdom. It tames "the fierceness of our corrupt nature."[57] It implants hope in our heart. The gospel dispels the darkness and brings the light of dawn to the eyes of the soul, exposing our self-love and our sin. For "even though one knew all Scripture by heart, unless we acknowledge our blindness there can be no real illumination, and knowing the Scriptures, we should be ignorant of their power."[58]

The gospels and the life of Christ must continually be before one's eyes as an example. "So too did the saints contempate this living divine image and imitate it." Because Christ lives in the gospels, they bestow, instead of the letter of the law, the act of grace; they are a healing against sin, "a vision of the mystery" to those who humble themselves and repent, for to receive faith from the gospels into one's heart one has to experience the power and fear of divine judgement proclaimed by the law.

Yet, wrote Tikhon, the word of God is also a judgement to those who listen to it in an unresponsive distracted spirit. Ignorance of the word often endangers the life of a society:

heresies, schism ("raskol"), all the struggles against the rule of faith grow, in Tikhon's opinion, from lack of knowledge of the Bible.

Above all, contact with the Holy Scripture is a personal spiritual experience:

> Blessed to me is the law of thy mouth, Ps. 118. 72, 103, 162. There is sweetness in the holy writ. It is like a letter from a king, it is a consolation, a thing to be admired, re-read, discussed: it is like the joy of a son far away from his father—and even more than that—for in the word of God we find God as our Father. . . .

Such joy is unknown to those who neglect to read it or who read it "for purposes of discussion and dispute, that they may appear clever before men."[59] He who would read profitably must experience an inward meeting with holy writ:

> Grow calm, grow quiet after harmful noise . . . you will experience a certain movement towards eternity; gradually, like a still, small voice, a thought will come to you as to who you are and what is your end and purpose . . . this is a sign of the approach of the word of God to your soul.[60]

He could not conceive of any one who loved God and did not love his word. With sorrow and irony he referred to those exterior signs of devotion that were paid to the book of the Bible. He inveighed against heavy gilded covers, against the kissing of the book by people who did not propose to follow its precepts. And he deplored the decline of preaching:

> Oh what a pitiful thing! Simple folk who cannot read go to church in order to hear soul-saving reading or hymns, but they are disappointed, poor souls, they are deprived of their wish and so they return to their homes, and the cause of this is the

sloth of bad popes and clerics who, closing their own eyes, hasten to hell and drag with them those who have been entrusted to them.⁶¹

By the word of God the Church was built and saved. One should go there in order to learn this divine word, striving that prayer be real, and not "mere noise and beating of the air." Attendance should be sincere, an outcome of love and not a hypocritical "politeness" towards the divine benefactor.⁶²

Tikhon spoke of the Church in evangelical terms: it is the Body, the Vine, the Ship, the Bride. But it was useless, he felt, to speak of "the members" unless they were fed and attended to; to speak of flocks and shepherds unless "the sheep were nourished by the word of God and the holy sacraments."

"Woe to clergy who do not preach!" It is even worse if they give scandal. In this life, "those who are placed at the helm must take more care; and those in whose hearts there is still a spark of devotion must pray and sigh." In the life to come, ministers of the Church will have to answer for "the thinking sheep entrusted to them."⁶³

A pastor, then, is an apostle and a prophet: he is also a priest. How is he to administer the sacraments?

Typical of this early period is Tikhon's first catechetical compilation, *On the duty of a Priest; On the seven Sacraments* [1765]. (At a later date Tikhon added the interpretation of the ten commandments as given in the *Catechism* of Platon Levshin, which came out in the same year, 1765.) He briefly defines the sacraments, and describes each one as to its matter, form, meaning, validity, and lays down the main conditions to be observed by the minister and the recipient. These instructions are followed by the decalogue without any interpretation.

Throughout this treatise Tikhon, in truly Orthodox fashion, uses the term "mystery." And he explains: "A mystery is a ministration which brings to the soul of a believer the invisible grace of God in some visible form." There are seven sacraments, some established by Christ, some through the apostles. They bear witness to God's love towards us and are the healing means of our salvation. Four conditions, writes Tikhon, are necessary in each sacrament:

1. The priest must be validly ordained.
2. The matter of the sacrament must be that which is regularly appointed.
3. The priest must both know the words through which the mystery is carried out, and have the firm intention of acting according to the canon of the Church and of performing the sacrament by the power of the Holy Ghost. For without such an intention, or if the priest does not know the words or acts without full consciousness of what he is doing, he does not perform the sacrament and is in danger of damnation.
4. The receiver of the sacrament must have zeal and a firm desire to partake of it.

> Baptism is a mystery in which, through the threefold immersion in water, and through the invisible grace of the Holy Ghost, the sins of the baptized are washed away.
>
> In Confirmation, power is given to us through the Holy Ghost, enabling us to confess with firmness the name of Christ and the Orthodox Faith.
>
> Penance consists in sorrow and pain for sins committed after baptism, and their remission through sincere and true confession, through contrition of heart and absolution by a priest.
>
> The Eucharist is a mystery wherein the true Body and the true Blood of Christ our God is given to us, Jesus Christ being present under the species of bread and wine truly, divinely and substantially.
>
> Marriage is the union of male and female persons in mutual consent and with the blessing of a priest.
>
> Ordination is a mystery whereby, through the laying on of hands by a bishop, special authority from God is bestowed upon the priest to officiate in the divine mysteries.

Unction is the mystery in which, through anointing with consecrated oil together with priestly prayers, the sick receive remission of sins, salvation of the soul, and healing of the body.

A noticeable feature of Tikhon's explanation of the sacrament of penance is that it goes into more detail and indicates three categories of sin not usually mentioned in subsequent Orthodox text-books. His definition of capital sin followed Moghila. In accordance with tradition, he mentions pride, cupidity, fornication, gluttony, envy, anger, and laziness or despondent negligence of salvation.

He enumerates six sins against the Holy Ghost:

> Despair, which means having no hope in the mercy of God; presumption—too presumptuous reliance on his mercy; opposition to revealed truth, of the Holy Scriptures and of the dogmas of faith confirmed by the apostles and the holy fathers; envy of the spiritual graces received from God by one's neighbor; obduracy in heresies and hardening in malice; negligence with regard to the salvation of the soul, till the end of one's life.

Finally, he defines as "four sins which cry to God for vengeance": deliberate murder; the vice of sodomy; embittering of the poor, of widows, and of orphans by offence and oppression; withholding or non-payment of wages to hired servants and workers. This attitude towards certain forms of social evil corresponds to the program for life outlined in St. James's Epistle.

In subsequent years Bishop Tikhon concentrated upon the three most frequent sacraments: the eucharist, penance and baptism with confirmation, performed by the baptizing priest who uses the oil consecrated by a bishop. Unction at this time was administered only on the death-bed.

A spirit of recollection, Tikhon taught, should accompany a priest throughout his ministry. Whether preparing himself for daily celebration, or for any sacrament, he ought to bear in mind the meaning of what he is about to perform. But, if the mystery is not clear in the light of reason, he must perform an act of intellectual confidence: "Be careful not to exercise curiosity, for some things demand our faith and are above reason. Believe as does the Church."

A priest should inwardly participate in the sacrament:

> When you perform a baptism, remember that you too have renounced the devil and his works. When you are hearing a confession and considering the conscience of a penitent—look to your own conscience, whether it accuses you of those same things in which you examine the penitent, and in all ways strive to cleanse your conscience, in contrition, humility and persistent prayer. At the burial of the dead, remember to what poor state we, who were created in the image of God, have been led by sin: and remember that dust thou art and unto dust thou shalt return.

The most striking feature of his teaching is his conception of baptism as a vital force. Though baptism of infants is in the tradition of the Orthodox Church, he repeatedly spoke to adults about the profound meaning and implications of this sacrament, and he continually enjoined them to the remembrance "of their baptismal vows."

> In baptism, the soul receives the cleansing from sin, or the token of cleansing from original sin. It receives the seed of faith. Through baptism, man rejects evil and enters, regenerated and renewed, into the realm of grace which leads to eternity; that is why he is called "a Christian"—a participant of the life of Christ with whom, in baptism, he died and of whose risen life he now partakes. That is why the power to live is given to him which makes him capable of a supreme love towards his brethren and towards his enemies.
>
> The baptismal vow is like the vow of marriage.

United to Christ in baptism, man becomes a partaker of the divine life—an image in human life of the two natures of Christ. In baptism the angels are given to us to minister to us. They keep us and guide us to the divine fatherland. It is ingratitude not to think of baptism as a spiritual benefaction: A Christian should remember baptism as the decisive step by which he has entered the Church and promised to lead a certain type of life.

They are not friends of Christ, they are his foes who, having been washed in baptism, fall again into sin.

Christ is no longer in the soul which deliberately chooses sin, though it has been regenerated through water and the Spirit. The spiritual life of such people is dulled, and baptismal grace lost to them even though they visit or erect and adorn churches and make a semblance of devotion. Aware of the shortcomings of Christians, Tikhon said: "The Church is a ship to which as to Noah's ark are brought both ferocious and gentle animals, so are we brought into it through baptism." To someone suffering from temptation Tikhon said: "Renounce the whispering slanderer, the devil, as you renounced him in your baptism."[64] The vivid images of the *Spiritual Treasure* again and again refer to baptism. A simple expression such as "Come with me" becomes a subject for meditation—and we are begged "to follow Christ in truth and righteousness as we promised in baptism."

Tikhon's symbolism is in itself highly suggestive. Thus the thought of the nets mentioned in the gospels reminds him that through baptism a Christian is set free from the devil, the words "Whose are you?" cause him to answer that he is Christ's through baptism; an oath recalls to him the sacrament's promise to a believer; the washing of the feet suggests our humble purification through baptism; renewal, washing, all these are so many images of the new creation. A girl betrothed to a bridegroom is "as we all are in Christ." One cannot over-emphasize the value which Tikhon attached to baptism, and this metaphor of bridal union clearly reveals his mystical conception of the sacrament.[65]

Bishop Tikhon had much to say concerning repentance in its treatment from the point of view of the spiritual combat, and in connection with the established practice of sacramental confession and a priest's part in it.

There are, according to him, two ways of appealing to a soul: the expository public sermon about sin generally or some particular case of injustice, and the private instruction of one who comes willing to repent. "When a man confesses his sin to you, you can say anything to him, so long as you speak affectionately, with compassion and not with anger; for he must realize that you speak from love and sincerely desire his salvation."[66] Tikhon stressed the priest's duty to keep the secret of confession. Then, in italics, there follow a few lines which one would gladly not meet there: the priest is under the obligation to "break this secrecy in a case foreseen by the *Spiritual Regulation*." This "case" was the duty incumbent upon all clergy to denounce to the civil authorities anyone who revealed his participation in a political plot. Did Tikhon write this, or was it added by the censor on publication? There are no means of verification now. In any case, a bishop of the Russian Church, especially whilst these regulations were still new (and strongly enforced), had to give place to them in a written document, if only half-heartedly.

> When giving instruction on the sacrament of Penance, speak to the penitent in this manner. . . . My child, you are confessing to God, who is displeased at any sin, and I, his servant, am the unworthy witness of your repentance. Do not conceal anything; do not be ashamed nor afraid, for there are only the three of us here, you and I and God, before whom you have sinned, who knows all your sins and how they were committed. God is everywhere, and wherever you said, thought, or did anything evil, he was there and knew all about it, and he is now here with us, and is waiting for your words

of repentance and confession. You too know all your sins; do not be ashamed to speak of all that you have committed. And I who am here, am just like you, a sinner, and therefore be not ashamed to confess your sins in my presence."

He next taught the clergy to explain that true repentance brings with it a true fruit of repentance—a firm intention to abstain from sin. Those who keep falling into the very same type of sin, or have a superficial view of sin, "only perform a ceremony instead of a true penance."[67] Tikhon, who was himself of sensitive conscience, and perhaps even suffered from scruples, was eager to foster hope. "There is more mercy in God than sins in us, provided we have sincere repentance; acknowledge, confess your sin at once, whatever it happens to be."[68]

He wrote for the clergy *The Figures of Divine Mercy*: "The loving-kindness of God is moved by the tears of men flowing from a contrite heart." God is waiting for and expecting human repentance, men's change of heart. All the Scriptures speak of this, "and God cannot lie." He calls us to repentance, through grace, in our consciences, through the death and humiliation of Christ, through his prophets and apostles, through the promise of temporal and of eternal bliss ("as a loving father can attract to himself a small child by holding out an apple"), through the warning of temporal and eternal punishment, through providential and edifying trials; through the spectacle of death around us.[69]

Tikhon constantly repeated such reflections. He said quite simply that the very ignorance of the hour of our death should call us to repentance. "And if now the heat that rises in your blood is unbearable to you, how much worse will be the flame which makes the demons shudder, which burns without consuming." He begged people to abstain from evil "if only to avoid the remorse of a tormenting conscience" in due time and not death. "Should we reject sin only when there is no more opportunity to sin? Shall we turn to God only when he is taking us to himself anyway? Shall we mend our lives only when there is no more life left in us to live?"[70]

Repent, he urged "for not abundance of sin causes a man to be lost, neither the magnitude of the evil committed, but an unrepentant and hardened heart." It is wrong to leave this supreme act till the hour of grave illness, "for in sickness you have no power left, nor a mind to withstand sin; you may even be unconscious, or in anguish, or in fear of death."[71]

As in all that he taught, his main argument and dominant motive was his personal love for Christ and his fear to offend him and to lose "his blessed and rejoicing presence in our hearts."

For Bishop Tikhon the eucharist was not "a rite." He taught the clergy that the altar was a holy place and demanded cleanliness in the sanctuary. He exhorted them to prepare themselves before officiating.

> Strive to obtain sincere awe and tenderness of heart by meditating upon the economy of salvation. Reflect how the Son of God and the Lord of all assumed the form of a servant; how the Unbegotten was conceived in the womb of the pure Virgin; how the eternal God became an infant. He who sits on the heavenly throne above the cherubim and seraphim, laid himself in a manger. The Lord of creation became poor and emptied himself. He who feeds all flesh, himself hungered and thirsted. The Invisible appeared on earth and lived among men. Reflect that when he was only an infant he was persecuted by Herod; that he fled from town to town, that he submitted to the Law and was circumcised; that he who is sinless was baptized by his servant; that, having himself been tempted by Satan, he helps those in temptation. . . .

Thus he dwelt upon the whole life of Jesus Christ—his suffering, death, resurrection and his future coming.

To the celebrant Tikhon pointed out that Christ himself is the centre, the One who offers and who is offered, and the moving power of the action which the priest is about to perform. The priest, as the liturgy proceeded, should identify himself in thought, prayer and humble aspiration with the episodes of the gospel narrative: at the preparation of the elements he should remember Bethlehem; at the Little Entrance of the Bible before it is read, he should remember the coming of Christ amongst people, still silent and unknown; at the Great Entrance he should remember Christ's triumphant entry into Jerusalem, preceding and already signifying his voluntary Passion. By such, words he familiarized the clergy and the laity with the meaning and symbolism of the liturgy. Tikhon was anxious for people to realize the grandeur of the eucharist, its close connection with the gospel story and its mystical power. He warned them against a superficial and purely formal approach to communion.[72]

Later he wrote more explicitly on *How Christians must approach Holy Communion.* "The apostle says: Let a man examine himself (1 Cor. 11. 28, 29).... Many read a great number of prayers, psalms and canticles. Such a preparation is insufficient." For prayer from an unrepentant heart is not acceptable to God.

> It is dreadful to approach communion without being purified by true repentance; dreadful, too, if one who has approached the eucharist is again soiled by the lusts of the world. Therefore meditation is necessary before and after communion, and mindfulness of this celestial gift. Before communion we must have hearty repentance and humility, we must put aside malice, anger and the caprices of the flesh. Be reconciled with your neighbor, have a firm intention and will to lead a new and devout life in Christ Jesus. After communion some manifestation of amendment of life is necessary; the reality of such amendment is testified by our love of God and of our neighbor, by gratitude, by a sustained effort towards a new, blameless, saintly life. To recapitulate: before communion we must have true repentance; after it we must bear the fruits of repentance, the good deeds inseparable from it. The

result, then, is this amendment of life, the newness of a God-pleasing life, so that communion be "not unto judgement and condemnation." One cannot be a Christian without having faith, there is no faith without love, and no love without good deeds. Otherwise a man is no more than a heathen even though he confesses the divine name. Everyone can see how terrible it is that such a man should approach the holy mysteries. It is because they partake unworthily that certain Christians not only do not become better, but become still more blind, bitter and callous; not recognizing their sin, they fall into worse sin and act as even civilized heathens do not act. They despise the divine grace and are thus deprived of it (Rom. 1. 28). Therefore, let everyone consider his own faults: let the fornicator change his heart and love purity, for he approaches the all-pure Lamb; let the proud learn that Christ is humble; let the malicious man change his heart, for Christ is the meek and angerless Lamb; let him who hates consider that the Son of God loves mankind; let the flatterer and liar remember that Christ is eternal Truth; let slanderers and those of venomous tongues remember that in the same lips they receive the all-pure Body; let lovers of Mammon love God, for his Son whom they approach is love; let the hard of heart remember that Christ is merciful; let thieves, robbers and extortioners remember that Christ is righteous; let the avaricious rich remember that Christ is generous, let drunkards amend their ways for the sake of the sobriety of the Crucified.[73]

Self-examination before and after communion is necessary: "Are we renewed? Do we persevere in the spirit of the new man? Let us strive that the living bread of heaven may become our sanctification, renewal, joy and consolation of soul."

Communion is a pledge on earth of life eternal.

See 1 Cor. 6. 17; John 6. 56 and 15. 5. Because such assurance is given by the gospels, Christians must know that just as the body grows and is fortified by natural food, so the Christian faith conceived in the heart grows through communion. For the Body and Blood of Christ is lifegiving and a remedy for spiritual disease.

The evident indifference of his flock and the decline in practice led Tikhon to urge a return to primitive Christian tradition.

The Christians of old frequently received communion as the cause and food of immortality, wherefore even up to our own time holy Church daily exhorts us to "draw near with fear of God and with faith." At the present day people have neither, as the facts abundantly prove; only once a year, and even then almost under compulsion, do they approach the table of immortality. And many by reason of ill-health leave it till their very death. How sad this is! Men hasten joyfully to banquets, but to this spiritual and most sacred table to which Christ invites them they come under compulsion![74]

Tikhon suggested that among the consequences of this lack of understanding of the eucharist and the decline in the practice of frequent communion were social injustices, for "are not the love of one's neighbor and the utter impossibility of offending and humiliating others the direct result of communion?"[75] Tikhon draws a poignant picture of the Son of Man who, in his earthly life, had nowhere to rest his head, and who is still knocking and trying to come to those for whom he shed his blood, and who enters meek hearts.[76]

Nowhere does Bishop Tikhon refer more openly to mystical union than in connection with the eucharist:

Blessed are those who saw Christ in the flesh. . . .
Still more blessed are we who see his image portrayed

in the gospels, and hear his voice from these same gospels, and confess him and call upon his name, and mystically partake of his all-pure Body and of his lifegiving Blood.

A deeply personal union of the soul with Christ is at the same time an essentially corporate sacrament: all mankind, all the members of the Christian body are "called to blessedness, for we all approach the same unique and only mystery of the most holy eucharist."[77] That is why Tikhon constantly uses such words as consolation, joy, bliss, pledge of eternal life, when speaking of communion. And he constantly relates the eucharist to its spiritual fruits.

Doctrinal Background

Except in a few pages of instruction to his clergy, Bishop Tikhon never attempted to evolve a system of doctrinal teaching. But the basis of everything he said on practical morals or pastoral duties was Orthodox dogma. His love of God and of people was more than an emotion of a pure and loving heart; it was part and parcel of his thought and of his whole outlook. He never moralized—he spoke as a Christian; and he never speculated without linking his thought with Christian life, feeling and will.

He himself, as we have seen, described his work as "speaking in parables." His doctrinal teaching was interwoven with moral exhortations couched in images from daily life. It was only between 1770 and 1772 that he began to elaborate a more comprehensive volume: *True Christianity*. His other doctrinal writings are contained in his *Private Letters* (of different dates).

True Christianity consists of four volumes:

1. On the Word of God—on spiritual wisdom;
2. On sin—on certain sins in particular;
3. On repentance—on the last things, death, heaven and hell; on Christian virtues;

4. On the Gospel and Faith; on the Church and Baptism; on the Christian's duty to God and to Christ the Son of God.

As the enumeration of the main sub-titles indicates, he had already dealt with many of these subjects in previous writings. The exposition does not follow any strict method; whole passages are repeated from earlier works; and in a later work (*The Spiritual Treasure*, 1777) he repeats many passages of *True Christianity*.

The analysis of a work which is essentially spontaneous, full of imagery and all-embracing is justified only by the practical purpose of study. For this purpose, and bearing in mind that Tikhon never separated doctrine from its devotional, moral and mystical implications, we shall examine only a few of his fundamental themes rather than analyze each work separately.

Tikhon's *True Christianity*, like his *Letters* or his pastoral exhortations, is much less a doctrinal treatise than the expression of a living and loving relationship with God. We shall, nevertheless, attempt to trace his teachings on God, on Christ and on the Holy Spirit; on the Virgin Mary and on the Saints; on Faith and Grace; on the Church and on the Last Things. To avoid repeating it later on, we must recall now that the whole of Tikhon's doctrinal teaching was based upon the Scriptures; his adoration of the word penetrated his every utterance. Just as his pastoralia would be unthinkable otherwise than on this basis, so would his *True Christianity*.

"God is Spirit," and can be apprehended only through spirit and truth. He is not good, but Goodness, and mankind is enclosed, encompassed in his love. He is the creator, the redeemer, the beneficent providence, and there is no event nor object in man's life which should not stimulate a loving remembrance of him. The soul, as a spirit created by God, finds no lasting pleasure, comfort or gladness except in God.[78]

It is interesting to note the importance which Tikhon gives to the veneration of the Divine Name. "This Name is in itself glorious and luminous," he writes.[79] In Tikhon's case one might suppose that his approach to the "adoration of the Name" was, also, purely biblical, for there is enough evidence throughout the Old and New Testaments to justify a mystical theology of the Divine Name.

Its glorification, writes Tikhon, does not affect the glory of this Name in itself—but man in his life on earth can either show it in its full light or dishonor it. We should remember it with awe and devotion, for God is a consuming fire. God alone is fullness of life, and to begin to apprehend this unique Life is to begin to love him and to glorify him "not in bodily rites and ceremonies but in spirit and in truth." The Name can only be truly glorified by understanding what it means—together with the other divine attributes.

How can such glorification be best expressed? By faith in the Holy Scriptures, by belief in Jesus Christ, by readiness to confess him; by firm hope, by guiltless forbearance and thanksgiving, particularly in affliction and injustices, and by the whole trend of a sincerely devout life—for "by such means are the heathen converted." In order that such a living glorification may be real, the Christian must not forget that our virtues and our thanksgiving, "though agreeable to God, do not affect his being, for he is like the sun which remains itself, whether we praise or despise it."[80]

The knowledge of God which we acquire by faith does not lead to "a pretence of learning," but to a sense of profound awe and a continuous feeling of repentance. The perception of God is a new birth: the soul, "like an infant, begins to grow and to walk"; without this perception there is no birth—"only the dream of a birth." The fruit of this new birth is imitation of God who created man in his own image. It is a process sometimes of sudden crises, sometimes of steady progress. Through the gospels, and by the road of continual repentance, man is called to grow again "unto the same image." Tikhon illustrates this teaching from: Eph. 5. 1; 1 Pet. 1. 15; Lev. 11. 44; 19. 2; 1 John 4. 11; 5. 1, 12-13; Gal. 3. 26-27; Matt. 5. 48.[81]

A sense of wonder in face of the economy of creation and of salvation overwhelmed Tikhon as he wrote "why one should love God." The thirteen points of this exposition may have been so many subjects of meditation. Man is drawn to love God "because God is clemency and goodness, and man himself is good inasmuch as he is a partaker of divine grace." God's love attracts our responsible love: "how beautiful it is, and how sweet. Those who love God even now experience a spark in their hearts." God is the creator, and he has called man to have dominion over creation, Gen. 2. 8; 2. 20. A yet greater honor—in man is the image of God; all creation is appointed for the service of man. God has raised fallen man, adopted him through the Spirit, calls back those who go astray and receives those who repent. All that comes from God is the outflow of love. He is the father. He seeks "our friendship, and such is this honor that no mind can even imagine it."[82]

The centre of all Tikhon's life and devotion was the person of Christ. There is hardly a sentence of his which does not refer to Christ. Through Christ he knows God; in Christ he meets and understands his fellow-men. Like his theology, his christology is inseparable from his ethical teaching and his devotional and mystical life. One may, however, distinguish three principal modes in his approach to the person of Christ. One is the loving contemplation of Jesus as portrayed by the gospels: "Jesus Christ, Son of God, son of the Virgin—a great mystery." This Christ of history is an example, an object of passionate devotion and admiring awe, a corrective to all the events and relationships of the world. Another aspect is the glorified Christ, the redeemer, the saviour, the future judge. The third is the Christ of the secret chamber of the soul, who is met in prayer, in acts of love towards people, in all those inexpressible moments which here on earth give man a foretaste of the life to come when God, and Christ, will be all in all. Christ is the only absolute necessity of the soul: "Let your first and utmost effort be to acquire him. All else is nothing, even though the whole world were at your feet."

The incarnate Son of God stands before the world like a pure mirror in which men begin to see their own vices. "Keep before your eyes the holy life of Christ"—force yourself to look upon it, even if you do not feel inclined to do so. Not only the sinless life of Jesus, but the whole "economy of salvation," is always the starting point of Tikhon's contemplation. "The condescension of the Son of God for our sake, which he accepted by his own will and by the benevolence of his heavenly Father and the co-operation of the Holy Ghost, is the cause of all our spiritual bliss." Christ, "the true image of humility," came into the world quietly "like rain upon the mown grass" (Ps. 72. 6). This humility of Christ moved Tikhon most deeply, as it moved many Russians before and after him. Christ, "who became poor in order to enrich us" (2 Cor. 8. 9), voluntarily accepted the manger, subjection to his mother and foster-father, temptation and finally suffering. As Jesus followed the way of human life and suffering, so now "a Christian must follow in faith and love him who was born in the flesh to enable man to be born in the Spirit." As he grew in stature—so must we, "not remaining always infants in Christ." Christ was tempted, he preached, he was hated. So a Christian must be able to renounce the world "wisely, with moderation"—not rejecting the world but rather offering it up and redeeming it.[83] Christ laid down universal standards: "The Son of God humbled himself for you—can you be proud? The Son of God took the form of a servant—can you seek to rule? He became poor—can you run after riches? He accepted dishonor—can you strive after honors? He had nowhere to lay his head—can you enlarge magnificent buildings? He washed his disciples' feet—are you ashamed of serving your brethren?

For Tikhon patience, forbearance, humility "even unto death" were not so many moral states of a soul but features which he saw in the second person of the Trinity (Phil. 2. 5-9) and in the incarnate Jesus. They were so many inward events, so many victories of Christ "which our faith allows us to make our own."

Christ's suffering, together with his humility, inspires Tikhon with words of sincere and loving sorrow; indeed, they sound like a participation in the suffering of a most loved person. One could well illustrate a "kenotic" trend in Russian religious thought by the words of Tikhon.[84] And he stands out among the Russians by the vivid, poignant language which he uses when speaking of the sufferings of Christ.

"To live in the world according to the example given by Christ" was the precept which he tried to follow himself and to teach others. He knew the power of sin, but trusted "Christ as the sun of the soul and the clarification of inward blindness." No sin, especially that of pride, can be conquered or even recognized "without the help of the meek-hearted Christ." A true Christian "works for Christ" in faith (John 6. 29) and, by fighting against sin and the devil, he carries Christ's burden and glorifies him—uninterruptedly, humbly, meekly and patiently, in fidelity and freedom. "This is our comfort, gladness and hope, that Christ is our Saviour, and this hope will not fail us."[85]

Tikhon used nouns, not adjectives, to speak of Christ: "Christ is our king, leader, helper, protector, strength, power, affirmation, victory and triumph." The relationship between Christ and his follower was to Tikhon as that of light to those it illumines; of life to those who receive life; of the shepherd to his sheep; of the way to the traveller; of the foundation to the building; of the indweller to his church (Eph. 3. 17; 2 Cor. 6. 16; 13. 5); of the firstborn of creation—the vine, the bridegroom, the head, the heir—with his co-heirs. Thus for Tikhon the thought of Christ was always projected beyond the present life. He never thought of Jesus without seeing in him the only-begotten Son of God and the glorified Christ, "author and finisher of our faith." Having heard of Christ from the holy scriptures, one becomes incorporated into him through baptism, one is sustained in this union through a life of active and loving imitation, with its suffering "even unto death," its prayer and its sacramental communion, till at last one reaches this consciousness of being a co-heir. In his last will, Tikhon wrote: "My hope sits at the right hand of the Father." His whole conception of this life of sorrow inevitable in "the body of suffering" was inseparable from his bold intuition of the triumphant state where, "delivered from eternal death, hell and torment, not through our own but through Christ's obedience, we shall receive eternal life" and where "the body of humility, like that of Jesus, will become the body of glory."[86]

Tikhon insisted that God is Spirit, and he meant the

Trinity, though his references to the Holy Ghost do not go beyond quotations from Scripture. It was mainly in order to emphasize the dignity of the soul or in connection with worship that he urged the adoration of the Spirit and the seeking of his gifts. "When fire touches the incense, there comes a fragrance: likewise, a heart under the touch of the Holy Ghost receives breathing and prayer." Not before we recognize our poverty do we receive the grace and the fruits of the Spirit. "It is folly to strive after the purest Spirit merely by various material means, through gold or silver, distinctive diet and clothes, and visible ceremonies; true worship of him is in awe, in love, in humility, patience, subjection of one's own will to his will. The sacrifice of God is a broken spirit. . . ." He often returns to the "sweetest gifts of the Holy Ghost," and frequently quotes Gal. 5. 22, 23.[87]

The Virgin Mary occupied a warm place in Tikhon's devotion. He had no inclination to speculate on the nature of the Virgin Birth and advised others to accept it as one of the mysteries of faith. He held in great reverence the coming of Christ into "the world of tears" and his birth from the Virgin. In Tikhon's thought Mary was the ever-blessed among women, and he cherished an icon representing her as a reminder of divine love. "Blessed be the womb that bore my Lord and my God!" Living in communities dedicated to the Blessed Virgin and celebrating or preaching in the cathedral, Tikhon followed the sequence of the liturgical year with its numerous festivals of Mary. When he spoke of her, it was either in terms of the scriptural angelic salutation, or of the liturgical hymns.

On the Orthodox festival of the Presentation of the Virgin into the Temple (the Gospel of the day is Luke 10. 38) he said: "Today the Mother of the Son of God is in the temple of God, she enters the holiest of the holy that she may become the holy temple and dwelling-place of the hypostatic word of God who is to become incarnate." On the day of the Assumption, in his famous expository sermon, he said: "On this day the living temple of God, the Mother of the unageing life, migrated from things earthly to things heavenly. On this day, the Queen appeared at the right hand of the King of heaven, adorned in garments of gold!" All those who attended the service, he hoped, were expressing their hope in the intercession of Mary, who "in the Nativity remained Virgin and in her Dormition did not abandon the world but intercedes for us before her divine son."

The intercession of Mary is for any Orthodox a natural expression of belief in the life and intercession of the saints. Thus, teaching his clergy how to approach a penitent, Tikhon wrote: "Bring before his eyes the pardon of the thief, and also remind him that the Mother of God is a strong defender of Christians, and that the other saints all pray for us to the merciful God and defend us by their prayers." He taught his flock always to have recourse "first to the protection of our Lady, the Birthgiver of God, common intercessor of all Christians, and next to call fervently upon all the saints." The saints, who experienced many human temptations, can share in our prayers and be full of understanding. Nevertheless Tikhon emphasized at the same time that even though miraculous help may come from the saints, "they perform miracles by prayer and in the name of Christ, Christ alone having this power in himself." These citizens of heaven form the unbroken and living link between the Church triumphant and militant, invisible and visible."[88]

In his early instructions to his clergy, Bishop Tikhon speaks of the earthly strivings, struggles and even failures of the visible Church. In his later writings he begins to elucidate the nature of the Church.

> The Church is one, (because she resembles) God in the Trinity. She is one because she stands on one sole foundation, Christ; on unity of teaching—the word of God; on belief in the Holy Trinity. She is one in the unity of the Spirit who leads her; in the hope of the resurrection. Thus, both militant and triumphant, she is one.

The Church is "the dwelling of God cleansed and sanctified by the blood of Christ." Tikhon often repeats the metaphor—and it was for him more than a metaphor—of the

Body; he uses numerous scriptural images to describe the Church: she is the house of God, the bride of Christ, the mother feeding her children by the word of God and the holy mysteries, the fold of the sheep, the vine, the ship, the Sion of the Holy Trinity. It was a consoling thought to him that we are all members of this Church. He begs Christians to cherish the purity of this sacred body and to show her a truly filial love. "Who is a true son? One who truly and heartily believes in God and in Christ, is baptized, lives in piety and, if he fails, repents." The Church here on earth is not perfect, for she includes sinners as well as saints, but she gives to both opportunity for amendment, growth, perfection and sanctification: "this ship, which is the Church, makes us peaceable and meek through baptism—so the fierce beasts become meek in the ark."[89]

Tikhon held the orthodox view of the nature of man, as created in the divine image and likeness and called to relationship with God. He did not go into the question of original sin but, as far as one can see, he thought of its consequences as an inheritance of evil inclinations: "We always carry evil in our hearts as a thing born with us." "Sin is everything that violates the law of God. It is disobedience to his will as well as a deterrent to good works. It is separation from God and an act of ingratitude to the creator and to the saviour who has suffered for us." All the evil of the world—sickness, war, death—come from sin.

Yet in spite of the "ferocious character of the old man," the incarnation and atonement have given us back the hope of divine adoption. The features of the Father have become recognizable in the children. New confidence has come with Christ.

> You see a beautiful person with the look of an angel. . . . Now raise up your mind to the inward man, to the soul, and think how much more beautiful is the soul, this divine image and likeness fashioned by God to abide in such a lovely dwelling. Learn from this to recognize and to respect the nobility, the beauty and magnificence of the soul, and to adorn

it as a thing immortal, more than this dust and these ashes—our body.[90]

In his social teaching Bishop Tikhon stresses man's dignity, the equality of "the sons of God and brethren of Christ." In his moral teaching he emphasizes the heroic virtues of which man is capable and to which he is called both by his nature—which is in the image and likeness of God—and by adoption as a Christian. One can see in his doctrinal pronouncements how deeply he values this conception of the nature and destiny of man: "All creatures are witnesses to the wisdom and power of God; but man is also honored by being created in the image of God and by his special counsel. Let us learn, brother, our initial nobility and prerogative." He also lays stress on the incarnation as a pledge of God's boundless promises to man: "Jesus assumed to himself a flesh equal to ours."

In a letter in which he allows his thought and feeling to run freely, he expresses almost ecstatically his views on the nature and destiny of man:

> Man is more beautiful than any other creature since he is in the image of God. Through the incarnation he is justified and is no more under wrath. He has become a member of the body of which the heavenly head is Jesus Christ. He mysteriously partakes of the lifegiving Body and divine Blood. He is made worthy to become the habitation of God and the temple of the Holy Ghost. He is in communion with the Father and his Son Jesus Christ. Through faith in Jesus he becomes a son, an heir, a co-heir with Christ. Read the Acts of the Apostles and you will see that all these titles are ascribed to man by the Holy Ghost. . . . And what will it be in the future life, according to the unfailing promise of God! What goodness, bliss, honor and glory! The uninterrupted flow of eternal blessedness will be like a river, incomprehensible to the present mind and inexpressible by the tongue, the blessedness which "eye

hath not seen" spoken of in 1 Cor. 2. 9. The children of God will shine like the sun in the kingdom of the heavenly Father, they will be as angels, like other gods. Glory be to the Trinity for having so honored and magnified our kind!"[91]

"The soul cannot live without grace." Grace and faith are the necessary conditions for the soul which strives to restore its innate nobility. "Our own strivings are powerless—read Psalm 118."

> Grace is the food and clothing of the saints. It wakens grief in a man's heart, making him dissatisfied and moving him to seek the reason of this dissatisfaction. Grace gives sorrow and grace comforts; showing us the poverty of all things, it engenders in us a repentant sorrow for having fallen short of the love of God. . . . One who is possessed by such sorrow will always grieve, for he thinks of God's offended love and not of the fear of hell. It is a grief of love.

This state, approaching what might be called perfect contrition, is propitious to the growing longing after God; through grace, the love of God is increased in the heart, and the soul "desires nothing more than it desires God." Humility, prayer, thanksgiving, assurance of divine mercy are gifts of grace.[92]

Faith—true, orthodox and living faith—was a theme upon which Bishop Tikhon expounded at length, opposing such faith both to the cold, theoretical knowledge of the Creed and to mere forms of worship and, still worse, superstitions.

> Faith is a spiritual gift; it enters the heart. It comes down from heaven and the heart of man is caught up to things celestial . . . . Faith is the comforting perception of the gospels produced in the heart by the Holy Ghost. It purifies the heart, endows it with joy and freedom, that gift of the Son.

Faith is intimately linked with hope, for "we hope in the One in whom we believe"; moreover, faith calls forth love for Christ, which leads to pity for all, love for all and—true fruit of true faith—acts of justice and sympathy. Tikhon went so far as to say: "Alone faith in the Son of God who died for us and rose again justifies us without regard to our works," but he was careful to add: "Nevertheless this faith cannot be idle but engenders love as its concomitant. Faith, this divine spark, is kindled in us and bursts into flame with the help of God through the reading of and listening to the word of God, through meditation on the acts of God in the past, through prayer, through the partaking of the holy mysteries—and, like a good tree, it reveals itself externally by sweet fruit of love."[93]

Faith, as understood by Tikhon, is not an emotion divorced from the logical powers of the mind. For him the creed was a matter of thought and conviction as well as of deep religious emotion produced by response to its historical and spiritual assertions. He never protested against the intellect, but only against the deadly theoretical knowledge of right dogma divorced from its expression in Christian life.

> True faith is the keeping and confession of right dogma, that is to say, it consists in true faith in Jesus Christ the Son of God: for knowledge of beliefs is one thing and real faith in Christ is quite another. The first often makes one haughty, arrogant, fruitless. Hence, many who possess a right knowledge of dogma live lawless lives; many even preach on faith, and teach and exhort others, but themselves do not move forward, as though they were mere signposts on the road. True faith in Christ is humble, patient, merciful, full of loving-kindness.

A traditional image best expresses it: faith is the root from which a Christian grows; good works of faith are its leaves and fruits and the more fruit there is, the lower do the branches bend, as true symbols of humility.[94] A questioning mind did not frighten Bishop Tikhon: "It is always good to enquire into one's faith, especially at the present time when there are so many phantasies." Yet he always made a clear distinction between the understanding of the facts and ideas which constitute Christian dogma, and the act of trust and confidence which pertains to faith. He besought Christians to defend themselves against the haughtiness of individual interpretation by an act of confidence in revelation and in the corporate mind and experience of Christendom: "Believe, together with the whole Church, what has been revealed by the word of God." But he understood and sympathized with those who had doubts or whose faith at times seemed dead— "as though it had never existed"—and he gave practical advice on "the keeping of faith."

Faith for Tikhon is inseparable from the other theological virtues. In the trinity of the acts of man's mind, heart and will, lies his total response to the perfection of divine love. And with the support of abundant references from the New Testament he affirms: "All Christianity and all Christian duty consists in faith, hope and love."

The person of Christ was everything for Tikhon himself and, in his estimation, the main obstacle to faith and spiritual growth is estrangement from the Christ of the Bible. He believed in the personification of evil, in the Evil One. We have seen how he spoke on the diabolical assault against man in his spiritual combat. It is "our only enemy, the Devil," he writes, who "sows doubt, disbelief, and despair of the goodness of God" in people's minds—particularly in the mind of a monk or of a man who is making spiritual progress. The Devil strives to tear the Church by schisms, by slanderous reports on righteous persons and, above all, by blurring the image of Christ in people's memory. It is the Devil "who turns our eyes away from the suffering of Christ" in order to prevent, or at least to endanger, our salvation.[95]

Yet the essential freedom of man remains—that freedom of which Tikhon speaks so much in connection with the spiritual combat. It is on account of this freedom that man can respond to divine love, to the sacrifice of Christ, and to the whole problem of the future life and salvation. The atonement has achieved the organic regeneration of man's fallen nature. But salvation has both its divine and its human side: God's love requires man's free response. "Are then all saved? Salvation is offered to all," but those who reject Christ, or false Christians, deliberately cut themselves away from saving grace, from the fruit of the incarnation—for Christ wishes to save all (1 Tim. 2. 4).

Salvation is both the content of Christian belief and the appropriation by man of Christ's saving life and death and resurrection; it is at once a belief and a mystical experience which has its beginnings here on earth and is to be lived and fully revealed in the life to come: "The beginning of salvation is to learn our own wretchedness. It is here that we must seek it—not after death. . . . But whilst we neglect it, Satan steals away our immeasurable treasure, the eternal salvation bought by the blood of Christ." Whilst he is alive a Christian must strive after that "which is his dearest hope."

> We were created and, having fallen, we have been redeemed for eternal life. We are renewed in baptism and through the word of God, and called to eternal life; to this end has holy scripture been given to us, to this end did Christ the Son of God, come into the world to live as a man, to suffer and die, that we should receive this everlasting life. The first duty of a Christian is eternal salvation.[96]

The token of salvation here on earth is true faith practised and expressed in acts of love, triumphant in its hope over all temporal tribulations and firm in its fidelity to Christ. Salvation in the future life can be apprehended through certain images and mystically experienced. The thought of eternity, one of the most dear and familiar to Tikhon, is best expressed in his occasional meditations and would be better studied in the context of his ascetico-mystical teaching, but it is essential to remember his biblical idea of the blessed and the damned eternity, of which he thought with fear until, with the passing of years he came to think of eternity, of the future life and of the resurrection "with some amazement, with transport, as it were beside oneself."[97] Natural phenomena and the events of daily life always turned his mind to expectations of eternity. "You see the rising of the sun—and yet when it goes down it seems as if it had never been there—and then again it appears." This reminds him of the death and resurrection of Christ, and of the resurrection of the dead. Victorious soldiers inspire him to contrast earthly triumphs with the "so much greater triumph of the saints whose souls are at peace and who contemplate the beauty of the Heavenly Jerusalem. What rapture overtakes those who put on the garment of salvation! . . . If here on earth people listen to sweet singing, and still desire to hear it, and are comforted by it beyond words, how much more so in that mansion where the voice of praise is ceaseless. There is peace, harmony and love, and his will, and the fellowship of the saints and angels, complete serenity and perfect wisdom."

The motive of beauty was very prominent throughout St. Tikhon's life and writings; it is part of his doctrine. Beauty is a reminder to man of his innate dignity; in nature it is a memory of paradise and an image of future harmony.

Transfiguration, a doctrine so dear to the Orthodox, creation's return to its own first image, were for him no mere metaphors. He copied out such passages as Rom. 6. 4; Eph. 5. 14; Matt. 13. 43; Phil. 3. 20, 2; Rev. 20. 6. His conception of transfiguration, of the resurrection, of the "resplendent appearance of the saints" was the fruit not of a dream but of a firm doctrine based on the scripture which for him was not a book but the true and living word "from the mouth of God."

Ascetic and Mystical Teaching

To classify Bishop Tikhon as a moral theologian or as an ascetic and mystical theologian would be equally inaccurate; he does not technically belong to either category; his doctrinal, sacramental, mystical and moral aspects are so many sides of one integral faith lived by a loving soul. His moral exhortations would sound almost flat outside their context of mystical love for Christ. That is why his writings on moral problems and virtues can be called "ascetic and mystical teaching." Yet such a term is bound to confuse those who look for a treatise on spiritual methods leading to mystical states. Tikhon left no such writings and did not study the spiritual life in separate chapters. He gave simple advice to monks, clergy and layfolk alike: reading of the Bible, individual and corporate prayer, watchfulness against sin and the practice of virtue and charity. In the light of his idea of the Bible as converse with God, of charity as life within the Body of Christ, of prayer as spiritual growth and of the sacraments as incorporation into the body of Christ, these simple precepts acquire a depth of true mysticism. He did not describe the stages of spiritual progress nor their accompanying psychological conditions; he seems to have overtaken a man in his daily life in order to lead him finally to heaven, "the fatherland of a Christian."

Christian action is presented by Tikhon in its inseparable, twofold character of active life and spiritual fight. His pastoralia and his sermons on social conditions are full of moral, ascetic and mystical teaching. He neither strove after, nor claimed, originality, but every now and then he allowed his personal thought and feeling to get the better of traditional forms and humbly offered his own spiritual experience as a possible help to others.

The title of one of his works, *The Flesh and the Spirit* (1765), illustrates best the way in which he approaches the subject of Christian life. He gives, the two sides as it were, of human life and nature: sin and virtue. His aim, as explained in the Preface, is not to speak "of abhorrent vices recognized as such by everyone, but rather of those which people scarcely regard as vice and sin: malice, envy, love of money, extortion, malicious talk, etc." Then he treats of virtues. He is anxious to write simply,

> so that most simple folk may the more easily understand it, briefly, so that the reader may not find it tedious. If, to some, this discussion should appear somewhat crude, I readily declare that its object is to profit, not to give pleasure; salvation rather than

the pleasing of men. Should any educated person find therein anything deserving of rectification, I beg him to ascribe the error to my lack of intelligence, not to my intention. Be saved in Christ, kind brother.

The ascetic precepts of Tikhon strike by their wise moderation: "to give the body food, drink, clothes, rest and all that is necessary. Only if and when the body begins to seek what is contrary to the will of God, man should not connive with it." Prudence, avoiding of idleness, respect for the opposite sex, were his main practical hints. Above all, he called all to vigilance and to the humble realization that "if even pillars have fallen, what can a reed expect of itself?"

He speaks of the flesh much less than of "the mind of the flesh—haughtiness, impurity, pride, cupidity, grumbling, slander, enmity, quarrels, rancour and vengeance and all that withstands the divine law." He warns all against that indifference to evil which gradually makes a soul unconscious of its estrangement from God. Such a soul is quite unaware of its condition; it is "like a drunkard till he wakes up."[98] People must cultivate a watchful conscience. For fear of being separated from God, the source of its existence, the soul must "break off sin as a dry branch."[99] Otherwise, it grows coarse, consenting to sin, it develops the habit of it, as so much inner idolatry. "Passion is like a fierce dog—when we run away from it it chases us, but if we stand and chase it, it turns away." Like Isaiah, he speaks of sin as blindness with regard both to God and to our fellow-men, whom we misunderstand, blame, calumniate. The most dangerous condition for a soul, he writes, is when it treats sin as a subject for joking.

Tikhon did not go into detailed admonitions on this or that type of behavior: he tried to quicken the whole life of the soul. That is why he continually reminded people of the presence of God and of the possibility of their own regeneration through the action of the Holy Ghost, through baptism and life in Christ. The gravity of an action lies in that it does not affect only the sinner—it always affects others. Every sin, intellectual or material, gives scandal; it is separation in the deep sense, ousting one both from God and from men: "Like heresy, which begins in one heresiarch, but, in spreading, ruins numberless others. A vicious life contaminates and, like a plague or epidemic, passes from house to house. Thus, in this or that family, town or village, certain particular evils abound."[100] Thus slander, luxury, cupidity, or feminine artifices bear in them a provocation to sin: "what the ears hear and the eyes see, stabs the heart."

Then, even if a man is aware of his fault, pride keeps him from acknowledging, and still more from allowing anyone else to notice it. "Pride is authoritarian, it interferes with others, it is envious, it refuses to be laughed at, it cannot endure to be despised."[101] The fight with pride belongs to the realm of spiritual combat.

> Confront your pride with the conviction of the omnipresence of God; with the memory of the suffering, obedience and humility of Christ (Phil. 2. 5-9); with meditation on your baptismal vows; with the thought that you belong to the Church where there is no room for uncircumcized hearts; with the consideration of the loftiness of Christian calling. Fight against it by holy communion; by prayer; by repentance springing from the contemplation of the unutterable mercy of God; by the thought of divine justice now and of future judgement; by reflecting that we do not know the hour of judgment and that we live in the hope of celestial bliss; by preserving a right and just measure of the things of this world and by examining the nature of sin and its origin.[102]

Against "the pride of life and the lust of the eye" there is only one effective remedy: "the love of God attracting us as an anchor from the depths."[103]

Another form of pride is "interference with others."

> Do not judge others, for you cannot know what is inside the other man. Do not condemn, for he may still rise whilst you may fall. Beware of even

talking about others, lest you start judging them. Enquiring into other people's sin is a curiosity hateful to God and man. It is often the origin of gossip and slander—transmission of contamination.[104]

This was abhorrent to Tikhon because,

> by judging, man usurps the powers of the only Judge, Christ, he interferes with one who is God's servant and not his own; and if people refrain from blaming a servant in the presence of his master, how much more should they refrain from blaming their neighbor under the eye of the Omnipresent; such people condemn themselves as well, both by constituting themselves judges over other folk and by often committing similar offences. It is wrong to judge at all, for both inward righteousness and secret sin are hidden from us, whilst rumors and reports about others are too often unfounded and untruthful. The commandment of Christ expressly forbids it (Matt. 7. 1). An injurious word is a sting to a soul, and sorrow is its consequence; such a pain and grief is the more keenly felt when a just man is its victim. If a person in authority is thus blamed and condemned, the way is open to anarchy. Above all, when judging another, we cannot know whether perchance he has not already repented and been forgiven by God.[105]

What surprised Tikhon was that people compassionate in regard to physical injuries, are so hard on the soul of another man, who "is your neighbor, your kinsman by nature."

Envy, anger, malice and impatience, together with pride, incite a man to judge others and make him burn with resentment at every rumor of another person's progress. They generate malicious talk, encourage gossip and slander. Like St. James, he spoke with horror of the evil produced by loose and biting tongues.

> Many abstain from meat, milk and other food which God has not forbidden and which was even given as a blessing to people who have learned the truth and know how to partake of these things with thanksgiving (1 Tim. 4. 34). But the same abstemious, devout-living people, give scandal by their action, and spread scandal with their tongue like an incendiary fire. It is good that they keep the traditions of the Fathers; but why do they abolish the divine commandment? With one and the same mouth they slander their neighbor and whisper their prayers, sing to God and partake of the Body and Blood of Christ!

Self-knowledge, active rejection of envy and stricter watch over one's own mind could be means of conquering this evil. He advocated prudence, avoidance of the company of slanderers, and prayer for others as a remedy against a haughty attitude towards them. But we must also pray about the guarding of the door of our lips.

> If you happen to witness your neighbor's fault, pray for yourself, lest you succumb to a similar evil, for we are all capable of it and ready to fall on any occasion; but, above all, seal your mouth by silence, and inwardly sigh to God about this brother, that God may straighten him.[106]

He saw Christian life as a valiant and continuous fight against self, against social evils and, deeper still, against the personal embodiment of evil. Tikhon believed in the devil and, without ever ascribing to him any pranks or miraculous apparitions, he spoke of

> our only real enemy, who turns our eyes away from the suffering of Christ, who profits by our idleness and takes possession of those in anger. If the devil does not succeed in undermining faith itself, he makes you despair of the goodness of God, or puts

fear into you, or makes you feel bored to death. Or he turns those around you against you, whilst stirring you either to despair or to pride, making you anxious to vindicate yourself.

Tikhon regarded as diabolical certain forms of despondency and those pretended virtues which conceal impure motives of self-seeking, such as leaving our immediate duty under the pretext of performing some kindness: "visiting the sick or serving our vanity under the appearance of a public service." This is especially true, said Tikhon, of a monk who leaves prayer to act in the world and loses prayerful recollection in the bustle of life. Hospitality as a pretext for self-indulgence, or its opposite, fasting, which leads to haughtiness, are so many openings to the influence of the Evil One.[107]

The spiritual combat should begin with self-knowledge, not as a matter of philosophical theory or of introspection, but as a practical necessity; in order to correct a deviation of the soul one must have a clear perception of what it is. "To know one's illness is the beginning of health, and the knowledge of one's plight and wretchedness is the pledge of bliss.[108] Such clear knowledge, however, cannot be gained without a deeper knowledge of God. For only by raising one's mind to him can one rightly measure one's own limitations.[109]

Often temptation is like an emetic, and shows what is in us. On most occasions, it arises from our own weakness, reveals our spiritual immaturity and teaches us to throw ourselves upon the protection and grace of God. Another form of temptation is created by our surroundings, or injustices by which others provoke one to self-justification or self-pity. A third and deeper form of temptation attacks the very core of the inward life: it consists in assaults against faith, in spiritual strife and confusion, scruples, despair and fear.

> At times, faith is evident and exalts the heart to the very heights; at others it is hidden as if it had never existed—yet against these waves which beat on and throw themselves against the believing heart, defend yourselves with the shield of faith.[110]

This state is often a proof that the soul is really alive; it is the struggle of the demon against the devoted servant of God.

> Even this is not without divine sufferance; Christ himself experienced it; it is for the benefit of the soul, which gains self-knowledge and learns humility, and, if victorious, gains the crown.

Physical fatigue is no excuse for relaxing from this inner struggle.

> It is painful enough to endure sickness, suffering, toothache, the desires of the flesh or palsy—anyone who has been thus tried knows it—but far worse for the development of the soul would be the weakening of the power of spiritual resistance and its consequence, eternal pain.[111]

Though different stages and types of temptation must be approached in different ways, the following general advice on how to deal with temptation was given by St. Tikhon:

> Direct the mind to some useful action. Say to the Tempter: "The Lord rebuke thee" and, protecting yourself with the sign of the cross, arm your soul by the power of the crucifixion; turn away from the Tempter, spit upon him as in the rite of baptism. Remember, it is a bad sign if the soul feels no temptation: it means hardening in sin. But those who strive are at times left alone by the Tempter—all the more reason that they should be on guard against an unexpected attack. The soul gains an experimental knowledge that its victory comes always from above. But if it happens that you give in, do not despair but rise at once, repent, make amendment and strive on with increased zeal by a continuous invocation of God: for this life is but a struggle, and now this side, now the other pursues, inflicts wounds and wins."[112]

Prudence, withdrawal from society likely to lead us into temptation, and increased recollection in solitude could help only in part for the confusion and revolt of mind and soul grow stronger in the desert and in solitude. *"Experto crede."*[113] Loneliness, desolation, the sense of being abandoned, all these he knew for himself, and he comforted souls who experienced such dark hours:

> As the sun, hidden by the storm, nevertheless continues its action and faintly directs its rays towards us, so does God in the hour of temptation and abandonment. . . . He is an experienced Christian who has passed through the fire and waters of temptation, trouble, tribulation and sorrow and who has steadfastly fought against the invisible enemy.[114]

He strongly stressed that a temptation is never isolated; like sin or virtue, it is dynamic. Consequently the slightest consent to the smallest sin generates a stronger evil. "Beat your enemy whilst he is weak"; and in the language of Heb. 12. 4 he urged people to "resist unto blood striving against sin." Man must strive after the inward integration of all his powers for, in his charming metaphor, although we have two eyes we cannot look up and down at one time.

Tikhon did not elaborate a system for progress in virtue. He taught in parables, "as is often done for the sake of simple folk in the sacred books." Yet, he felt, "nothing is ever quite similar to any other thing." Faith and reflection illumined by it lead one "both to understanding and to practice of the Christian virtues."[115] He laid down as a general rule that a Christian should be in the habit of "frequent and attentive reading of and listening to the word of God"; that he should also read the lives of the Saints and strive to follow their example; that he should cultivate "pure and frequent prayer from a broken heart" and, with all the powers of his soul, deliberately set out upon the "narrow way," with a firm intention to subject his will to the will of God and "not to crucify Christ again, for this is terrible and woeful."[116]

For daily life he advised: "Every morning make a fresh

good intention—that is, think every morning that you wish to be a Christian, and look upon the past as time wasted." Such an intention would put daily activities into their proper perspective and would give every action a Godward direction. For whatever our activities, they can become either "the sapient flesh" or the expression of divine love.[117] His fundamental ideas on the means of avoiding sin and progressing in virtue can be summarized as a certain direction of mind and will:

> Attend to the things that can free you from sin: the omnipresence of God; prayer; communion; the suffering of Christ; the judgement of Christ; our ignorance as to the hour of our death; eternal pain; sin in itself as a deed of the devil; sorrow and grief for offending our Father. If nothing else avails to stop you, abstain from sin if only for fear of remorse in your conscience. And pray for the gifts of the Spirit.[118]

These injunctions can be supplemented with his precepts on the education of a Christian: memory of the baptismal vow; thought of death, judgement and the kingdom of heaven; meditation upon the nobility of the Christian calling; thought on the passion of Christ ("Be not his tormentor, O let it not happen!"); vigilance ("cut off the first thought of sin"); the argument that sin, though sweet, is brief, that it lastingly wounds the conscience and leads to eternal torment, and that in practice it is easier to withstand earlier than to fight against habitual sin.[119]

He taught people to educate their conscience which "coincides with the law of God in nature," even though the events of daily life are differently apprehended by different types of conscience: "So in nature warmth melts wax, oil or snow whilst it dries up grass or hardens clay." A pure and sensitive conscience is the main instrument for gauging one's inward progress or stagnation. Beware of a heart insensitive to the pricks of conscience; cultivate that responsiveness in which, hearing some general criticism, we recognize our own faults. Conscience is in a man "like a fair witness." When at peace, it is the "seat of hope," but how easily, too, is it stricken by a mortal blow! "Refrain from all that would torment your conscience at the hour of death. . . . For then each one enters bitter or blissful eternity. True faith and life, and a firm hope in Jesus, the conqueror of death and hell, triumph at such an hour."[120]

Increase of active exercise of virtue and a growing life of prayer are "the school of the Holy Ghost," where we acquire "true spiritual philosophy." This teaches one the fear of God ("for if we accomplish the law of an earthly Tsar—how should we not obey him who speaks to us both as the Almighty and as a loving Father?") and it "consists in nothing else than true knowledge and worship of God and of Christ the Son of God. . . . The end of spiritual wisdom is God and eternal bliss."[121]

St. Tikhon did not use the words "heroic virtue." But their reality made him demand of himself and of every true Christian to resist sin "unto blood" and to follow Christ the Saviour "unto death." He called to conversion; not merely to abandoning sin, but to a truly new birth. Repeating Jeremiah 2. 27, he said that people live with their backs to God. A soul turned towards him would "set the Lord always before itself" (Ps. 16. 8). To desire conversion is to seek the personal God who, whatever one's inner state or outward walk of life "is always near thee."[122] A converted soul goes through daily renunciations, and overcoming of evil, till finally it reaches the state of forgetfulness of self at which Christ becomes its centre and moving power. Renunciation springs from the longing for God. One becomes different not outwardly but inwardly; "so a good harp produces a lovely sound, so a good bell chimes melodiously."[123]

"Beware of everything that turns us away from the love of God: possessions, family, work or our health." In the world and amidst objects "man is the mediator between God and creatures, and while these exist to serve man, man exists to serve God" through them.

What are the marks of true detachment? Mortified self-love, indifference to riches, honors, glory, or the company of exalted personages. A man who is detached is not afraid of poverty or insult, though he is grieved by them. Indifferent to praise, forbearing and compassionate towards those who hate him, he perseveres in the desire to unite his will to the will of God and lives in constant memory of the celestial homeland.[124]

Our attitude to our fellow-men is a check upon our conscience. "Take great care not to offend a man by word or deed, for thus you offend God who loves him. If it happens that you do hurt him, humble yourself at once before him, beg his forgiveness."[125] If, on the other hand, it is you who are the victim, remember that any injustice, like temptation, reveals our inner state: "thus a heated stone or iron is silent till a splash of water makes it hiss."[126] However hard the wrong, "no one as yet has spat upon you"; consider the scorn and pain endured by Christ. Listen not to self, nor to the spirit of pride but, "looking towards the meek-hearted Jesus, remember that an undeserved accusation cannot really cause us harm." And "if anyone hates you or is angry with you, conquer him by love, seek to be reconciled with him; and even if he should not desire peace, seek peace yourself, prepare peace yourself; though our heart may not wish it, we must convince and bend our heart to peace. To conquer anger and vexation by love is the most glorious victory."[127]

Forgiveness, Tikhon said, comes to us like reading to a child: first we learn letters, then syllables, at last whole words. "First, try to render good for good; then, not to render evil for evil; finally, learn to love your enemy. Try to pray for your offender without ill-feeling, thus imitating Christ." He summarized the reasons why one should forgive: because God and the love of Christ command it; for sometimes a revengeful person is himself sorry, albeit too late, because we realize divine mercy to ourselves; if you cannot forgive for love of God, try to do so for your own profit, since a forgiving heart is more likely to be attracted by God, "the doors of whose mercy are opened to publicans and harlots but locked to malicious people": because an unforgiving spirit (Ps. 109. 4, 7) is an obstacle to prayer: because we all sin against each other: because if everyone were to take vengeance, society would crumble: because an injustice already committed cannot be effaced, whereas it would be an effort, and perhaps an unsuccessful one at that, to try to answer back.[128]

But no utilitarian or even moral consideration, no effort of will, can produce what only grace can generate in man, which alone enables him to "keep the wholeness of love towards our Bridegroom without return to the unchaste love of the world." Freedom, inseparable from this love, is not only the initial freedom of choice between good and evil. Tikhon meditated on John 8. 36, and Gal. 5. 1:

> Every man has a natural inclination to freedom. But a Christian has another such inclination all his own: to be free from sin, death and eternal damnation; from condemnation by the Law and the Jewish ceremonial, since Christ fulfils what is lacking in the Law; from that Law itself, for in Christ there is no slavery but sonship.

Thus freely man turns to Christ and labors for him who has attracted him and who helps him by his grace on the freely chosen, narrow way of perfection.

"As a bird without wings, as a soldier without arms, so is a Christian without prayer."

In his sermons Tikhon dealt with the formal aspect of prayer, and gave warnings against a prayer "that is without understanding—a fruit of the art of the tongue alone. For the word is a messenger of the heart and mind, the overflowing of what can no longer be withheld. Otherwise it would be no more than the voice of a trumpet or a bird or an animal."

> Prayer does not consist merely in standing and bowing with your body or in reading written prayers: it is possible to pray at all times, in all places, by the mind and spirit. You can lift up your mind and heart to God while walking, sitting, working, in the crowd and in solitude. His door is always open, unlike

man's. We can always say to him in our hearts: Lord! Lord! have mercy![129]

Tikhon taught people first not to indulge in gross, unforgiving, materialistic prayer; then how to pray for temporal things "if such were God's will"; then to seek "things profitable to their souls," and finally disinterested prayer for spiritual gifts to the glory of God. He emphasized that prayer should be made "in the name of Christ," as the expression of a true and confident faith and that it should be offered up to be purified by the Holy Ghost.[130]

Tikhon's teaching on prayer must be studied in relation to his writings on the sacraments and on a Christian's duty to God, to himself and to his neighbor. Prayer, he taught, should be not for oneself alone but always for others too; for grace for every moment of the day; for the gift of the Holy Spirit and for his spiritual gifts; for lively heart-felt faith; for understanding of the holy scriptures; for the renewal of the soul; for the salvation of all. Above all, he taught that one should "fix one's mind on God" at waking, on entering a church, on going to sleep. "Read the psalter and meditate at all hours of the day. Read the doxology and repeat attentively: Glory to God in the highest. . . . I beg you also to remember me before God, the fervent servant of you all."[131]

His meditation on the Lord's Prayer well illustrates his teaching.

> Father—true Father, adoption and sonship through Christ. Unity of all Christians. Love. Prayer for all. Equality of Christians. Seeking after the divine likeness. Repentance if one has lived as a prodigal son. God is everywhere, but he also leads us to heaven.
>
> Hallowed be . . . that is, be glorified. Seek to praise Him. Also hallowed in ourselves by preaching the glory of God and living accordingly; ask for the grace to do so. Therefore we begin to understand our frailty. Not to seek glory for ourselves.

Not to live against the Word of God.

Thy Kingdom . . . kingdom of heaven. To despise earthly kingdoms; to foster a pure conscience.

Will . . . that we may become capable of doing his will. We can do nothing without it. It is accomplished through devotion. To live peaceably, lovingly, angelically. To renounce one's own will.

Bread. Daily. All that is indispensable, but not luxury. Not to strive after riches. We confess our poverty; we beg for others too; "our" expresses care and love. God tends the pagans too, but the Christian knows the donor.

Forgive. Our sins. Forgiveness through meditation on Christ. Prayer for all people. *This is the prayer of the saints.* By sins we mean not the coarse and deliberate ones but those which come from frailty and weakness. Forgive your brother. He who wishes to pray for sinners must first abandon his own sin.

Temptation. Not that which comes from God but that which comes from the devil. God does not tempt by evil (Jas. 1. 13, 14). Prayer for preservation in grace. Even if we succumb to temptation, that we be not conquered by it. We see our lack of power. We learn to turn at once to prayer. Not to trust in ourselves. Spiritual virility: that of our own will we should not give in to sin.

Evil. The devil. Ask to be defended. And at the hour of death. We are delivered in and through prayer. Pray the same for other people. Without sloth, in watchfulness.[132]

For a Christian the life of prayer is in direct relation to historical facts and the historical person of Christ. Therefore as people look at paintings of battles in order to remember them, so "an icon and a picture represent not only to the inward eye but also to our physical vision the story of Christ," thus touching our hearts.

> Keep in your house a picture of the passion of Christ, look at it often and with reverence: it will be to you a substitute for continual reading and visible history. Throw away those masquerading pictures which weaken and tempt and burn your flesh; paint instead the tribulations and victories of Christ; the whole deepest content of the gospel is portrayed in the passion of Christ and incites us to imitation.[133]

St. Tikhon's teaching on prayer can thus be summarized under a few main headings: warning against formal and "unpurified" prayer, whether corporate or individual; discursive prayer; meditation.

It is important to emphasize the novelty to most of his contemporaries of his precepts on meditation, especially those so intimately linked with the prayerful reading of the Bible, on the reminder of baptismal vows and on the practice of frequent communion.

One can discern next his own ejaculatory prayer, which he advocated without laying it down as a definite method of prayer. Certain allusions lead one to think that these ejaculations were connected with the cult of "the Name of God" and "the Name of Jesus." But it would be unfounded to draw from them any conclusions as to his knowledge, practice of, or still less teaching on "the prayer of Jesus." One gains the impression that he himself strove, and taught others, to achieve a permanent state of prayer through the memory and exercise of the presence of God. And this meant the presence and memory of Christ. He seldom used the word "contemplation," but he spoke of "fixing the eye of the mind" on Jesus Christ. The most direct approach to the idea of contemplation and union with God are to be found in his words on eternity and the love of God.

To turn the inward eye to the person of Christ is to be devoured by loving zeal to follow him. Like most Orthodox writers, St. Tikhon more often speaks of "following" than of "imitation" of Christ, but he does use both terms, for with all his humility he had the boldness of a saint:

> We Christians are disciples as were the apostles. We must be followers both of the teaching and of the example set by the life of the Master. . . . And what is it then, to follow Christ? To do good and to suffer for the sake of the will of God who desires our forbearance; to endure all, looking upon Christ who suffered (Phil. 2. 8; I Pet. 2. 19-21); for many wish to be glorified with Christ yet few seek to remain with the suffering Christ. Yet not merely by tribulation but even by much tribulation does one enter the kingdom of God.

Let not the conscience be troubled by the seemingly humble question: how can one walk in the steps of One who sits at the right hand of God? For the answer faces every Christian:

> By the way of the Cross, for thus have followed him all the saints, who have been led into the celestial homeland. We must choose this way of humiliation if we, too, desire to reach that land, which I wish both to you and to myself. Be saved![134]

The way of humiliation is traced in Phil. 2: it is in this light that one must read St. Tikhon's words on poverty, humility, obedience and patience. These were neither the stoical ideas nor even the ascetical exercises of a mortified will. It was a conscious, free choice and a growth in spiritual apprehension of those qualities and merits of Christ "which faith allows us to appropriate." One can thus distinguish between mere theoretical knowledge of Christianity and true living faith sustained by grace. "My God and Saviour. Faith clings to him as an infant to his mother."[135]

Christ "became poor that we might become rich." In the active life the response to this is in acts of charity; in one's personal life, detachment; spiritually, it becomes the emptying of a soul in an act of perfect obedience. This heroic offering of one's will makes prayer, preaching, daily works, acceptable to God. Without it, St. Tikhon said, even the confessing of God's name or the very gift of miracle-working are of no avail. With it goes its corollary, patience. "In patience one possesses one's soul." The point is not to "experience and bear with many calamities but to meet them generously—thence, amidst misfortunes, arises a sweet quiet."[136]

"Patience is the Christian's coat of arms. In it we are likened to Christ as members to the head." Far from being a passive state, patience is a fruit of the will and is never learned without sorrow. It goes together with a pure conscience and can "quiet and tame a stirred agitated heart, thus grounding a man in calm."[137] But it is sincere and lasting only if based on humility.

> God descends to the humble as waters flow down from the hills into the valleys. God creates out of nothing; and if we sincerely recognize ourselves as being nothing, he will recreate our hearts. This new creation (which has nothing in common with the covering of the body with a black habit without clothing the heart), produces as it were a ceaseless hunger and thirst after the grace of God; for humility does not consider what it already possesses but seeks what it has not yet.... Humility is a learning compared with self-satisfied ignorance; for one who learns in this school of divine wisdom, the more he partakes of divine gifts the better he sees his spiritual misery and, out of real want, he seeks in sighing. (Then) the lowly path of humility leads man to the Highest.[138]

This seeking is a sign of humility and there are practical ways of acquiring it.

> Try to know yourself, your own wickedness. Think on the greatness of God and your wretchedness. Meditate on the suffering of Christ, the magnitude of whose love and suffering surpasses our understanding. Ascribe the good that you do to God

alone. Do not think about the sin of a brother but about what in him is better than in yourself. . . . Flee from glory, honors and praise, but if this is impossible, be sorry that such is your lot. Be benevolent to people of low origin. Be freely and willingly obedient not only to those above you but to those below. . . . The lowlier we are in spirit, the better we know ourselves, and without humility we cannot see God.[139]

The supreme act of obedience "unto death" was for St. Tikhon the corner-stone of the inward life.

> Remember often, especially during the night, the suffering of Christ. It will kindle in you love for the Sufferer; this love will preserve you from sin. Meditate upon his Passion: it helps the fulfilment of Christian duty. . . . The suffering of Christ is like a saving book from which we learn all the supreme Good: repentance, faith, devotion to God, love of our neighbor, humility, meekness, patience, detachment from worldly vanities; like a spur it stimulates one.

A note of personal adoration pierces through when St. Tikhon wonders how one can torture and crucify Christ afresh by certain acts of sin or injustice.[140] With moving simplicity he points throughout his writings to the person of Christ, stressing the voluntary self-emptying of the Son of God, the humble manger and all the earthly humiliation of the "meek-hearted Jesus."

In Jesus he saw and loved God. The moral precepts scattered through his sermons or letters stop short at the theme of divine love. It is in this theme that one is justified in speaking of his mystical theology. He uses the metaphor of marriage. "If for the sake of marriage we leave father and mother, how much more so for the love of God; by this we can verify in ourselves the ardor of our love for God."[141] He tried to express in the language of reasoning and argument the causes why one ought to love God: because he is the highest good and the source of goodness; because he is our creator; because he has created man to his image and likeness; because he has lifted him up again through the Incarnate and Crucified; because he has given us guardian angels; because he waits mercifully for our repentance; because he has created everything for us—the sun, all nature and beauty; because he is our providence; because he is our Father.[142]

Yet it is in the ecstatic language of a lover that he interrupts these arguments over and over again.

> The human heart cannot be void, and all creation preaches to us the benevolence of God. . . . Love! insatiable desire and spiritual delight! Give us light to see thee, hearts to love thee. . . .
>
> And whom else would we love if not God? Love cannot hide, but expresses, itself in signs. But let us see what are the signs of the love of God, in order to make sure they are not illusion and dreams rather than love—for in no other thing does man so err as in love. These signs are: the keeping of the commandments; a heartfelt joy in God and because of God, which is the spiritual joy and foretaste of the sweetness of life eternal; contempt of worldliness: for there is only one precious pearl. He who loves God remembers him constantly, and thus is enraptured by God. His treasure is God, therefore his heart abides with God permanently; he desires to be always with the Beloved. Many Christians who desire to be glorified with the Lord but who do not wish to be with him in dishonor, to carry the cross, to suffer in the world, show by this that their heart is wrong, that they do not truly love Christ and, to be frank, that they love themselves more than they love Christ. Love of God is shown in the love of our neighbor.[143]

Throughout his personal life and in all his writings he

emphasized that the love of God is inseparable from the active, prayerful, forgiving, forbearing and generous love of people. Who is my neighbor? everyone, particularly Christians. We must never do evil, never hurt others; we must love and help the poor, for "he who loves is moved even physically, so that he cannot help giving assistance." And however much man may try to deceive himself or others, true love "cannot be hidden, any more than the bubbles under the water which reveal the air." Therefore "be simple and without flattery with others, as with yourself. Such as you appear to man on the surface, so be inwardly." Take him more to your heart than he ever expected you to do.

> For love does not seek its own, it labors, sweats, watches to build up the brother; nothing is inconvenient to love, and by the help of God it turns the impossible into the possible. . . . Love believes and hopes. . . . It is ashamed of nothing. Without it, what is the use of prayer? What use are hymns and singing? What is the use of building and adorning churches? What is mortification of the flesh if the neighbor is not loved? Indeed, all are of no consequence. . . . As an animal cannot exist without bodily warmth, so no good deed can be alive without true love; it is only the pretence of a good deed.

Likewise, he says with profound penetration, "without love there can be no gratitude, only a hypocritical one." Truth and sincerity of love for him are centred in worship and adoration of the Trinity, outside and above man. In him they would recognize each other as members of the same body, and holy communion is the visible sign on earth of union with men.[144]

Love of our enemies, "though hard to nature," can be learned by "looking upon Jesus." St. Tikhon insists most particularly in this connection on the aspect of voluntary humiliation, suffering and forbearance of Jesus Christ, who reconciled us to the Father whilst we were yet enemies. He who loves his enemy is truly a son by grace. "Love and meekness provoke even the fiercest enemies to contrition." To him who loves his enemy is given boldness in prayer. To learn and acquire this love may be a matter of long years but is the final proof of love of God and the token here on earth of celestial joy.[145]

The motive of joy appears in all St. Tikhon's writings, though to a casual reader it is less apparent than his words on suffering, sorrow and the spiritual combat.

> In the morning you see the sun which comes up brightly and amazes everyone. Think, then, what great gladness will be experienced by souls resplendent in the eternal sun of righteousness, Christ, the Son of God. Pray that in your heart too may shine the beneficent light of his grace![146]

St. Tikhon taught that "thanksgiving and gratitude is a heartfelt joyous recognition of the divine benevolence and mercy towards us, unworthy ones, shown by him freely and testified by our heart and mouth." It grieved him that Christians who ought to see what fills the whole history of the Church do not see God in the flesh walking on earth in the form of a servant, working miracles and suffering and risen.

He made special thanksgivings for being preserved from sin and the devil, for being called to the light, for faith, for redemption and for the hope of eternal life.[147] Consolation for a true Christian begins in this life. Blessed is the death of sincere and devout people who pass from sorrow to joy. Let those frightened by death recall

> the guiltless passion of Christ; the resurrection of our bodies; the angels who carry our souls to God; the beginning of a new and better life, where we shall see God, where there will be the amiable society of the Queen of Heaven and of the saints; where we shall become free from this world into which we were born with a cry—for a devout soul feels always like a stranger till it reaches its homeland of

heaven. There will it rest from strife and labor—and it will be in eternal rest.

The beatific vision begins here on earth. A Christian is given to know the bliss of pure joy in the love of his neighbor, in the thought that he is a child of God, in earthly rejoicings which too should be referred back to God, in communion—"for the presence of God cannot be without consolation and joy." Here—if only as a hope—we experience the triumph of spiritual victory, we have a foretaste of the bliss of eternity. "My heart and my flesh rejoice. Rejoice in the Lord!" These exclamations of the psalmist fill pages of *True Christianity*. Joy for him is inseparable from love of God and love of people. "They call God their Father! They have the Son of God for a King!" Above all, a true Christian is led "to the gladdening thought of eternal bliss in the contemplation of God face to face." This fatherland, open through the Son of God's obedience unto death, is such "that man could have agreed to endure everything to gain this treasure, which the mind is not capable of apprehending, which is beautiful, sweet, magnificent and which is so variously described through the Holy Ghost in the Scriptures...."[148]

The thought of eternity was one of the most dear and most familiar to Tikhon. He counselled frequent meditation upon it, "especially at night." He did not make light of the idea of the last judgement; and, closely following the gospels, he taught others, and himself practised, the essential conditions for facing this judgement: belief in Christ (John 6. 29) and active love of people who are inseparable from him (Matt. 25. 37 ff.). If sin is separation from God, how much more so is hell! In this sense Tikhon had a true fear of hell, for even the shortest period of separation from God in his moments of despair was unbearable to him. Torment of conscience, dissatisfaction, "despair of the goodness of God," inability to change—it seems that he thought of such states of mind when, in his *Waters which Flow By*, he wrote about those who, "in the fatal eternity, will die all over again and will long for death, and will be unable to die fully, and will suffer and find no comfort." In his early writings he said:

> Meditate more often, O Christian, on eternity, that you may the better escape sin. One cannot think of eternity without sighing and fear. Meditation upon eternity makes weeping and tears sweet, it lightens every toil, it teaches us to accept with thanksgiving any temporal punishment, sorrow, offence, dishonor, banishment and death itself; it prevents us from falling into the snare of lawlessness. He who thinks of eternity will seek the word of God and instruction to salvation more than he seeks his daily food.

St. Tikhon adapted the imagery of the gospel to the circumstances of everyday life: he spoke of citizens expecting their Tsar; of one being left, another taken; of the gardener cutting down a tree, and so on, and he exhorted people "with zealous hearts to seek eternal bliss, where everything is like the earthly festival, yet everything is celestial: friends, food, singing, praise and love."[149]

His later metaphors have an unforgettable touch of poetry and vividly picture Russia with its contrasts between the dreary months of cold and the blossom of spring.

> Winter has come, the earth is covered with snow, frost has chained lakes, rivers and marshes, and thus a free road has been made so that there is no longer any need for bridges or other means of crossing. This is divine benevolence, serving your need: bless him who gives snow (Ps. 148. 8). Winter passes and spring approaches. You can regard this as a resurrection of all nature which died by frost: bless him who thus appointed it. Spring has burst out; it reveals a new treasury of divine gifts; the sun shines and warms pleasantly, the air is filled with scents; the womb of the earth brings forth its riches; the fruit of seeds and roots appears and of-

fers itself for the use of all; the meadows, the cornfields, the woods deck themselves with green, they adorn themselves with flowers and pour out fragrance; the springs flow and the impetuosity of the rivers gladdens not the sight alone but also the hearing; everywhere the diverse voices of a variety of birds make sweet melody; the cattle stray over meadows and steppes, no longer asking food from us but fed and satisfied with what the hand of God spreads before them—they eat and play as though thanking God for his mercies; in a word, all things under heaven change into a new, beautiful and gladsome form; both animate and inanimate creation is so to speak born anew.[150]

And again:

The trees which in winter nearly all look alike under the snow, blossom in spring. So shall it be with our bodies when they rise again. Now we do not clearly distinguish between good and evil, but in the resurrection all things will be clear. As trees put out leaves in spring, so, in the resurrection, will the goodness concealed in the hearts of the saints be revealed in their bodies; their risen bodies will be clothed as in gorgeous vestments. They will be likened unto the glorified body of our Saviour (Phil. 3. 21). And just as dry grass and dry branches are ugly, so will it be with sinners. All that is true in us is hidden. Praise not, neither judge, for you know not a soul from within. And seek goodness with faith, that you may adorn your soul and make it beautiful.

And from this spring which you perceive with your senses, let faith lead your mind upwards to the fair and desired Spring which God has promised through his word. That Spring, in which the bodies of the faithful who have slept like seeds since the beginning of the world, will bud forth and rise and clothe themselves with beauty. Then will they receive the crown of goodness from the hand of God; they will shine with beauty like a bride and will flourish like the earth bringing out its blossom. And their heads shall be crowned with eternal joy. So this corruptible shall put on incorruption. Thus, rapt in spirit to this desired Spring, sow now in faith and hope, and with the help of God, the seeds of the blessed harvest, that then you may reap with joy."[151]

Tikhon's beloved prophet, Isaiah, together with the gospels, expresses the longing and hope which inspired him for himself and for all who are prepared to believe in Christ and to learn the active and the ascetic mystical way of true Christianity.

My soul shall be joyful in my God; for he hath clothed me with the garment of salvation, he hath covered me with the robe of righteousness as a bridegroom decketh himself with ornaments, and as a bride adorneth herself with her jewels. For as the earth bringeth forth her bud and as the garden causeth the things that are sown to spring forth; so the Lord God will cause righteousness and praise to spring forth before all the nations.

7

Growth of Veneration

CERTAIN STAGES MAY be noted in the development of the position Tikhon was to hold in the hearts of men after his death: the translation of his body on 14 May 1836, the publication of his *Works*, the spreading of their influence in the ecclesiastical world and among the masses, his canonization on 13 August 1861 and, finally, his impact upon the great Russian novelist.

It is often said that canonization in Russia is the result of popular devotion to the memory of a man of holy repute and of popular acclamation. Tikhon presents a striking example of such loving and living memory. Ever since his solemn burial there had been a continuous stream of pilgrims to his grave. The wife of a Major, Anna Ivanovna (born Khluzova), ordered an engraved silver tablet in his honor (its date is unknown). It was still on the tomb in 1835.[1] Memorial services were held at his grave annually (on 16 June and 13 August), and attended by a great concourse of people; many "observed the touching habit of writing Tikhon's name on a diptych."[2] The two wells dug by Tikhon became places of pilgrimage. In 1813 a landowner, A. Th. Vikulin, built the church of the Virgin Mary on one of them, and in 1820 an almhouse was erected there for retired soldiers. Then a women's community was established (1833, called "Of the Grave," Kladbishchenskaya), officially recognized and named after Tikhon (1860). The water from the well was conducted into an outer reservoir and into a separate bath-house, the pilgrims coming there in search of healing. By 1871 there were three churches and a hospice for 12 women.[3]

Round the other well was constructed "a skete"—a more secluded extension of the Zadonsk monastery, for twenty brethren and twenty novices, called Zadonsky-Tikhonov (1871).

The large number of pilgrims contributed to the growth of the premises; Zadonsk built a wing in 1798 and later, two-storied hostels; six churches as well as wings were added to the old ones; altars were dedicated to Tikhon's memory after his canonization. The community's feast-days became those of his memory. After 1861, when he was canonized, they were: 14 May, anniversary of the discovery in 1846 of his relics, and 13 August, the day of his death and canonization. In addition, four times a year his relics were carried in procession from the winter to the summer building of the church and back, and on 13 August round the monastery. The "third class" monastery of 1764 grew by 1851 to the rank of "first class." The whole diocese was enriched by the pilgrims. There were some forty thousand of them annually.

As works of charity, the monastery built a free hostel for poor pilgrims; a hospital with twelve beds; in 1818 a boarding-school for twenty-four boys—with ten scholarships in memory of Tikhon's love of children; and two small almshouses—one for a dozen gentle-women, another for twelve simple folk. In Voronezh the Annunciation - St. Mitrophan community (founded in 1836) developed a Brotherhood in the name of St. Tikhon, with a library, a parish school for 150 boys, a hospital with ten beds for monks and ten for pilgrims, and two hospices.

After the canonization all the places in which Tikhon had lived, with the exception of Tolshevo, erected churches or altars to his memory; that of Otroch represented on its rear wall the murder of St. Philip.[4] Korotzk, Tikhon's birth-place, opened a monastery in 1871.[5]

One curious case of veneration recorded (unfortunately undated) is the story of an apparition of Tikhon, in a dream, to a retired officer, Mamonov, who wrote three times to the

Synod urging Tikhon's canonization. Dressed in episcopal garments (except for the color of the slippers, they were described by Mamonov, who was not present at the burial, as those given by bishop Malinovsky for the funeral), Tikhon stood with his hand pointing to an icon of the Virgin with Child. The officer asked a friend to make a picture, and honored it as an icon; venerating a picture of a non-canonized person was prohibited: the image was "arrested" by the authorities, but eventually smuggled away by a devout old woman, finally to hang as an icon over the entrance to a women's community.[6]

When, in 1832, Voronezh celebrated the canonization of St. Mitrophan, its first bishop, it was thought that Tikhon also would be proclaimed a saint. People mentioned cases of miraculous healing. The Tsar was approached, but was reported to have said that one canonization in one reign was sufficient. The case was officially raised in 1836 by the Archbishop of Voronezh, Antony. His two reports to the Synod explained that whilst preparing to rebuild the church he had to move the coffin of Tikhon. The cover was scratched by the bricks, and the coffin was nearly rotten. The body was found in good condition, "like the relics of Kiev," the vestments whole and hardly changed in color. He also spoke of cases of miraculous healings. A few hours before his death, on 20 December 1846, he signed a testimony concerning the miracles and expressed the hope that Tikhon's cause would be promoted. This document was addressed to the Tsar, Nicholas I.

The famous Metropolitan Filaret of Moscow described these events to a head of the St. Sergius-Trinity monastery.

> I have good news from an eye-witness about the translation of the relics of Bishop Tikhon. The Rt. Rev. Antony had an impulse to do it after a repeated apparition in a dream. He felt at first different about taking this action or about raising the case before the Holy Synod; then he said: "I must do it. If they are discontented, let them prepare a place for me somewhere in Solovki!" He thus went

to Zadonsk. He ordered three priests to open the grave. In order to lift the coffin, they found it necessary to call a fourth. As they tried to lift it, they saw that the side boards of the coffin were rotten. They borrowed from an ascetic a coffin that he had prepared for himself, and they lifted the relics on the bottom board which had remained strong, put them into the ascetic's coffin and thus transported them into the church. This was in the night before the Ascension. The bishop and those present sang the Easter canon, or a requiem, I do not know which exactly, I only know that they did sing: Christ is risen! The eye-witness, together with the others, kissed the uncorrupted hand of the departed bishop. Then the bishop (Antony) sealed the coffin.[7]

A cautious, highly intelligent theologian and statesman, Filaret, was both drawn to the example of Tikhon and afraid of following it:

It would be good to escape from everything, especially in times like ours. . . . But the prospect of following in the path of the blessed Tikhon and of standing firmly in it, does not appear to be without obstacles. . . .[8]

He followed with keen interest, but with due reserve and critical sense, the records that were coming in. "There are many apparitions, many healings, but one does not see anything really decisive. . . . May God give wisdom to the Synod."[9]

On 18 November 1860 he opposed the authorization, by the Synod, of a service of praise to some sixteenth-century monk locally venerated in the North, and bitingly wrote to the Ober-Procurator, Count A. P. Tolstoy:

It would not have been superfluous for the Holy Synod to consider whether it was useful for the Church to print these newly compiled services and akathists in which there are many words but little spiritual edification, and to occupy with such things people of small discernment, whereas time and zeal are lacking to carry out with exactitude the substantial church services transmitted by the divinely inspired Fathers. . . .

The Orthodox Church acknowledges saints after a reverent investigation, and by a corporate decision.

Everybody is convinced of the saintliness of Bishop Tikhon, but one cannot print a service to him before he is canonically and solemnly recognized as such by a corporate decision.[10]

Other churchmen also waited for this solemn decision. "Someone writes to me that the cause of Bishop Tikhon has been raised, and probably his relics will soon be open to veneration," wrote Platon (Fiveysky), Bishop of Kostroma.[11]

The records referred to by Filaret were those mentioned by Bishop Antony, and forwarded to the Synod and the Tsar by his successor Joseph in 1860. A commission was appointed to investigate the case: it consisted of Bishops Joseph of Voronezh and Isidor of Kiev, Paissy, the Archimandrite of the Moscow-Pokrov monastery and two co-opted priests and monks of Zadonsk.

They studied forty-eight cases of healing, of which nineteen originated in the monastery. The record of 1827 strikes one by its vagueness: "A young lady, A., saw St. Mitrophan accompanied by an honorable elder who was taking the book of the gospels from his hands, and the young lady was assured that this was Tikhon of Zadonsk."[12] The cases reported between the thirties and the canonization resulted either from prayer for the intercession of the saint, or from pilgrimages to the monastery, which were accompanied by communion there. A case of healing from cholera in 1837 was ascribed to an icon of Tikhon (one more proof of the existence of his icons before the canonization); one person touched his cloak in 1850, another was anointed with oil from the lamp on his tomb; a monk, racked with fever, called out: "If only you would help me!" whereupon he recovered. Some illnesses were classified as demoniac posession or eye-trouble. On 14 October 1874 the surgeon Dr. Orlinsky certified the healing of dropsy after six year's illness; a physician and a University Professor Edward Maremy certified in Kiev 1847 the healing of haemorrhage; there were cases of hysteria and head-aches. In 1854 an official, about to undergo an operation for as polypus, was found to be in good health. His name is given as Stepan Vikulin (unless the name has been incorrectly quoted, in which he may have been identical with Semen, a son of Vikulin who built the enclosure round Tikhon's well). Then cases of cholera, of fever and even one case of tooth-ache.[13]

Let us mention, by anticipation, healings related at the time of the canonization solemnities. Two out of six seem to be the same that had been included in the previous record—the Christian names, places of birth and symptoms are similar, though the surnames are given differently—which might have easily happened since uneducated folk often gave their nicknames or patronymics instead of the surname. They describe "head-aches, faintings, hysterical blasphemous cries, paralysis of one leg, probably from a chill," and a case of a girl who was normal as a child, grew mentally deficient and half-dumb at adolescence, and her body became bent; she was not healed completely, but was able to stand upright.[14] One of these sufferers possessed an icon of St. Tikhon which her parents had received from their mistress (Evdokia Mikhailovna, daughter of the Colonel Parenov, whose estate was situated near Tolshevo and whom Bishop Tikhon had often visited). They remembered Tikhon exhorting their masters "not to prevent their servants from having a chance to work for God."

On 25 May 1860 the Synod reported their support of the cause to Alexander II, recommending that the saintliness of Bishop Tikhon should be testified and his uncorrupted body recognized as holy relics to be laid open to veneration; that a service should be compiled to St. Tikhon, who was meanwhile to be celebrated according to rubrics for saint-bishops; that 13 August should be considered as his festival, as well as a day which the Tsar should fix for the opening of the relics; that a public announcement should be made by the Synod.

The Tsar wrote on the same day: "I am in agreement with the Holy Synod."

The canonization was fixed for 13 August, with the bishops of Voronezh, Kursk (Sergius) and Novgorod and St. Petersburg (Isidor) presiding.[15] The rite of canonization was taken from the *Book of Occasional Services* (*Trebnik*) of Peter Moghila.[16] Officials, gentlefolk, the Tsar's brother, Grand Duke Nicholas Nicholaevich, and three hundred parish clergy, as well as many monks, attended the ceremony. Among the celebrants was the Bishop of Tambov, Theophan (Govorov, 1815-94); the saint's personality produced a deep spiritual impression on him. Five years later he retired, to devote himself to a life of seclusion, theological writings and spiritual direction by correspondence. He painted an icon of St. Tikhon for his cell.[17]

An eye-witness speaks of devout crowds on pilgrimages in his honor from all parts of Russia. In carts and on foot, peasants hastened to venerate one who was their protector and defender. Some people drew attention to the fact that Tikhon was canonized in the year of the emancipation of the serfs (19 February 1861).

> I shall never forget that moving sight witnessed in early youth, when an almost uninterrupted chain of pilgrims was moving along the roads, and at the question of a passer-by: "Where do you go? There?. . . ." they all answered as in a choir, as if they were answering in the affirmative by a corporate decision of the whole Orthodox world: "Of course, we are going there."[18]

The roads were strewn with tangible signs of their feelings: gifts of home-spun crush, towels, leather, lace and money. The colonel of police said that literally cart-loads of goods and heaps of money were gathered then by the monastery—a fact sarcastically commented upon by the opponents of the clergy.[19]

The sixties was the most notable period of aggressive materialism among the intellectuals of Russia, and Tikhon was left to become mainly a saint of the uneducated masses. A certain legendary element grew round his name. In his good biography (1865) the priest Lebedev found it difficult to speak of the saint because nothing miraculous seems to have taken place in his life! After the canonization one can trace a "supernaturalizing." Thus one heard of a monk who was suddenly awakened by an apparition and led to the church. There three holy men were moving about in the light from invisible candles.[20] It was remembered that on the day of the birth of the future Alexander I, Tikhon had foretold his victory over "a Goliath"; Efimov claimed to have written down this prophecy of Napoleon, but regretted having mislaid the note.

There was nevertheless the solid fact that this righteous and loving man's memory remained undying. Small booklets on him or extracts of his *Works* (not always well chosen) spread in thousands, and were for long the favorite reading matter of the people.[21] His spiritual influence and the belief in his prayer were unshaken. The popular devotion to St. Tikhon did not diminish with the times. Only the revolution produced a definite break in this side of Tikhon's after-life story.[22]

A different, though no less important side of veneration, and a continuous means of prolonging St. Tikhon's influence, is to be found in the spread of his writings. No outstanding churchman seems to have overlooked them. Evgeny (Bolkhovitinov, Metropolitan of Kiev, 1767-1837), gave in his *Dictionary of Russian Ecclesiastical Writers* a detailed bibliography of Tikhon's *Works*, and compiled a short *Life*.

A warm appreciation of Tikhon is given by Filaret (Gumilevsky, Metropolitan of Kiev, 1805-66) in his *Survey of Russian Ecclesiastical Literature*. Filaret (Drozdov) gave Tikhon as an example of a good writer—"the real simplicity of the Church."[23] It was he, above all, who ordered (15 February 1832) that all church libraries should contain

Tikhon's writings; he indeed considered them as indispensable (to the Synod, 3 February 1867).[24]

In 1848 the Synod entrusted some higher clergy with the compiling of a list of publications for the masses. Tikhon's *Works* were commended by all, in particular by the well-known scholar and founder of the journal *Sunday Readings*, Innokenty (Borisov, 1800-57, Archbishop of Kherson) and Gregory, Bishop of Kazan. It is curious to notice that the latter wished the books to be printed in the old Slavonic alphabet![25]

A book of extracts from modern Russian bishops published in 1861 was criticized for the omission of Tikhon, "whose every thought is warmed by deep Christian feeling, and whose every word breathes the fragrance of unction." Another author exhorted clergy to fight the superstitions, and wrote: "Let us remember St. Tikhon's eloquent exposure of the superstitious people of his time."[26] Still another writer compared him with St. Cyril of Turov.[27]

Tikhon was held in great esteem by A. M. Bukharev (Archimandrite Theodore, 1822-71, who resigned his rank in order "to sanctify" the non-monastic way of Christian life). A great believer in Russia, whose particular calling, according to him, was "to serve in the purification of thought and knowledge, literature and civilization of the Christian world in the spirit of the Lamb, in a sacrificial and lowly spirit," he was aware of the imperfections of Russian life, past and present, but added:

> Even during epochs of spiritual dreariness such as the seventeenth and still more the eighteenth century, holiness never disappeared; there was the monk Paissy, there was Dimitry of Rostov, Mitrophan of Voronezh, Tikhon of Zadonsk ... true ministers of the Word and pastors of the Church.[28]

One could find any number of such appreciations. Tikhon was commended as pastor and as moral and doctrinal theologian.

His personal love of Christ and his conception of the

mystical life within the Church stirred some minds. It would be an optimistic inaccuracy to speak of his provoking a liturgical revival, but his pronouncements on sacramental worship, and especially on the practice of frequent communion, were heard by some.

Michael (Desnitzky) made a habit of reading in Lent to his flock Tikhon's exhortations to those who were preparing themselves for communion. Innokenty (Borisov), too, advocated the more habitual partaking of the sacrament.[29] A well-known spiritual writer, Bishop Ignaty of the Caucasus (Bryanchaninov, 1806-67), strongly recommended Tikhon's *Works*, advocated the return to weekly communion and remembered (in connection with his own experience) Tikhon's inward voice, which told him of the day of his death.[30] One hears Tikhon's voice—although he is not referred to in the context, which is not at all unusual in a sermon—when the missionary Bishop Innocent (Veniaminov-Popov, 1797-1879, who succeeded Filaret in the see of Moscow) called Christians to a weekly partaking of the Lord's Supper; there is a similarity in some of his other remarks.[31] Filaret (Drozdov), who in his early *Catechism* (1824) speaks of the duty of approaching the sacrament four times a year, in later years privately advised a more frequent practice.[32]

The famous modern preacher, priest and healer who brought about an unusual revival in confession and communion, Father John Sergiev (of Cronstadt, 1829-1908), preached on the day of the opening of the relics of St. Tikhon, the return to frequent communion, which renders us holy by the holiness of Christ through sacramental union with him.[33]

It may be of interest to notice that reverence for Tikhon was observed even by some foreign visitors to Russia. R. Pinkerton, who visited the country in connection with a branch of the British and Foreign Bible Society, spoke of the publications of Tikhon's works by the Princess Meshchersky and of his books found in a cell of some monk of good repute.[34] William Palmer (Fellow of Magdalen College, Oxford, 1811-79), who came to seek reunion with the Russian Church, heard in 1840 rumors of Tikhon's apparitions and healings and, although in his own strong views concerning Protestantism and Erastianism he criticized all clergy who did not protest against the establishment or existence of the State-controlled Synod, he admitted that "they (Mitrophan, Dimitry, Tikhon) seem to have been good and pious men, and the belief in their sanctity was of spontaneous growth, not by any means caused or suggested by the Synod, or by the civil Government."[35] The writings of Tikhon, of which contemporary Russians spoke as "almost our only model of practical piety," struck Palmer (who clearly did not quite grasp them in their entirety) as "remarkable for the almost total omission of everything that is ecclesiastical, so that their spiritual piety would seem to Protestants akin to their own, though they might not discover in them any positively Protestant statements."

An ironical remark on the subjection of the Russian Church to the secular powers was repeated by another traveller, a Frenchman who recorded the story of the Tsar's deferment of the canonization: "Tikhon had to wait a score of years. His turn came under Alexander II."[36]

8

St. Tikhon in Russian Literature

TIKHON HAD no direct contacts with secular writers of his times.[1] Indeed, it was precisely in this historical period that the secular and the ecclesiastical worlds drew clearly apart, when the almost medieval unity and simplicity of the Russian conception of the world began to crumble, to be gradually superseded by a diversity of conflicting ideas. If, in the late seventeenth and the early eighteenth centuries, verse, drama or satire came from clergy or the ecclesiastical schools, the post-Petrine period emphasizes the contrast of the old and the new worlds. Clashes between the high clergy and Antioch Kantemir (1708-44) or Michael Lomonosov (1711-65) are good illustrations of this separation of secular and ecclesiastical culture. The development of secular schools, introduction of the new alphabet, increase in private printing and the growing penetration of western technical knowledge and philosophy produced a new type of educated Russian whose intellectual premises would appear not only unfamiliar, but even hostile to a member of the traditional Orthodox clergy. Yet, as far as Tikhon's ideas are concerned, he may well be compared with other great and creative men of his times. His criticisms of and his injunctions to the clergy and the lay folk remind one of Pososhkov (1652-1726), who in his *Testament to his Children* exhorts them to defend the weak and to be "like a lamb in one's own

215

cause, but like a lion in God's cause, however small." His social consciousness, his pity for the peasant ("The peasant's brow is covered with bloody sweat. Is there anyone more despised in our midst than the laborer?") could find parallels in some of the novels by Fedor Emin (1735-70), and even in the revolutionary *Journey from Petersburg to Moscow* (1790) of Alexander Radishchev (1749-1802). Tikhon's sensitivity, his interest in an individual man and his sensitiveness to nature and beauty forestall the sentimental and humanitarian literature of the period and the poetry of pre-Romanticism. As a reaction to the materialistic type of enlightenment religious problems were pondered anew. Some pietist literature penetrated into the country, people were seeking the "Inner Church," personal regeneration and the change "of the wild stone of the heart." Then, like a "paroxysm of conscience," as the historian V. O. Klyuchevsky aptly remarks, came Freemasonry. One of its first adherents, whose sincere Christianity was testified by Platon Levshin, was the great martyr of the Russian Press, editor and printer Nicholas Novikov (1744-1816). His concern for social justice, for education and charitable activities, as well as for the need of spreading true Christianity among the masses, in spite of the difference in form, has much in common with the leading principal ideas of Tikhon.

We have found evidence that the writings of Bishop Tikhon were well known and appreciated in these circles. The champion of the reforms in the courts of justice, though a political conservative, one of the leading figures of the Moscovite freemasonry, the Senator I. V. Lopukhin (1756-1816) helped Novikov in subsidizing several students and in his publishing activities. "Defender of all heretics," as an enemy once called him, Lopukhin was open to all spiritual currents. His famous English garden in the village Savinskoe, near Moscow, contained an "island of Yung-Stilling" (with whom he corresponded), statues of Fénelon, of Madame Guyon and a symbolical monument to the memory of Tikhon, representing a burning candle, as a reminder of his love of God. When praising the works of a bishop (that same Michael Desnitzky who, as a parish priest, read to his flock Tikhon's books), Lopukhin, in his *Memoirs*, compared them to those of Dimitry of Rostov and of "Bishop Tikhon I of Voronezh."[2] It is curious that Lopukhin himself tried to write a masonic catechism on true Christianity. This shows an undercurrent of sympathy and understanding uniting contemporaries widely separated by space, culture and social surroundings. It creates further an unacknowledged but existing link with all those great literary figures of the next generation who were connected with Lopukhin, as were, in particular, the famous essayist, poet and historian N. M. Karamzin (1766-1826) and V. A. Zhukovsky (1783-1852), poet, translator of western poetry, and tutor to the future Alexander II, in whose reign Tikhon was canonized.[3]

The religious revival and the mystic, somewhat syncretic atmosphere of the reign of Alexander I (1800-25) gave way to the growing interest in political and social problems. At this time the intellectuals were not concerned with Tikhon, but by the forties in some educated circles his name had become familiar.

The first writer who, in quest of God and "the soul," showed a direct interest in Bishop Tikhon was N. V. Gogol (1809-52). He asked his friends to send him Tikhon's writings, and advised Count A. P. Tolstoy (the future Ober-Procurator) to read them. Among Gogol's manuscripts remained some notes made after the reading of the *Memoirs* of Chebotarev. Gogol's own complex religious history, his ascetic, even morbid, attitude to Christianity and his fear of the devil reveal no trace of Tikhon's influence. More connection may be found, perhaps, in the ideas on the liturgy which Gogol expounded in his *Meditations on the Divine Liturgy*. It would be premature to speak of direct influences, since we have no proof as to what works of Tikhon's Gogol had actually received and read. He studied, moreover, general traditional interpretations and *De Hierarchia* of Pseudo-Dionysius, the latter not congenial to either himself or Tikhon.[4]

There is no evidence as to whether Tikhon was known to the peasant poet of Voronezh district, Alexander Koltzov (1808-42), but in the next generation the poet Ivan Nikitin

(1824-61), himself a former seminarist of Voronezh, on the eve of his death "spoke much and at length about the spontaneous religious feeling which had sprung up before Tikhon's canonization; he spoke with understanding of Tikhon and of the memoirs of Chebotarev just published in *Pravoslavnoe Obozrenie*."⁵

It is often not easy to find a link between St. Tikhon and the secular writers for lack of detailed documentation about their reading or sources. It is therefore of value to find a direct mention of him in the correspondence between two leading Slavophils. A. I. Koshelev apparently was asking I. V. Kireyevsky's advice on religious literature; in the latter's reply there is a significant line: "If you have so much delight in reading Basil the Great, Chrysostom, and Tikhon of Voronezh, you will undoubtedly read all the holy fathers in Slavonic translations." It is worth noting that Tikhon is already placed among the holy fathers.

The letter is dated 10 June. The year is not mentioned, but it could be either 1846, 47 or 52, for it has reference to "our Almanack" ("The Moscow Literary and Scientific Almanack"); or it can be 1856 when Koshelev edited *Russkaya Beseda* ("Russian Conversation") to which Kireyevsky contributed (he died of cholera on 11 July 1856).⁶

The general current of opinion, however, did not receive favorably any ideas from the Church, or indeed from Christianity. The Slavophils who called their nation back to the Church were looked upon as pleasant but rather eccentric people. The leaders of the intelligentsia were convinced Westernizers, and, like the West, underwent the influence of positivism, were affected by the writings of Strauss and Darwin, turned towards socialism and felt proud of calling themselves "thinking realists" or "nihilists." At the time of Tikhon's canonization, the exiled revolutionary A. I. Herzen (1812-70) published in London, in his periodical, *The Bell*, on 15 August 1861, an article on "A fossil of a bishop, an antediluvian Government and a deceived people." Though ready to admit that "Tikhon was perhaps and honest man," he took this opportunity of pouring scorn on the clergy "who only have beards in common with the peasants" and who by boosting their miracles extort people's hard-earned gains. "Who believes in them, anyway? Not the clergy who investigated the miracles which only happen for their benefit, or rather are manufactured by them. I wish one could know who examined them and how they carried out the examination." The paradoxical state of affairs in Russia made it possible for the majority of the intellectuals to read this paper, which, though officially prohibited, was largely circulated in the land; but the Church had no means of answering such accusations, for, officially, no one was supposed to have read them.

The canonization could not have passed unnoticed. It is tempting to regard as an echo of it the reference to "some man of rank who had asked to be buried under a stone" in the *Strange Story* by I. Turgenev (1818-83), written in Baden in 1869. The author, a Westernizer, a liberal and a sceptic, had often rendered in his writings the religious craving of the Russian peasant soul.

The emotional and political emphasis of the seventies was on "the people," the popular masses. It was during this decade that the youth of educated classes went to live among peasants and factory workers, some as a means of political propaganda, others urged by conscience to make in this way an attempt at expiation of social injustice. The conscience-stricken Gleb Uspensky (1840-1902), with his burning desire to improve the lot of the poor classes, thought that the courageous and disinterested service of the "populist" teachers or doctors was not quiet adequate, for it lacked that spiritual character which was to be found in "St. Tikhon or St. Stephen of Perm . . . who shared with the people all their knowledge, all their enlightenment, who poured out the treasure of their souls to all who needed them." He pointed out that in spite of the conventional manner in which they were written, the lives of the Russian saints revealed that realistic and active character which he considered as typical of true Russian spirituality.[7]

A remarkable though unwilling tribute to Tikhon's popularity comes as it were from the opponents' side when Tolstoy or Gorky cite him as an example of goodness and sincerity. It almost seems that these writers, divorced from the religious life of those same peasants whom they love, have to accept Tikhon whom these masses hold dear. Indeed, it was to some extent a similar process that compelled some Russian intellectuals, including Dostoevsky, to seek religion and even Orthodoxy, after they "rediscovered" the inner life of the Russian popular masses.

Leo Tolstoy (1828-1910), in one of his most anti-clerical works, *The Kingdom of God is within us—Christianity not as a mystical teaching but as a conception of life* (1893), spoke of some men, like "Francis of Assisi, our Tikhon of Zadonsk and others (who) were good in spite of the fact that they served a cause hostile to Christianity (i.e. Church) and who would have been worthier still and better had they not succumbed to the error to which they ministered."[8]

Tikhon's sincerity had also impressed Maxim Gorky (1869-1936), who in his earlier life was well versed in popular religious literature and was interested in the seekers of the spirit—this early phase differed in this respect from his later anti-religious period.[9]

Ivan A. Bunin (b. 1870) was born in Voronezh, and spent his youth on his parents' estate in the Yeletzk district. Zadonsk monastery forms a background to some of his stories: *A Lucky Life* (1911), *The Gay Household* (1911), where a peasant woman treasures the only present from her son, a large handkerchief from Zadonsk, with a black skull and cross-bones pattern, and an inscription around the edge: "Holy God, Holy and Mighty..." In *Spring* (1913) an old prince, fearing that he may succumb to loneliness and begin to drink, sets out for Zadonsk, accompanied by an old peasant. The realistic accuracy of Bunin's works throw an interesting light upon Tikhon's popularity even in recent times.[10]

Above all, it is the recent research in the U.S.S.R. on the literary sources of Dostoevsky that brought St. Tikhon to the forefront.

It is with Dostoevsky (1821-81) that St. Tikhon gains his unique place in literature. He becomes important for any student of the novelist. Whatever Dostoevsky's treatment of the historical figure of Tikhon, it is of the utmost importance for the history of Russian literature and religious thought that he should have found in the simple Russian saint his initial idea of perfection. For various reasons, those who wrote on Dostoevsky often disregarded Tikhon or dismissed him in a few words. Some maintained that the portrait of the elder Zossima in the *Brothers Karamazov* (1881) was taken from Amvrossy (Grenkov, 1812-91), the monk of Optino. There is some justification for this claim: Dostoevsky visited the community three times, together with Vladimir Solovyev (1853-1900), and conversed with Amvrossy. Certain external features on his reception by the elder, the background, the crowds, as well as the fact that he spoke about the death of his son (as a peasant woman does to Zossima) caused people to believe that he tried to portray the famous spiritual director. K. N. Leontiev (1831-91), who lived near Optino, and was secretly professed, spoke ironically of his mistaken representation of an ascetic. Bogdanov supported this theory, and as late as 1921 it was held by Metropolitan Antony (Khrapovitzky, 1864-1936), who also suggested another possible name—that of Makary (Ivanov, d. 1860)—as the original of Zossima.[11]

Dostoevsky, however, left an implicit statement on the subject, and his attraction to the personality of St. Tikhon goes farther back than the period of writing the *Karamazovs*.

"A child of his age," a sceptic, a "western liberal," Dostoevsky lived through arrest, threat of capital punishment and awaiting of death on the scaffold, and years of hard labor and exile. He had gone to Siberia with a copy of the gospels and the ecstatic hope of regeneration. He had passed through and triumphed over "the whirlwind of doubt," and had discovered the simple Russian folk with their faith, wisdom and integrity. He became anxious to communicate this faith to educated Russians "in the grip of some madness of negation"; he grew convinced that the vocation of Russia was to reveal to the world a Russian Christ as yet unknown to it, and the Orthodox faith of the masses embodying the hidden image of Christ.

We do not know the exact date when Dostoevsky first heard of or read Tikhon; it may have been in Siberia, whither

Tikhon's writings had already penetrated; but on 31 December 1867 he wrote to A. N. Maikov:

> There is a thought which has haunted me for a long time, but I have been afraid of turning it into a novel, because it is too difficult. And I am not prepared for it, though this is a tempting thought and I love it. It is *to portray a wholly good man*. Nothing is more difficult, I should say, especially in our time. . . . It has already appeared before in flashes, in certain creative images, but only in part, whereas the whole is necessary.

A year later he returned to the theme of the "Russian Christ," rejected by the educated, who nevertheless, he ardently believed, "will be healed like *The Possessed*" and will sit at the feet of Jesus.[12]

It is impossible to follow here the complex and fascinating process by which Dostoevsky evolved the "perfect man." We see him appear in a novel, only to be replaced by another figure or to become two personages. The first drafts of *The Idiot* (1868) show such an attempt. The figure was soon to require a new setting.[13]

"I put all my trust in this novel, and all the hope of my life—not only from the financial point of view. This is my innermost conviction which I have evolved only during these last years. . . . This idea is the only thing for which I live. . . ." So Dostoevsky wrote (14 December 1869) to his niece, Sophie Ivanova.

And at last he pronounces the name of Tikhon. On 25 March 1870, writing from Dresden, he confides to Maikov:

> This is my last novel: the size of *War and Peace*. You have approved of the idea. The novel will contain five great stories . . . (in two years the whole plan had matured). Each story is quite separate, so that they could even be sold separately. . . . The action takes place in the forties. The general title is *The Life of a Great Sinner*, but each story will have

its own title. The main problem which will run through the whole is the one by which, consciously or unconsciously, I have been tormented my whole life: the existence of God. The hero, in the course of his life, is now an atheist, now a believer, now a fanatic and a sectarian, then again an atheist. The whole of the second story will take place in a monastery. I have fostered all my hopes upon this second story. Perhaps it will at last be said that I have not written only trifles. To you alone, Apolon Nikolaevich, I make this confession: I wish, in this second story, to portray as its main figure Tikhon of Zadonsk, naturally under a different name, but he will also be a bishop and will live in retirement in a monastery. A thirteen-year-old boy, who has taken part in a crime, and who is precocious and vicious (I know the type), is placed there for training by his parents (of our class, educated). This boy is the future hero of the novel. This little wolf, this child-nihilist, becomes a close friend of Tikhon (you know the character and personality of Tikhon). Then, in the same monastery, I shall place Chaadaev (also of course under a different name).... Friends could visit him—Belinsky, for instance, Granovsky, even Pushkin. (For this is not really Chaadaev—I simply want to put this type into the novel.) ... I know the monastic world, I have known the Russian monastery since childhood. But the main thing is Tikhon and the boy. For God's sake do not tell anyone about the content of the second story. I am making a confession to you. Even if for others it should be of no value, for me it is a treasure. Do not tell them about Tikhon. I have written to Strakhov about the monastery but did not write about Tikhon. If only I could depict a *positive* holy figure. This is no Kostanzhoglo, nor the German in *Oblomov*, neither the Lopukhovs nor the Rakhmetovs. It is true that I am not going to create but only to portray a real Tikhon whom long ago, with deep delight, I received into my heart. If I succeed I shall account it a great achievement. Please do not let anyone know. But for this second novel I must be in Russia. P.S. How do we know—perhaps it is in fact Tikhon who represents our *positive* Russian type, which is so sought after in our literature—and not people like Lavretzky, Chichikov, the Rakhmetovs and so on?[14]

Meanwhile, in 1871, *The Possessed* was published. A whole chapter—which was not included in the novel—was called "At Tikhon's," and the hermit of that name meets the power of negation, in the person of Stavrogin, who threatens the whole life of Russia. This "confession of a great sinner" did not, however, express much of Tikhon. The hermit, the "fool for Christ's sake," is not suggestive of the retired Bishop of Zadonsk, though a few minor features, such as the opposition of the monks or the name of the Bogoroditzky monastery, might have some connection with him. Nevertheless, the author noted: "The most important thing about Tikhon is Tikhon."[15]

Dostoevsky returned to Russia from the West and was obviously eager to gather fresh impressions of places of pilgrimage. "Perhaps I shall go this summer to Voronezh and Kiev," he wrote from St. Petersburg on 4 February 1872.

The godly Makary, in *A Raw Youth* (1875), was yet another attempt to portray Russian holiness. "I am my own censor: my pilgrim who quotes in his speech the scriptures speaks very cautiously."[16] A comparison of the intricate drafts of the novels of the period 1868-60 shows clearly that the *Life of a Great Sinner* and the person of a saint were in the mind of the author all the time. The names were as yet unspecified; thus Zossima at first appears as "Makary," as in the *Raw Youth*, while Alyosha Karamazov is foreshadowed in the person of *"The Idiot."*

Meanwhile Dostoevsky developed the themes of Russia's vocation, of God and of atheism in his *Journal of an Author* (1873, continued 1876-7). The person of Tikhon was identified in his mind with the best aspirations of the Russian people. In the *Journal* of 1876 he bursts into that emphatic and polemical strain which was so typical of this *Journal*:

> Do not judge our nation (people) by what they are but by what they would wish to become. For their ideals are lofty and holy, and it was these that saved the nation through centuries of torment; rooted in their souls they had for ever endowed these souls with simplicity, honesty, sincerity and a broad, open mind.... I am not going to remind you of their historical ideals, of their Sergius, Theodossy of Pechersk, not even of Tikhon of Zadonsk. And by the way: are there many who do know about Tikhon of Zadonsk? Why then should you not know of him and why should you promise definitely never to read him? Is it that you have no time to read? Believe me, gentlemen, to your surprise you would have learned beautiful things.[17]

In April 1878 he began to write *The Brothers Karamazov*, this final form of the *Life of a Great Sinner*. At the end of June he went to Optino for three days. The first book of the novel—*The Breath of Corruption*—appeared in September in the *Russky Vestnik*, whose May issue contained the *Pro and Contra*. Its theme is the denial of God and of the purpose of his creation; there was to be a refutation of this theme "in the last words of the dying man."[18]

The Russian Monk appeared on 31 August. "I have written this book for the few and consider it to be the culminating point of my work," wrote Dostoevsky to the Ober-Procurator, K. N. Pobedonostzev (1827-1907; they first met in the winter 1871-2). And he added in brackets, with a *nota bene*: "Biographical information on the life of the Elder Zossima and some of his exhortations." Did he want to convey who Zossima really was? Or did he conceal it from this new friend as he concealed it from Strakhov? Pobedonostzev claimed to have had much influence on Dostoevsky. "Zossima was thought out with the help of my suggestions."[19] Possibly he found the chapters on denial more powerful than those of the apology. Dostoevsky wrote from Ems on 13 September 1879:

> My main worry and care just now is with regard to the necessity of refuting the atheistic thesis. I intend to give the answer to the whole negative side in *The Russian Monk*. I tremble for it and wonder whether it will be a *sufficient* answer, not to the statements made before (in the *Inquisitor* and earlier), not point by point, but only indirectly. I shall show the opposite so to speak in a picture which serves as a contrast. That is precisely what worries me: shall I be comprehensible enough? Shall I, even to the smallest degree, approach my purpose? There are also the exigencies of art. It was necessary to portray a figure both of modesty and of grandeur. Meanwhile, life is full of comical things and is sublime only in its innermost aspect, so, willy-nilly, for the sake of art I had to touch on the most trivial sides of the life of the monk, so as not to detract from artistic realism. A few of the monk's exhortations will be decried by everyone as absurd; perhaps they are in the usual sense, but in their inner meaning they seem to be right.[20]

Mentioning the name of Tikhon in the first draft, Dostoevsky noted separately: "The dream, like Tikhon's, about the emancipation of the peasants." On 10 May 1879 he again spoke of this novel as the refutation of Ivan Karamazov; on 8 July he wrote to Lyubimov: "Pater Seraphicus. The death of the Elder. I consider this the climax of the novel."

It is clear that he did not propose to write a biography. The censorship would not encourage such a thing in the form of a novel; his own artistic sense prevented him from turning a novel into a life of a saint. Yet there are many more affinities between Zossima and his historical prototype than appear at first sight. In this respect the first drafts and notes of Dostoevsky are more revealing than the novel in its final version. It is not the purpose of this study to make a detailed comparison. One can simply point out a few parallels, while keeping in mind that Zossima was "a refutation," and that his words and actions were to some extent a direct antithesis to the discourses and activities of Ivan.

Among such parallels are the following: the teaching that active love is a means of finding God and that prayer is education; Zossima's denunciation of the clergy's financial demands and complaints; Tikhon's denunciation of their greed; their teaching on and attitude towards children; their exhortations on the relations between masters and servants, on judging fellow creatures, on admonition or consolation, on words which, though spoken unawares, may offend a young soul; their description of hell as the place where men burn in the fire of their own wilful hatred and yearn for death and annihilation. Many expressions sound the same note. There is also a long passage in the *Life* of Father Zossima on holy scripture. It is to be noted, moreover, that Alyosha also comes into the picture, for, as Rozanov has, with sharp insight, pointed out, Tikhon is both in Zossima and in Alyosha.

There are other parallels in their life-stories, however different. There is the mother who has to part with her adolescent boy. The monks who surround the living saint and the saint of fiction seem to have something in common, and the monk of Obdorsk reminds one of the critical Gavrilov with his moustaches. There is the episode of Zossima's humiliation before the man whom he had offended when he was an officer. (This idea of humiliation and Tikhon's prostration before the landowner who struck him in the face haunted Dostoevsky. We find it in *The Idiot*, where the humble and loving Prince suffers because he foresees how ashamed the offender will be of his brutality; and in *The Possessed*, where the supreme act of pride is for Stavrogin to bear Shatov's blow.)

Dostoevsky hoped to make the dying man's last words a refutation of the denial of God. Does the death of Zossima bring Tikhon nearer to us? The atmosphere conveyed by Zossima's parting from his spiritual children is reminiscent indeed of the scenes at Zadonsk. But the exhausted and smiling Staretz of the novel is unlike the silent Tikhon in his last retirement. And their deaths—the one kissing the ground in joyous ecstasy, the other begging for communion and dying without it—differ very deeply.

One cannot but linger over the pages in which Dostoevsky describes the "breath of corruption" which follows Zossima's death. Zossima and Tikhon both lay stress on the pure act of faith: "Children, seek no miracles, miracles will kill faith." And, as a contrast to, and an illustration of, the type of faith which clings to material things, Dostoevsky speaks of the decomposition of Zossima's body, and of the scandal which this physical condition produces in the minds of so many people. Even Alyosha is shaken and, through sorrow over this event, is almost driven to sin. It is after death that they seem to join in the realm of the spirit. Their certainty of future life and joy, and the effect it has on those around them, cause one to realize very clearly the power of personality and of faith. Alyosha's vision of Cana and St. Tikhon's meditation on *The Spring* stir us as something greater than poetry. In the ecstatic Pater Seraphicus the novelist revealed something at which St. Tikhon, out of the depths of his hidden spiritual life, only hinted.

We must point out certain fundamental differences between the image of a saintly man of fiction and the real Tikhon. The figure of Zossima represents the "Starchestvo," an almost charismatic ministry of spiritual direction suspected by many of the clergy of endangering sacramental confession. Inasmuch as the life of Bishop Tikhon was not directly affected by these problems, they are irrelevant in this study. Another, and notable, difference is in their general attitude towards a Christian's life. Zossima is presented to the reader at the height of his spiritual achievement—indeed, a seraphic vision. But his childhood, too, and even his brother, are described in similar tones of jubilation. "Life is a paradise, the keys are in our hands!" Such words are precious, but they reveal not Tikhon, or even Zossima, so much as Dostoevsky himself. They came to him after his experience of the death sentence, followed by his liberation. Henceforth they resound throughout his correspondence and his works. Tikhon, in spite of his deep love of nature, has none of the almost cosmic mysticism of Zossima. Nevertheless, it is significant that Dostoevsky should have seen an ecstatic and joyous personality in the sober and somewhat veiled figure of St. Tikhon.

A fundamental difference between St. Tikhon and Dostoevsky lies in their attitude towards the Russian people. Not that Tikhon did not love his countrymen. His life bore witness to his love. But never did he say anything that could justify the theories so dear to Slavophils and, to a considerable extent, to Dostoevsky. He spoke neither of the triumph of the Orthodox Church transforming the whole life of the nation, nor of the glorious "messianic" vocation of Russia among the nations. In *The Possessed* God is hardly separable, in Shatov's mind—and in the mind of the author—from the masses: "the soil, the God-bearing people." The *Journal of an Author* is full of such ideas. The religious conception of *The Brothers Karamazov* is more pure, but there, too, the destinies of Russia are a prominent feature. As for St. Tikhon, he loved every creature, every sufferer, humbly and firmly; he did not encourage national any more than personal pride. He regarded the monasticism of Mount Athos with loving respect; he protested against social evils, but did not engage in politics. He was for ever content with the single standard of the Bible and Christ. For him to live was to die with Christ; to die was to enter one of two eternities; and hope and faith enabled him to catch a glimpse of the light of celestial joy in which there is neither Jew nor Greek.

9

Historical Significance of St. Tikhon

WHAT DOES St. Tikhon stand for in the life and religious consciousness of his nation?

There are, it seems, certain tides in the influence and attraction exercised by this or that saint. One could almost say that there are "fashions" in saints in different places and periods. From this point of view one must recognize that at this present moment the person of Tikhon is not in the forefront of Russian religious consciousness; he is less "popular" than in the past—indeed, he is for the most part only vaguely and inaccurately known.

This effacement of his image is probably largely due to the absence of the kind of literature on him which would satisfy an educated modern mind, as well as to the fact that even old-fashioned Lives have long been out of print. It may also be due to the tendency of many Russians to seek extremes, maximalism, paroxysms, even in spiritual matters. Russia's historical destinies have done little to stabilize or to counteract this tendency. Tikhon is very remote from such things; he speaks of a contrite heart, but he means something quite different from the smitten heart of Dostoevsky's heroes, which so many people have superficially described as "Russian characteristics," or even as the "Russian soul."

Russians who stress the connection between religious and national consciousness are more attracted by such figures as

St. Alexander Nevsky or St. Sergius of Radonezh. Those who are more preoccupied with the purely spiritual side have turned increasingly during the last hundred years to the ascetic, mystical teachers of the school of Paissy. Significant in this connection are the revival and development of certain methods of orison borrowed from the Byzantine hesychasts ("the Prayer of Jesus"), as well as the recent interest in St. Seraphim of Sarov. Though our knowledge of the latter is based on insufficient historical documents, it is evident that St. Seraphim, with his eremitical individualism, his insistence on the joy of the resurrection, his ecstatic and thaumaturgical gifts, his outspoken striving after these gifts and the "acquiring of the Holy Ghost," differs profoundly from Tikhon. Significant, too, are the currents of neo-platonic thought, the speculations of thinkers such as Vladimir Solovyev, Paul Florensky, N. Berdyaev, S. Bulgakov. The theories of the "holy flesh," popular in the beginning of the present century, whether in their semi-judaic presentation—for instance, by V. Rozanov—or in the light of comparative religions of antiquity confronted by Christian gnosticism—as was the case with D. S. Merezhkovsky—have little to do with such a person as St. Tikhon. And little attention was paid to him even by educated Russians who returned to the Church with their famous and controversial manifesto of 1909, *Vekhi* (Landmarks). This group later took an energetic lead in the summoning of the Russian Church Council of 1918. One cannot help feeling that St. Tikhon's evangelical, sacramental, enlightened and social churchmanship could have been of great inspiration to them. Perhaps he was that inspiration to Tikhon, the Bishop of America who was then elected Patriarch, for he was named after St. Tikhon—"who preceded him and who is gratefully remembered and venerated," as was pointed out by the Anglican bishop, H. Bury.[1]

In the history of the Russian Church Tikhon is neither an innovator nor the head of some school or party. He did not fight theological battles or direct important movements of ecclesiastical learning and policy, as did Peter Moghila; he did not open new vistas to Russian monasticism, as did St. Nil of Sora or Paissy Velichkovsky, nor was he a great ecclesiastic and statesman, as were Patriarch Nikon, Metropolitans Platon or Filaret. The popularity of his *Works* bears witness to his influence, but it was a spiritual and moral influence of a non-combative, non-spectacular, silent type. One can only guess to what genuine heart-searchings his booklets stimulated many a parish priest or simple Russian layman.

Though he had absorbed all the cultural treasures available in his epoch, Tikhon could have repeated the words of a sixteenth-century monk, Philotheus of Pskov:

> I am a villager. I have learned to read and to write but I have not examined Greek subtleties. I have not read the rhetors and astronomers. I was not born in Athens and have not conversed with the philosophers, but I have read the books of the Sacred Law.

Tikhon was simply a monk and a bishop who had read the books of the sacred law, who pointed to the need of having the Bible in Russian translation, and who took it as the substance of his own thought and action. These are the features which determine his place in the history of Russian religious thought.

One can define him as a religious reformer grounded in the Scriptures. For he certainly belongs to the current of reformers of the Russian Church. Even a brief outline, such as we have given in the chapter on his sources, shows this spiritual kinship. In the "non-reformed" Russian Church not a century has passed without producing some ecclesiastical reformer who has left his mark and whose efforts have borne some fruit. Even the *Spiritual Regulation*, in spite of its dangerous and polemical spirit, contained elements of truthful criticism. There is a risk, in the modern reaction against the eighteenth century, of forgetting altogether that the thought of this epoch, though in many ways limited and superficial, also contained true and progressive features in the best sense of the word. Tikhon belonged to his epoch and to the eighteenth-century reforming current which inspired the Synodal Russian Church in the persons of her best representatives.

Accordingly, his place in the Orthodox world is not in the metaphysical line of the great Alexandrians, nor in that of the desert fathers or the Byzantine mystics; his place is among the bishops of the "humanistic" and evangelical school of St. Basil and St. John Chrysostom. With St. Basil, he believed in the "reasonable sacrifice" of an asceticism which respects and sanctifies the entire human person. He sought salvation not in dogmatical speculation or through certain techniques of contemplation, through ritualism or unusual deeds of asceticism, but through meditation, prayer, love and the practice of the gospel of Jesus Christ. And like St. John Chrysostom, he was a bishop—that is, a dispenser of the word and of the sacrament—and a pastor who applied himself to the teaching, the social and individual reform and guidance of his flock. His denunciation of social evils has a lasting value.

Nor is this all. Together with the two liturgical doctors of the Orthodox Church, St. Tikhon goes back to the fullness of the New Testament doctrine of the Church and to a lofty sacramental teaching. A modern reader familiar with the development of mystical ecclesiology and with literature on the Church as the Body of Christ is in danger of under-estimating the value and importance of Tikhon's teaching on this subject. One must keep his background in mind. The doctrinal controversies of the seventeenth and early eighteenth centuries undoubtedly won a place in the general history of Russian religious thought and expressed a certain development in doctrinal teaching. They still remain of interest and importance for students of theology. These detailed discussions on points of doctrine or liturgy went back to the scholastic period; but from Peter I onwards attention was focused on the relationship of Church and State. In the period of the *Rock of Faith* and the *Spiritual Regulation*, Tikhon's words come with a refreshing vigor. His scriptural doctrine of the Church transcends the polemics of the time. It enables an individual steeped in his teaching on Christ to incorporate this ideal into the life of the whole Christian body. Therefore, too, his writings on the sacraments of baptism and of the eucharist have a living appeal, and remain to this day one of the best

Russian exhortations on the subject. A liturgical revival in the Russian Church which seems to have begun in this century would be justified in claiming Tikhon as its patron saint.

St. Tikhon was not a dogmatist. Yet he has made a definite doctrinal contribution. It must not be forgotten that as late as the thirties of the nineteenth century some of his books were used in the seminaries as doctrinal text-books. He claimed no originality; he wrote what belonged to the tradition. But he was the first to attempt to produce an accesible and integral presentation of Christian dogma in its application to the life of the individual and of society. Thus an intellectual approach to Christianity was intimately united with moral theology. The difficulty of appreciating and analyzing Tikhon's thought lies precisely in his unified presentation of doctrine, morals and mystical life. The novelty and strength of his writings were all the more striking in that he did not use the language of the seminaries—theological terms couched in a heavy style, and often tedious, owing to the latinized forms of words and the polonisms of the previous generation—he wrote in a beautiful and picturesque language accessible to any reader.

Fr. G. Florovsky writes:

> St. Tikhon was a great writer. His books fascinate by their light yet plastic images. His *True Christianity* in particular has a historical significance. It is not a dogmatic system; it is rather a work on mystical ethics or asceticism. But it was a first attempt to formulate living theology and experimental theology in distinction, and as a counterbalance, to the schools devoid of authentic experience.

This experimental aspect of theology links St. Tikhon, as we have seen in studying his sources, with the pietists. One cannot lay too much stress on his insistence that personal feeling and a personal act of faith are necessary for one to become a real Christian. He is a true contemporary of the eighteenth-century secular and religious western writers, by the place he gives to feeling and to religious experience. The

Slavophils, who so strongly advocated integrity of mind, feeling and will, and believed Russia to be the embodiment of such "existential" religious philosophy, could have found their best example in St. Tikhon.

Dostoevsky was right when he turned for this integrity to St. Tikhon. He found in him the emphasis on freedom and beauty which was so dear to both of them. One might say that Tikhon is the first Russian ecclesiastical writer who can be called "modern." His language, style, thought and feeling are not only those of their century; they foreshadow developments of the future.

St. Tikhon was a living reply to the anti-religious ideas generated in eighteenth-century Russia. Dostoevsky must have felt this when he so persistently tried to portray him as an answer to and refutation of the denial of God, when he pointed out that his last novel was to be the answer to atheism, with its climax "in the last words of the dying man." His appreciation was particularly true when he added that "the most important thing about Tikhon is Tikhon."

For not only is Tikhon linked by every fibre of his being with the Russian tradition so that he could be identified with the piety of his people; it is his personality which is most striking. There is in him that solid and natural character, that nearness to nature, that "soil" for which Dostoevsky himself expressed his longing through the tortuous and passionate minds and destinies of Ivan or Dimitry Karamazov, and of so many others. The Russian novelists had often found such integrated characters among the people. A modern writer, Boris Zaitzev, insists on the calm naturalness of St. Sergius of Radonezh; and, to use his metaphor, we find the same "odour of freshly planed wood" in St. Tikhon.

This would not, however, have been enough to make a lasting impression. Neither during his lifetime nor after his death could Tikhon pass unnoticed. His personality could not but influence others through the sheer force of his generous, disinterested love and his truly holy poverty, which overflowed into the lives of his fellowmen in the continual giving of his possessions and in his endless compassion. Love of God and love of man were the motives of his reforming zeal. Without violence, though with vigor, without striving to break or change any systems, he said simply and sincerely what he wished to say, instructing and edifying rather than protesting and demanding. Symbolically, the leaflets which he circulated in his diocese were for display not in public places, but inside churches, for the use of his clergy and people. His reforming spirit and ideas were based on humility, on personal repentance, all the more deep in that it emanated from a life wholly reformed according to the Word of God.

Tikhon's pastoral teaching is quite outstanding. In a land where spiritual progress was mainly conceived in the form of monastic life, he revived the Christian appeal to men of all conditions, and he enlivened it by examples of failure and virtue within his own Russia. Tikhon's teaching on true Christianity in each walk of life opened new vistas before every struggling soul. He left no precise spiritual method, but he was the first Russian writer to deal with the obstacles and progress of the Christian soul in its bearing upon everyday life. His readers cannot fail to recognize throughout his works the personal experience of one totally given to God. They are the revelation of the supernatural life of a soul, with its trials, despondency and fear, and with its triumph, "the token here on earth of eternal life."

Christians of all traditions can recognize in his experience and writings the essential values of their faith, striven after, lived and loved by him with utter sincerity. The Catholic may be attracted by his faithfulness to the tradition of the Church, his sacramental mysticism, his devotional emphasis on the Crucified. The Protestant may appreciate his love of the Bible, his freedom, his social Christianity and his message for everyday life. Perhaps it is exactly this blending of many-sided experience that makes the person of St. Tikhon a living expression of Orthodoxy at its best. In spite of historical and national differences, one can hardly fail to recognize in him, transcending his human difficulties and history, that "gift from above," which, coming from the One Source, remains in all its diversity one: saintliness.

Appendix

Note on the Canonization of the Saints in the Russian Church

THE PROCESS OF canonization was received by Russia from Byzantium: together with the acceptance of Christianity, Russia adopted the calendar of the Greek Church and the list of saints commemorated every day by Constantinople, "the great Church of Christ."

Since the eleventh century Russia developed her own veneration of national saints, such as Boris and Gleb—two young princes who allowed themselves to be murdered without offering any resistance. There were some twenty-one Russian saints between the eleventh and the sixteenth centuries.

The Council held in Moscow in 1547-9 under the Metropolitan Makary ratified the anterior canonizations and introduced thirteen more names.

After 1721—date of the institution of the Holy Synod—and till 1917, canonization became more rare, and was regulated by a definite procedure. (There were about six canonizations of a universal character and about fifteen local ones.) A local inquiry had to be followed by the Synod and submitted to the imperial approbation.

Throughout the whole history of Russia there were two groups of saints: those whose veneration extended to the whole country, and those approved only for a definite local part of the Church (monastery, city, diocese). There were also persons dead "in odour of sanctity," not canonized, but whose memory was piously kept by the faithful. Before the sixteenth century no strict rules existed on the subject of canonization. Sometimes a saint was canonized by the popular devotion, *vox populi, vox Dei*. Sometimes a metropolitan or a council issued some official act of canonization or disapproval of some local case of veneration. Sometimes the Muscovite Tsar intervened. Thus the Council of 1547 was the first attempt at legislation on the subject. The canonical inquiry as instituted after 1721 was bearing on the personal holiness (or the martyrdom) of the person concerned and on the miracles performed by him or her in their lifetime or ascribed to their intercession. The state of conservation of the body of that person was also taken into consideration, but although it never constituted a condition *sine qua non*, it was a popular belief of the masses that the preservation of the body or relics was a necessary attribute of holiness. Golubinsky, Professor of Church History in the Academy of Moscow, in his *Canonization of the Saints in the Russian Church*, draws attention to the fact that neither the incorruptibility of the body nor the miracles were necessary requisites for a canonization. He gave the example of St. Vladimir as a "non-miracle-working" saint. He also pointed out that the word "relic" was at different times interpreted in different ways, so that at one time bones clear of flesh were considered a proof of holiness, whilst at other times people looked for the preservation of the body. This thesis, known in the ecclesiastical circles, did not sufficiently penetrate the wider groups of the faithful.

Generally speaking, the procedure for the canonization was less rigorous than that followed by the Roman Church in similar cases.

The ceremony of canonization consisted in the solemn transfer of the relics of the new saint into a church, where they were, for the first time, officially offered to the veneration of the faithful.

NOTE ON THE NON-POSSESSORS

The name of "non-possessors" has been given to a group of Russian monks who, in the fifteenth and sixteenth centuries, opposed the conception of a wealthy Church and of monasteries endowed with huge land property and serfs. They were also striving towards a more interior and spiritual religion. This movement was a protest against the ideas of Joseph Sanin (St. Joseph of Volokolamsk, 1439?-1515), abbot of the monastery of Volokolamsk, and his partisans (the "Josephites"). The chief of these were the Metropolitans Daniel and Makary; they advocated an uncritical traditionalism, the extension of ecclesiastical property, the strong repression of heresies and more generally a close link between Church and State, but they also believed in social work by way of help to the peasants and colonization of undeveloped areas. The "non-possessors" had their centres in the monasteries of Beloozero and Vologda, and were often called, therefore, the "elders beyond the Volga." The main leader of the "non-possessors" was St. Nil (Maikov, of Sora, or Sorsky). He raised the question of monastic property in the Council of 1503, and was defeated. He also recommended tolerance towards the heretics. His disciple, Prince Vassily Patrikeev, became a monk in 1499 (and is better known under the name of Vassian Kossoi); he fought energetically for their cause, was condemned in 1531 by a synod of the "Josephites" and imprisoned in the monastery of Volokolamsk, where, according to his contemporary, Andrew Kurbsky, he found a violent death. The monk Artemy (the Elder) was also their supporter. The scholar and reviser of liturgical texts, Maxim the Greek, sympathized with the non-possessors and suffered for it. So did Metropolitan Varlaam, who was replaced (1522) by the "Josephite" Daniel.

The "Josephite" conception became officially sanctioned by the middle of the sixteenth century, and the independence of the Russian Church was greatly infringed upon by the State.

NOTE ON MOUNT ATHOS

Mount Athos—an Aegean peninsula about thirty-five miles long, rising at the outer end to a peak of more than 6,000 feet—shelters twenty Orthodox monasteries forming a semi-autonomous republic within the Greek State. Most of them are Greek—e.g. Vatopedi, Pantokrator, the Great Lavra; a few of them are non-Greek—e.g. Zographou (Bulgarian) and St. Panteleimon (Russian). Besides these monasteries there are minor monastic settlements, called sketes, kelia, etc. Only the twenty major monasteries have a voice in the governing assembly of the peninsula, which has its seat at Karyes. The present number of the monks is about five thousand. No woman is allowed, even as a visitor, on the "Holy Mountain."

At the present time the peninsula is annexed to Greece, but the Patriarch of Constantinople retains sole and immediate spiritual jurisdiction over the Athonite monks.

There were hermits on Athos in the ninth century, and possibly earlier. The real start of Athonite cenobitism was the foundation of the Great Lavra by St. Athanasius in 963. The Byzantine Emperors favored the development of monasticism on the Holy Mountain. The monasteries managed to survive under the Turks. Many legends and sacred traditions are connected with the Athos. The Virgin Mary is said to have appeared there. From an artistic standpoint the churches and icons of the Athos constitute an invaluable treasure.

Mount Athos played a considerable part in the development of the Orthodox spirituality (though one often underrates the part played by the Sinai, Jerusalem and Constantinople monasteries and exaggerates the Athonite contribution). The mystical movement called "hesychasm," so important in the history of the Byzantine Middle Ages, did not start on the Athos, nor did the "Jesus prayer" or invocation of the Name of Jesus. But they had eminent representatives on the Holy Mountain, such as Nicephorus and Maximus of Kavsokalyvia (fourteenth century), Nicodemus the Hagiorite (eighteenth century). The Russians, Nil Sorsky (by the end of the fifteenth century) and Paissy Velichkovsky (eighteenth century), visited the Athos and were influenced by it. They accepted, in particular, the tradition of mental prayer as handed down from the desert fathers and some of the hesychasts. Eugenius Vulgaris (1716-1806), the greatest Greek Orthodox theologian of the period, lived a few years on the Athos as the head of a theological academy founded by the

Patriarch of Constantinople Cyril V, but he left because of internal quarrels there. The Academy did not survive his departure. Generally speaking, the intellectual element seems to be on the decline at the present stage, although the libraries contain precious manuscripts.

The daily life of the great monasteries is very severe. The monks are submitted to strict rules of fasting, and attend long services, including at times the all-night vigil. Their work is mostly manual. Contemplative prayer exists side by side with the ritual observances, but remains more free, less regulated than in the Western religious orders. Dogmatic rigidity even in small matters (the question of calendar) characterizes the *milieu*. Great communities are ruled by abbots, smaller ones consist of some elder surrounded by his disciples. There are no organized novitiates in the Western sense: each beginner is entrusted to the care of some elder. The majority are "monks of the little habit," while the fullness of monastic perfection is the lot of the small minority of strictest ascetics, called "monks of the great and angelic habit." Besides regular community or hermitic life, there are also so-called "idiorhythmic" houses, whose inmates retain some personal property and practise only an attenuated form of monastic life.

PUBLICATIONS

The collected *Works*, sent to the Synod on the eve of Tikhon's death, met with approbation. "His *True Christianity* is a real spiritual treasure, it should be put before everybody's eyes," said Platon Levshin.[1]

Sermons came out in 1784—St. Petersburg, Shnore Press; the second edition, 1794, by the Synodal Press.

The Works, issued by the Breitkopf Press, 1784, in one volume, were re-edited in 1794 by the Synod. This work, a compilation from twenty-seven dogmatical and moral exhortations, was mainly intended for "monastic and ecclesiastical readers."

The Instruction on the particular duties of every Christian was circulated by the Synod to all churches, to be read to their flocks. It is known that crowds attended such readings of his works in Moscow in the parish of Ivan Voinstvennik, where Michael Desnitzky read them aloud (d. 1824 as Metropolitan of Novgorod and St. Petersburg).[2]

The Works were recommended to the students of St. Petersburg Seminary (1788-99), and introduced into the schedule (1809-84) first at St. Petersburg, then throughout the country. Up to the thirties *True Christianity* was often used as a treatise of dogmatic theology.[3] Thus, whole generations of Russian clergy were brought up on Tikhon's works.

Publication was delayed by long discussions over copyright: it was not clear, owing to the double system of censorship, whether it belonged to the Synod in St. Petersburg or to the Moscow Ecclesiastical Censorship Committee. The matter, settled in 1832, was raised again in 1834 and 1838. Meanwhile, private printers and editors brought up small booklets of extracts from the *Spiritual Treasure*. One of these was a lay-woman, editor of Russian and translated religious writings for the people, Princess S. S. Meschersky, sister-in-law of the Ober-Procurator. Her choice of Tikhon's works was supported by the Metropolitan of St. Petersburg and by the scholarly Bishop Innokenty (1785-1819, died as Bishop of Penza and Saratov).[4] In 1835 Gregory, Archbishop of Tver (Postnikov, d. 1860), approached the Synod on her behalf. There were such delays owing to "human passions" and to censorship, that the Princess finally entrusted the work of editing to foreigners, Merillius and Anne-Sarah Biller.

The Spiritual Treasure collected from the World came out in St. Petersburg, 1825, in 4 volumes.

Private Letters, in Moscow, 1830, 2 volumes.

Works edited by the Synod, in 1836, 5 volumes.

Biographical Notes

St. Alexander Nevsky (1220-63). Prince of Novgorod and, since 1236, of Kiev. Was esteemed for his wise policy, obtained from the Tartars permission to collect taxes instead of their own men ravaging the land. Supported the famous Metropolitan Cyril III of Vladimir. In the North, defended the border against the onslaught of Germans and Swedes. Surnamed after his victory over them in 1240 on the River Neva (p. 23).

St. Alexis (Byakont, d. 1378). A learned nobleman. He visited Constantinople. Tried to retranslate the gospels from the Greek with corrections of the early Slavonic version; his texts were used in the seventeenth century by the Moscow revisers of the Bible for its first printed copy. Metropolitan of All Russia (1345), he transferred the see from Kiev to Vladimir. Supported the political development of Moscow. Founded Chudov Monastery. Visited the Tartar centre and healed the Khan's wife (1357). Obtained from the Tartars several privileges for the Church. Was a friend and admirer of St. Sergius of Radonezh (p. 267).

Amvrossy (Grenkov, 1812-91). Son of a church reader. Was a schoolmaster, then entered the Optino community (1829) and was directed by Makary (Ivanov) and Leonid (Nagolkin, 1768-1841). Became a famous spiritual director; was visited by all classes and knew many writers (p. 221).

Amvrossy (Popel). A Dominican (nationality and dates uncertain). Joined the Orthodox Church (1736) together with a Carmelite, Jacob Turansky. Both were sent to Alexandro-Nevsky Lavra. Went to Kharkov Collegium, taught philosophy, brought his pupils to a theological class, which was not started owing to shortage of students. Returned to Alexandro-Nevsky Lavra. "To avoid his idleness," was put under the charge of Archbishop Amvrossy Yushkevich (1741) (p. 31 n. 12).

Amvrossy (Yushkevich, *c.* 1690-17 May 1745). Pupil and teacher of the Kiev Academy. Professed in 1731. Was Superior of the Vilensky Svyatodukhov Monastery. Suffered from Prokopovich for his sympathies with the *Rock of Faith*. Archimandrite of the Moscow Simonov Monastery (1734) and later of Ipatiev. Consecrated Bishop of Vologda (1736), but lived in St. Petersburg since 1739. Member of the Synod and Court Preacher. Archbishop of Novgorod (29 May 1740). A great educationalist. Wrote a Memoir (1742) against the Synodal system under the lay Ober-Procurator; protested against theft in the Economic College; wrote on the means of overcoming the Raskol [1744] (p. 28).

Amvrossy (Zertiss-Kamensky, 1708-71), of Kiev Academy. Was called to St. Petersburg Alexandro-Nevsky Lavra (1736); professed (1738), taught in the Seminary. Took part in translation of the versified *Historical Mirror of the Russian Tsars from Rurik to Elisabeth*. Consecrated Archbishop of Moscow and Kaluga (January 1768). During the plague of August-September 1771 advised the population not to crowd when kissing the venerated icon, to prevent the spread of the epidemic. Had to hide in the Chudov Monastery, but was assaulted and killed by the mob. Left many possessions, including 252 shirts of fine linen, nine eye-glasses in golden frames, etc. (p. 79).

St. Antony of Pechersk, eleventh century, a hermit, possibly first professed at Mount Athos. Was living in a cave (hence the name) near Kiev, where other men joined him. Together with his disciple Theodossy he is regarded as the founder of Russian monasticism. Is believed to have introduced the Rule of Studion into Kiev Pechersk Lavra, cf. Theodossy (p. 271).

St. Antony the Roman (d. 1147), according to the tradition arrived miraculously at Novgorod. Possibly a man from the West. The historians are so far not agreed about him. Founded a monastery (1117 or 1119), left a Rule. Novgorod claimed a last will of his concerning the election of the Superior, whom he "commended to the Blessed Virgin and to all the Christians. Let him be accursed if he is chosen by brethren for a bribe or enforced on the community by a Prince." His life was written in the twelfth century by order of the Novgorod Bishop Niphont "for the affirmation of the Orthodox Faith and to the Romans who had abandoned the right faith unto shame and reproof and curse."

Not to be confused with St. Antony of Novgorod (in the world, Dobryina Andreikov), author of the *Journey to Constantinople* in 1211 (p. 23).

Antony II (Smirnitzky, d. 1846), Bishop of Voronezh (January 1826). Introduced before the Synod the cause of canonization of Tikhon of Zadonsk.

Antony (Vadkovsky, 1846-1912), Metropolitan of St. Petersburg, was previously in the Seminary of Kazan and Inspector of St. Petersburg Academy. Was popular as a pastor, and advocated the closer union of ascetical and pastoral ministry (p. 247).

St. Arseny (d. 1409), Bishop of Tver, founder of Uspensky Zheltikov Monastery (p. 37).

Artemy (Elder, d. 1575). Monk of the Cyril-Belozersky Monastery, then Superior of Troitzky Monastery in Moscow diocese. Was in touch with Maxim the Greek; supported the Non-possessors. Was accused of sympathies with the heretics Kossoi and Bashkin and with the Protestants; after the Council of 1553-4 was arrested, escaped, fled to Lithuania, where he proved a defender of Orthodoxy. He kept in touch with the lay brotherhoods, was mentioned with admiration by Prince A. Kurbsky. There remain nine Epistles of his, striking for their conciliatory spirit and intelligence (p. 241).

Athanassy (Vol'khovsky, d. 1776). Born in Poltava, student of Kiev, Archimandrite of Pecherskaya Lavra, First Prefect in the Moscow Troitzkaya Seminary (1745), Rector (1748) and the Bursar of the Lavra (1749). Began his course of theology (November 1751); *Summa Theologiae, Salutarem fidei Orthodoxae doctrinam sincere et perspicue proponens ac improbe in eam congestis tum infidelium blasphemiis, tum haereticorum calumnis et cavillationibus vindicans, pro varietate materiae in vario tractatus dispertita, et pro studentium* *usui dictata, in Seminario Lavrae Sacrosanctate Trinitatis caepta anno incarnati Verbi* 1751. Archimandrite of his Lavra (1753); Bishop of Tver (April 1758), of Rostov [May 1763 till his death] (p. 36).

Berynda (Paul or Pamva, seventeenth century). A Moldavian, a member of the Kiev brotherhood. Author of the *Lexicon or Interpretation of the Sloveno-Rossic nouns* (1627). (p. 33 n. 17).

Cyril (Florinsky, d. 1744). Pupil of the Kharkov College. Sent to study abroad (1729). Returned (1732), professed same year. Taught in his College Poetics. Ordained (1733). Teacher of Philosophy, Prefect (1735). Transferred to Moscow (1736), taught theology in Slavo-Greco-Latin Academy; became Prefect. Was to be sent to London. Remained instead the head of Simonov Monastery. Rector of the Moscow Academy (1741) and Archimandrite of Zaikonospassky Monastery. Tried to supersede or renovate scholastic methods. Took part in the revision of the Bible. Organized Moscow Troitzkaya Seminary (1742). Wrote a *Dogmatic Theology*.

Not to be confused with his namesake, Cyril (Florinsky, c. 1729-95), of Kiev Academy, professed (1756), taught in Novgorod Seminary; Embassy chaplain in Paris (1760), where he quarrelled with everybody. Bishop of Sevsk and Briansk (1768); after complaints brought against him before the Synod (1773) was forced to retire (p. 33).

St. Cyril (Veliaminov, d. 1427), in spite of his longing for monastic life, acted for some time as administrator to his relation, a Moscow boyar. Professed in Moscow Simonov Monastery (founded by St. Sergius of Radonezh and often visited by him). St. Sergius singled out this monk, who, to avoid popularity, acted as a "fool for Christ's sake." Cyril became Archimandrite, but his ascetic ideal compelled him to retire beyond the Volga as a hermit on the White Lake (hence the name Cyril Belozersky). Gradually a monastery grew there. St. Cyril stressed obedience more than asceticism, and personal and communal poverty. Though his community became famous, and soon after his death, very wealthy, it was there that was still cherished the ideal of the "Non-possessors" (p. 241).

St. Cyril of Turov (1130-82). Ascetic, then Bishop of Turov. Famous for his sermons, of allegorical and rhetorical character (p. 119).

Daniel (Metropolitan, d. 1547). Was Superior of Volokolamsk Monastery, then Bishop of Moscow with the title Metropolitan of All Russia (1522-39); deposed under Ivan the Terrible. He made preparations for the correction and translation of liturgical books, but found fault with the criticisms made by Maxim the Greek, whom he condemned at the Council of 1525. Was also an opponent of the Nonpossessors. Under him took place the divorce of Prince Basil III from his childless wife Solomonia (p. 241).

Dimitry (Sechenov, d. 1767). Preacher and teacher in Moscow Academy (1738-9) and Archimandrite of Sviazhsk. When the Seminary of Kazan was founded (1740) he was sent there to preach among the heathen. Converted the half-Asiatic tribes, not without help from the secular arm. Destroyed a cemetery of the people of Mordva and was attacked by them, but protected his converts and possibly bribed them by various privileges, freedom from taxation and serfdom. Consecrated Bishop of Kazan (1742), member of the Synod, then Bishop of Riazan and Archbishop of Novgorod (1757). Was in disfavor for a short time for protesting against restrictions of Peter III, which put him into prominence under Catherine. He crowned her (1762), made several orations in her presence. Received the title of Metropolitan. Was member of the Commission on Ecclesiastical Property and presiding member of the Synod (p. 36).

St. Dimitry (Tuptalo, 1651-October 1709). Son of a wealthy upper-class cossack. Pupil of Kievo-Bratsky school. Professed (1668); acted as a preacher; ordained (1675). Superior of Buturino (1681-3); stayed at Pechersk Monastery and began to work on the Lives of the Saints (1684); returned to Buturino (1686). Began printing the *Lives* (1689). Visited Moscow with the Hetman Mazepa (July-September 1689). Lived in seclusion, writing (1690); became Superior of Glukhov (1694). By decree of Peter I went to Moscow; appointed to go to Siberia as a diocesan (March 1701); for reasons of health released and nominated Bishop of Rostov

(1702 till his death). He was a friend of Stephen Yavorsky and in touch with Eudoxia, the first wife of Peter I. Received orders to go and preach in Moscow and Yaroslav (August 1708). He was renowned as a scholarly man who fostered schools in his diocese, a bold preacher and a man of holy poverty, gentleness and charity.

He left several religious dramas in verse and devotional writings. In his works on the Virgin Mary he inclined to believe in the Immaculate Conception. His *Chronicle or the Sacred Church History* begins from the refutation of Greek mythology and turns into a doctrinal and theological treatise (1707). His *Findings on the Brynsk beliefs* (1709) is an argument against the Raskol. His *Calendar of Saints* is the first attempt to produce a critical edition. His *Diary*, incidentally, was found in one of the monasteries of Yeletz and was edited, together with his *Chronicle*, in Moscow 1784, in the Free Printing Press of I. V. Lopukhin.

Bishop Dimitry of Rostov was canonized in 1757 (p. 31 n. 13).

Epiphany (Slavinetzky, d. 1676). A learned monk from Kiev. Came to Moscow as teacher (1649); translator and corrector of the liturgical books, compiled *Lexicons*. Used Western sixteenth-century editions of the Bible in his work of preparation for the new edition of the Bible, though he was an expert on Greek language and took a distinctly Greek point of view in his disputation with Simeon Polotzky on the Eucharist (1673; the controversy continued after their death). His love of erudition went together with the quiet and devotion of a good monk (p. 21 n. 3).

Evgeny (Bolkhovitinov, 1761-1837), son of a priest of Voronezh, pupil of local Seminary, sent by Bishop Tikhon III to Moscow Academy (in 1778, as a boy). Returned to teach rhetorics in Voronezh Seminary, French and Church history. Was married, ordained (1796). Widowed (1799), professed (1800) and made Prefect of St. Petersburg Academy. Archimandrite of Zemnetsky Monastery. Bishop of Staraya Russa [suffragan of Novgorod] (1804); Bishop of Vologda (1808), of Kaluga (1813); Archbishop of Pskov (1816), Metropolitan of Kiev (1822) and member of the Synod.

A keen bibliographer, member of numerous historical and archaeological societies; a statistical rather than a creative mind. Left many writings and fostered historical research; a new approach to Russian history through the study of regional chronicles, etc. He thus described *The History and Geography of the Voronezh province* (1792) and the Novgorod, Pskov and Vologda regions; described the Cathedral of Kiev and the Pecherskaya Lavra (1826). Though subject to verification, his works remain an important source of information; and so are his *Dictionary of the Russian Ecclesiastical Writers* (begun in 1805; came out, 1818 and a verified and completed edition, 1827) and his *Dictionary of the Russian Secular Writers* [edited by Pogodin in 1825] (p. 9).

Filaret (Drozdov, 1782-1867). Studied in Kolomna and in Troitzkaya Lavra. Became there teacher of Greek and Hebrew, then of poetics, rhetorics, preaching. Professed in 1808. Taught philosophy in St. Petersburg Seminary. Ordained (1809); Rector of the Alexandro-Nevsky Seminary. Taught in St. Petersburg Ecclesiastical Academy exegesis and philosophy (1810); Archimandrite, then Rector of the Academy and its virtual creator (1811); D.D. (1814). Took part in the creation and work of the Biblical Society. Bishop of Reval (1817), suffragan to the Archbishop of St. Petersburg; member of the Synod. Bishop of Tver (1819), of Yaroslav (1820), Archbishop (1821) with residence at Moscow. Metropolitan of Moscow (1826 till his death).

Main works: *Catechism* (1824, re-edited with corrections 1839); *Exposition of the differences between the Orthodox and the Western Church* (1811); *Dialogues on Orthodoxy* (1815); *Introduction to the Old Testament* (1871-76). Especially renowned for his *Sermons*, remarkable both by their beautiful language and by the doctrinal teaching. Able administrator and the most outstanding figure of the nineteenth-century ecclesiastical world (p. 205).

Filaret (Gumilevsky, 1805-66), died as Archbishop of Chernigov. Was teacher of Moscow Academy, biblical and patristic scholar, new in his introduction of some critical methods of the sources and of philological references, fostered by historical method. Author of *Historical Teaching on* the *Fathers of the Church* (1859) and the *Survey of Russian Ecclesiastical Literature* (1859-61). His work on the *Edition of the Works of the Fathers in Russian translations* developed into an academic magazine entitled *Pribavleniya k izdaniyu sviatiykh Otzev* (p. 10).

Gabriel (Buzhinsky, d. 1731) studied in Germany. Teacher in Moscow Theological Academy (1706); preacher (1709); Ober-Hieromonk of the Russian Navy (1718); Archimandrite of Sergieva Lavra and the Counsellor of the Synod; supervisor of schools and of the printing press. Translated the *History* of Puffendorf. Bishop of Riazan [1726] (p. 33).

Gabriel (Gregory Kremenetzky, 1711-93 or 1783). Began his studies in Kiev, then in Kharkov Collegium, finished in the Moscow Academy. Was invited to Alexandro-Nevsky Lavra (1736), and taught Latin and Greek. Professed (1740), ordained deacon (1741) and priest (1742); continued teaching in lower forms. Archimandrite of Spassky and member of the Synod (1748); Bishop of Kolomna (1749); transferred to Kazan (1755). Bishop of St. Petersburg (July 1762) and resident member of the Synod. Attended the coronation of Catherine II. Gave order that the clergy should preach (1769). Organized book-shops in Kazan for the spread of religious literature. Accompanied the Empress and preached on solemn occasions. Received the title of the Bishop of St. Petersburg and Reval (May 1764); Metropolitan of Kiev (September 1770), though he still remained in the capital and in the Synod. Took leave in May, moved to Kiev, where there was a plague epidemic. He supported the Academy and left big endowments to it (p. 40 n. 2).

Gabriel (Peter Petrov, 1730-1801). Student of the Moscow Academy. Finished his studies (1753), refused to be professed "out of respect," not feeling a vocation, asked to be allowed to bake loaves for eucharistic use; was made main corrector in the Moscow Synodal printing press; then taught rhetoric in Academy (1758). Was professed by order, at Karpovka House, by Archbishop Dimitry (Sechenov) on 28 June 1758. Rector and teacher of theology in the Lavra Seminary (July 1758). Ecclesiastical Judge (August). Member of the Moscow Synodal Office and Archbishop of Tver (December 1763). Called to St. Petersburg to work on various Commissions (1765): that on ecclesiastical schools (1766) and the one projecting the new Code of Laws. Went to Moscow to meet the Empress (1767); returned to Tver. After Dimitry Sechenov, was the Deputy of the clergy on the Ecclesiastical Commission. Member of the Synod (1769). Archbishop of St. Petersburg (1770-1801); laid foundations of Troitzky Cathedral in the Alexandro-Nevsky Monastery (1778)—with sculpture in it, work of Flemish and Italian artists, dedicated in 1790. Additional rank of Archbishop of Novgorod and Staraya Russa (January 1775-80). Rank of Metropolitan of Novgorod, St. Petersburg and Olonetzk (1783-96).

Supporter of monasticism, he left a Rule of cenobitic life and was in touch with the group round Paissy (Velichkovsky). He founded several schools; joined the St. Petersburg Seminary and the Nevsky into one main seminary. Had every possible distinction and great wealth, which he distributed to some churches and to the poor. (He deposited in St. Sophia Cathedral of Novgorod a medal with which Paul I decorated him, a favor resented by the clergy as a worldly affair.) His last year was spent in ascetic strictness, in spiritual reading and in daily confession and communion. He was respected by the clergy, was a member of the secular Russian Academy, and was loved by simple folk. There was a continual pilgrimage to his grave long after his death.

Apart from his works as a corrector of the Synodal Press and reviser of the Bible, he published his *Sermons for every Day collected from the Fathers* (1781) and his *System of theology*, in Latin; corrected the *Rubrics for the Week of Orthodoxy*; worked for the Dictionary of the Russian Academy (both letters "i"). Wrote an explanation of rites and ceremonies of the Church (1792); his *Interpretation of the Beatitudes* remained in manuscript; the *Interpretation on the Epistles* came out in 1784 (1 Peter excepted). He wrote also on the rite of sick-visiting (p. 36).

Gedeon (Krinevsky, *c.* 1726-63), pupil and teacher of Kazan Seminary; was professed and ordained deacon; eager to study, he fled to enter the Moscow Academy (1751). Was heard as preacher by Elisabeth and appointed Court Preacher (1753). Archimandrite of Savvin-Storozhevsky Monastery (1757). Member of the Synod (March 1758) and Archimandrite of Troitzko-Sergieva Lavra (April). Bishop of Pskov, though remaining Court Preacher (1761), was in his diocese only March to June 1762. Returned to the Synod, attended the coronation of Catherine II. Begged to return to his diocese (June 1763), died on his return journey.

His congratulatory sermons were new in their direct and simple style. He often spoke against the neglect of the Bible by the clergy and much against calumniators. Was easygoing, friendly to younger and talented men, but liked to excess good clothes, jewellery—up to the buckles on his shoes—and money. His Sermons were published in 1754-9, 1860 and 1855. He was a protector of Platon Levshin (cf. Platon, p. 265-66).

Georgy (Konissky, 1717-95) of Kiev Academy. Professed (1744), taught poetics (1745) and philosophy; Prefect (1747), taught theology (1751). Rector and Archimandrite of Bratsky Monastery (1752). Gave catechetical instructions to the students, teaching them how to deal with biblical materials. Consecrated Bishop of Mogilev (1755), organized schools and printing presses, studied history and legislation of the region and the difficulties of Orthodoxy in White Russia. In 1762 he visited Moscow and gave an oration in the presence of Catherine II. Sent to Poland (after 1763), he begged Poniatovsky's support of the Orthodox, wrote *On the Rights of the Orthodox in Poland*. When Russian armies occupied Poland, the Catholic Bishop was arrested on his insistence. His diocese became in 1772 "Mogilev-Mstislav-Orshansk." Paid a visit to St. Petersburg, addressed the Empress. Published *A Historical Study of the diocese of Mogilev*. He built schools and the Seminary (1780). Was nominated Archbishop and member of the Synod (1783). Fighter against the Catholics and the Uniats, he allowed the Orthodox to fill the vacancies after the death of Uniat clergy, and claimed that the mass return to Orthodoxy of the Uniats was a spontaneous movement.

Historical works apart, he wrote verse in Russian, Latin and Polish and a "tragicomedy," *The Resurrection of the Dead*. Wrote a *Philosophia peripatetica*, and was the first to attempt a course of systematic theology. His *On the Duties of Parish Priests* was written in co-operation with Parfeny (Sopkovsky). In his sermons he spoke against social injustices, called cruel landlords "Cains and fratricides" and exposed vigorously the slackness of the clergy (p. 122).

Gregory (Postnikov, d. 1860), Rector of St. Petersburg Academy (1819), later Metropolitan of Novgorod and Archbishop of St. Petersburg. Founder of the magazine *Christianskoe Chtenie* (1821). Published part of his theological course (1822). Taught in Russian language, and even used the Russian translation of the Bible for his course. Liked a popular style of preaching and writing for the masses. Author of a non-polemical, conciliatory book written with the purpose of convincing the Old Believers: *The Truly Ancient and Truly Orthodox Church* (1855). He was an admirer of religious and moral English pamphlets (p. 211).

Ignaty (Bryanchaninov, 1806-67), a nobleman, a student of the Mikhailovsky School of Engineering. Early felt a monastic vocation, but had to overcome the resistance to it of his family and of the authorities. Was a monk in Optino, then Superior of the Sergiev Posad near St. Petersburg, later Bishop of Caucasus. Politically an extreme conservative, he was also in religious reaction against the mysticism of somewhat Protestant type characteristic of the early nineteenth century. He stressed asceticism and was the expounder of the Optino mystical tradition not without originality. Author of *Ascetical Exercises* and advocate of frequent communon (p. 212).

Innokenty (Borisov, 1800-57), pupil of Orel Seminary (till 1819) and of Kiev Academy. Its first M.A., professor of Church history and Greek; transferred to St. Petersburg Seminary and professed monk (1823); ordained. Became professor of St. Petersburg Academy and Archimandrite (1826), taught dogmatics and symbolics ("expository theology"). His orthodoxy was suspected, but a Commission rehabilitated him. Rector and professor of Kiev Academy

(1830). Introduced teaching in Russian instead of Latin language and a course in the history of dogma. Bishop of Vologda (1841), and, after nine months, of Kharkov (till 1848). Then Archbishop of Kherson. During the Crimean War made in Odessa ecclesiastical foundations for Bulgaria. A vivid, emotional orator and a moralist more than a theologian. Author of *The Moral Character of our Lord Jesus Christ* (1823), *Sermons* (1825, in the collection made by students), *Life of St. Paul* (1826), *The Last Days of our Lord Jesus Christ* (first ed. 1847), *Life of Cyprian, Bishop of Carthage.* Founder of the periodical published by the Kiev Academy since 1837, *Voskresnoe Chtenie* (p. 212).

St. Innokenty (Kulchitzky, d. 1731), student of Kiev and (1714-18) professor of philosophy in Moscow Academy. Then the Cathedral Hieromonk of the Alexandro-Nevsky Lavra. Appointed to the mission to China. Could not penetrate there, but instead carried on missionary work among the primitive peoples in Siberia. Consecrated Bishop of Irkutsk (1725). Organized schools, and especially fostered the learning of Chinese, thus preparing missionaries for the future and some famous orientalists.

Innokenty (Migalevich, d. April 1744). Teacher of St. Tikhon. He was a student of Kiev; then of Novgorod; taught poetics and rhetorics. Prefect (1740), Rector (1743) and Public Catechizer. Archimandrite of Antoniev Monastery (10 July 1743); released then from teaching duties (p. 31 n. 12).

Innokenty (Smirnov, 1785-1819), son of a village subdeacon, surnamed in the Moscow Seminary for his gentleness and quiet "Smirnov." Teacher (1806) and Inspector (1809) of that Seminary. Professed (1810), moved to St. Petersburg (1811), took a degree in Church history (1812). Professor (1813), D.D. (1814), Archimandrite (1816), Bishop of Orenburg and Saratov (1819), where he died mainly from overwork, accompanied by ascetical strictness.

Author of a *Survey of Church History from the Biblical Times till the Eighteenth Century; Theology* (in Latin); *An Essay of Interpretation of the First Psalms; Explanation of the Creed; Sermons; Letters.*

He was a man of sincere devotion, "converted" through the epistle to Timothy (p. 244).

Innokenty (Veniaminov-Popov, 1797-1879). Son of a church bell-ringer from Siberia. Childhood of great poverty. Seminary of Irkutsk. Married, ordained deacon (1817) in Alaska; priest (1821). Worked among the Aleutians. His wife died (1839). He went to St. Petersburg to discuss the translation of the sacred books into Aleutian. Professed (November 1840); consecrated Bishop of Kamchatka, Aleutsk and Kurilsk (December). Carried on his missionary work and wrote his *Journal of the Travels* (1842, 1843 and 1846). His *Way into the Kingdom of Heaven* (1833) had several editions in Aleutian and Russian, likewise his *Sermons*. Nominated Metropolitan of Moscow (1868). Founded the Orthodox Missionary Society (1870) and a school of icon-painting (1873) with the purpose of helping the missions. Founded almshouses and the Filaretsky school for girls (p. 212).

Ioanniky (Pavlutzky, d. 1763) monk of Turuchansky-Troitzky, Monastery in the diocese of Tobolsk; Archimandrite (1754-7). Same in Savvin-Storozhevsky Monastery near Zvenigorod in Moscow diocese (1758). Bishop of Voronezh (December 1761). Had the reputation of being a money-loving prelate who even resorted to usury (p. 42).

Isidor (Nikolsky, 1799-1892), student of St. Petersburg Academy; Bishop of Polotzk and Vilna (1837), of Mogilev (1840), Archbishop (1841); Exarch of Georgia (1844), Metropolitan (1856). Transferred as Metropolitan of Kiev (1858); and from July 1860—of St. Petersburg (p. 209).

Ivan (Vishnevsky or Vishensky, d. about 1630). Born in Galicia. Was monk at Zographou Monastery on Mount Athos. Known for his Epistles with their defence of Orthodoxy, warning against the union with Rome and their energetic protest against the evils that permeated church life, against the high clergy and the oppression of the poor (p. 119-20).

Joakim (Strukov, 1674-1742) was a parish priest; when widowed became professed (1712); was Chaplain to the Navy (till 1715). Subsequently Superior of Selizharovo

Monastery, in Tver diocese, Bursar of Chudov and Archimandrite of Donskoy Monastery in Moscow diocese; Bishop of Pereyaslav (1727) and of Voronezh and Yeletz [June 1730] (p. 274).

Joasath (Khotunzevsky, d. 1759), was member of the Mission to Kamchatka (1754-7). Wrote a Catechism. Was Archimandrite of Vysokopetrovsky Monastery and Novgorod suffragan [1758].

Joasath (Mitkevich, d. June 1763). Teacher of St. Tikhon. He was a student and teacher of Kiev, then of the Novgorod Seminary. Author of a drama performed by the seminarists (1742). Became Prefect (1748); taught theology (1750), and was the Archimandrite of Antoniev Monastery. Introduced Hebrew into the program of the Seminary. Archimandrite of Khutynsky Monastery (February 1756). During 1755 was working on the re-editing and correction of the Kiev Paterikon. Consecrated Bishop of Belogorod and Kursk (1758). Supported learning and helped to develop the Kharkov Collegium. Offered a post of teacher to G. S. Skovoroda (p. 31).

Job, Metropolitan of Novgorod (d. 1717). A monk of Moscow, Troitzkaya Lavra; Archimandrite of Vysokopetrovsky Monastery and (1694-7) of Sergieva Lavra; Metropolitan of Novgorod (1697); obtained the liberation of the brothers Likhudi and founded two schools (1706): a Slav and a Greco-Latin one; having trained there future teachers, organized fourteen schools in the diocese. Obtained the right to organize a printing press, but the plan was finally upset. Founded three hospitals and a home for foundlings and illegitimate children (1706). Fought against the Raskol. Consecrated the first church of St. Petersburg (1704) in the fortress of St. Peter and St. Paul (p. 26).

John (Maksimovich, d. 1715). Hieromonk of Pechersk Monastery; Archbishop of Chernigov (1697); founded there a seminary. Metropolitan of Tobolsk (1712). Author of the *Latino-Russian Lexicon*, of *The Edifying Mirror* and, in verse: *Spiritual Thoughts, Meditation on the Beatitudes* (1709), *The Alphabet of the Saints, The Lord's Prayer, The Hail Mary* (p. 31 n. 13).

John (Sergiev, 1829-1908), son of a village subdeacon. Went to a school in Archangelsk, had difficulty in learning. Pupil of St. Petersburg Academy (1849). Ordained parish priest of Cronstadt (1855 till his death). Taught in city school and (1862) in the College.

Man of devout life, outstanding in his love and pastoral care. Since his ordination received communion daily. Great gifts of healing. Crowds came to see and hear him. He introduced corporate confession because the crowd was too big for the individual ones. Called people to frequent communion. Had a widespread spiritual influence.

His diary, *My Life in Christ*, had several English editions, and his *Works* had a wide circulation in Russia. He is considered by many a saint, and a group of his followers has begun collecting materials on his life, influence and miracles (p. 212).

Joseph (Yamnitzky, d. December 1748). Teacher of St. Tikhon. Was a student of Kiev. Transferred to Novgorod (1741); taught Latin. Professed monk (1743) and became Prefect. Taught philosophy (1748), then theology. Became Rector and in January 1748 the Archimandrite of Antoniev Monastery (p. 32).

Kliment (Smoliatich, *c.* 1114-54). A Bulgarian, put on the see as Metropolitan of Kiev by the Russians without Greek authority. Left some written sermons, like his *Word on Kiev Caves*. Was reputed a learned man "who wrote from Homer and Plato" (p. 120).

Kozlovsky, Alexey Semenovich, Ober-Procurator (April 1758) and previously to this post a major in the Body-Guard. Had no influence. Dismissed by Catherine II in June 1763 (p. 41).

Lazar (Baranovich, d. 1694), Rector of the Kiev Academy 1650-8. Archbishop of Chernigov. Took an energetic part in the struggle of Roman Catholics to unite the Ukrainians to the see of Rome. Wrote in Polish, Latin and Russian, in the fashionable manner of the time, with references to mythology and with witticisms. Main works: *A New Measure of the Old Faith* (1676), *The Sword of the Spirit, The Trumpets* *of the Words, On the Queen of Heaven, The Lyre of Apollo* (p. 21 n. 3).

Lev (Yurlov, 1678-1755). Consecrated Bishop of Voronezh (March 1727). Tried to organize a school. Spoken of as a grasping man; he used to breed horses in the Voronezh steppe and to bribe the authorities with them. He mentioned Eudoxia, first wife of Peter I, in prayer, and was banished. Then Anna Ioanovna learnt in 1730 that he had refused to take the oath until her accession to the throne had been confirmed to him by the Synod. For this offence he was carried to Moscow, tried, deprived of his rank and of the monastic habit, flogged and as a layman "Lavrenty" banished to Arkhangelsk. He was restored in rank and freedom under Elisabeth (p. 49).

Likhudi (Ioanniky, d. 1717; Sophrony, d. 1730). Learned Greeks invited to Moscow as correctors of sacred books. Took an energetic part in polemics against the Catholics, the Protestants and the Russian heretics, also in the Eucharistic controversy. Had many enemies; were accused of heterodoxy and ejected from Moscow (1701), but continued in Novgorod schools. They were also practically the founders of the Moscow Theological Academy (1687). Compiled Grammars and a series of apologetical and polemical writings: *Akos* (against the Pope), *Dialogues with a Jesuit*, a *Spiritual Sword*, *On the Luthers and Calvins*, etc. (p. 26 n. 2).

Lopukhin, Ivan Vladimirovich (1756-1816). Born in Orel province. Nominally, joined the Preobrazhensky regiment (1775). Keen student of law. Retired (1780) and became councillor and president of the Moscow criminal court and Senator. Went through a "conversion" (1779). Joined the masons, supported Novikov, carried on the Free Printing Press. Author of *On the Inner Church* (1789-98) and of the *Memoirs*, etc. Had difficulties with the authorities (1792) concerning the part taken by the heir in masonry. Produced a very contradictory impression upon his contemporaries (p. 216).

Makary (Glukharev, 1792-1847). Pupil of St. Petersburg Academy, influenced by Filaret (Drozdov), and wholly under his direction. An Old Testament and Hebrew scholar.

Well read in mystical literature of the West and tolerant to Christians of other churches. Advocated before the Synod the need of a Russian translation of the Bible from the original languages (1834). Was misunderstood and had difficulties with the Synod. He did missionary work in Siberia, with only two other monks, in great poverty. Wrote on the organization of missions within the Russian Empire (1839). He returned to study natural sciences as useful for helping his converts; had obtained for a woman the permission to do missionary work. The Alatai mission sprang entirely from pure motives and zeal. Makary continued his translation of the Bible. He obtained permission to travel to the Holy Land, but died when just about to set out on this pilgrimage (cf. Filaret, p. 251).

Makary (Metropolitan of Moscow, 1481-1563). While Archbishop of Novgorod (from 1526) he taught and baptized the Karelians and helped the Tartar prisoners. Became Metropolitan of Moscow (1542), had a good influence on Tsar Ivan IV. Makary was a great scholar, and remained famous for his encyclopaedic labors. His *Chetyi-Minei* was a compilation of the lives of the saints and of "all the books that are being read in the Russian land." A similar attempt was the Code of Canon Law (*Kormchaya*, 1527) and the Code of the Bible—the Old Testament story given partly in the form of a free narrative. He also made an attempt to collect the Chronicles, from Rurik to 1559 (*Stepennaya Kniga*). Makary took lead in several church councils, including the famous *Stoglav* (1551); he promoted the canonization of many national saints [1547-9] (p. 239).

Markell (Rodyshevsky, d. 1742), student of Kiev, where he knew Prokopovich, whom he strongly opposed. Supporter of the *Rock of Faith*, he was arrested for his *Life of the Heretic Prokopovich* and persecuted like his friend Theophilact. Liberated in October 1740, sent to Novgorod. Archbishop Amvrossy nominated him Archimandrite of Yuriev Monastery and Rector of the Seminary, then consecrated him his suffragan [January 1742] (p. 22 n. 4).

Maxim the Greek (*c*. 1475-1555). A learned monk from Mount Athos. Studied in Western Europe, especially in Italy.

Was invited to Russia as translator and corrector of the sacred books. Knew hardly any Russian; dictated in Latin to scribes who knew no Greek and retranslated into Russian; hence, various mistranslations, which allowed his rivals to accuse him of heresy. Politically opposed Russian *rapprochement* with the Turks. He was tried (1525), deprived of communion and sent to Volokolamsk Monastery, a stronghold of his opponents; tried again (1531), transferred to Otroch Monastery. During the controversy on monastic lands strongly supported the Non-possessors. Had a great pastoral and spiritual influence. Mentioned with admiration by Prince Andrey Kurbsky. Though still a prisoner, he was consulted in matters of theology and allowed to write. Came again into prominence under Ivan IV; asked to take part in the Stoglav Council (1551). Spent his last year in Troizko-Sergieva Lavra under the sympathetic and enlightened Superior Artemy. Apart from his translations, especially of St. John Chrysostom, is famous for his apologetic writings against the contemporary rationalistic "Judaizers"—which were later inscribed "Against the Lutherans." Wrote also against Rome. His *Works* were collected and partly edited for the first time in 1860-97, in Kazan (p. 37).

Melety (Smotritzky, d. 1633). Archbishop of Polotzk. He supported the Orthodox lay brotherhoods. His *Verses to the Apostates* (1597-8) were addressed to those who passed into the Roman jurisdiction under the agreement of Brest-Litovsk "Unia," i.e. an agreement by which the Orthodox were reunited to Rome, recognizing the Pope but retaining their rites and their canon law (1595). The *New Roman Calendar* (1597) is against Rome, and so is his famous *Lamentation* (1610, in Polish, signed Theophilus Ortholo-gus). He went to Constantinople and, disappointed in Orthodoxy after finding Calvinist ideas in the *Orthodox Confession* of Cyril Lukaris (1629), he became a supporter of the union with Rome, and, after repeated returns to Orthodoxy, finally joined the Roman jurisdiction. To this period belong his *Description of the Journey to the East* and the *Apologia* (1628). Renowned especially for his *Grammar* [1619] (p. 28).

BIOGRAPHICAL NOTES 263

St. **Mitrophan** (d. 1703). There is a great scarcity of historical information on him. Superior of Makariev Unzhensky Monastery, he was consecrated first Bishop of Voronezh and Yeletz (1682); was a supporter of the policy and ideas of Peter I. Canonized in 1832 (p. 205).

Nikon (Patriarch, d. 1681). Of peasant origin; began as a parish priest; then a monk; Superior of Solovetzky Monastery (1643); Archbishop of Novgorod (1649); Patriarch of Moscow (1652). A learned and authoritarian prelate, he fostered the correction of the liturgical books. His clash with the Tsar and with the clergy brought disfavor upon him. The refusal of many to accept the drastic measures of liturgical revision proposed by Nikon brought about the Raskol, the Schism of the Old Believers (1654; 1665-7). Nikon abandoned his see, retired, then returned again (1658); was tried (1660); returned to claim his dignity (1664), but was ordered to withdraw to Voskresensky Monastery. Was condemned after a two-year-long synod of the Eastern Patriarchs resident in Russia (1666-8) and exiled to Therapontov Monastery, on the White Lake. After the Tsar's death (1676) was allowed to return to his original community, Solovetzky, but died on the journey. Whilst the Patriarchs of the East condemned Nikon, they supported the cause of the liturgical reform (p. 20).

St. **Nil of Sora** (1433-1508). His surname in the world was Maikov, his origin disputed. Went as a monk to Mount Athos. Was influenced by the ascetico-mystical tradition of the desert fathers. Returned and lived in Kirilo-Belozersky Monastery. Took a leading part in the controversy on monastic wealth and was the leader of the "Non-possessors." A man of learning and deep spiritual life, he emphasized evangelical poverty, love of the Bible and the practice of mental prayer. Left a *Rule* which reads more like a treatise on the spiritual life. In English, see G. P. Fedotov, *Treasury*, pp. 85-133 (p. 120).

Paissy (Velichkovsky, 1722-94), son of a Kiev priest and of a Jewish-Christian mother. Ran away from the studies with their "pagan mythology" and, after many difficulties and wanderings from one to the other community (1739-

46), eventually reached Mount Athos. Professed there, and ordained (1758), he soon became a spiritual leader. He collected, copied and retranslated (sometimes literally) the writings of the ascetic and mystical fathers. His labor was the heavier, as he had no full knowledge of Greek or Syriac, and had to deal with defective Slavonic manuscripts. He had to move to Moldavia (1763), and after more peregrinations with his disciples became Superior of Niamets (1779), and after the Russian occupation of Yassy (1790) was made Archimandrite by the Archbishop of Poltava, who visited him. He fostered a school of translators: over 200 manuscripts of the Niamets Monastery were their work. He was in correspondence with the Russian monasteries; Platon Levshin wrote to him. The followers of Paissy brought back to Russia the almost forgotten writings of the desert fathers and the Byzantine ascetics, and helped the revival of contemplative monasticism.

Paissy's main stress was on obedience to the Elder and on the practice of constant prayer. The Russian "starchestvo"—spiritual direction as distinct from sacramental confession—goes back to Paissy and was a matter of controversy. He wrote little of his own; his main works are his letters of spiritual direction (practically, his Rule, 1776) and *Chapters on the Prayer of Jesus*. He was the first Russian translator and compiler of the collection of ascetic and mystical Fathers known as the *Dobrotolyubie* (Philokalia). A copy was presented by his monks to Archbishop Gabriel Petrov (p. 31 n. 13).

Parfeny (Sopkovsky, 1716-95). Student of Kiev. Taught in the Novgorod Seminary (1744); Prefect (1750); Rector and the Archimandrite of Antoniev Monastery (February 1756); then of Khutinsky Monastery (April 1758). He professed St. Tikhon. Consecrated suffragan to the Archbishop of Novgorod with the title of the Bishop of Keksholm and Ladoga (October 1759). Transferred as Bishop of Smolensk and Dorogobuzh (March 1761), then member of the Synod. Co-operated with Georgy (Konissky, Bishop of Mogilev) in the book *On the Duties of Parish Priests* (p. 32).

Peter (Moghila, 1596-1646). A Moldavian nobleman (his true name was Movila), he was brought up probably in Lvov, and had travelled in the West. Had connection with the Polish upper classes, which helped him in his organizing of the life of the Orthodox in Poland after the troubled times produced by the Union with Rome. He became early the Archimandrite of the Pecherskaya Lavra in Kiev. Supported the lay brotherhoods, and together with them laid foundations for the school which developed into the Kiev Academy (Kiev Collegium, 1631). The teaching was done in Latin, and was not without Roman influence. Since 1633, Peter was the Metropolitan of Kiev and Exarch of the Patriarch of Constantinople. (Kiev, cut away from Russia, had independent church life till in 1685 its Metropolitan came under the Patriarch of Moscow.) The main work of Moghila, approved by the Eastern Patriarchs, is the *Orthodox Confession of Faith* [1642] (p. 31).

St. Philip (Kolyshev, 1507-69), monk of Solovetzky Monastery. Agreed to become the Metropolitan of Moscow on condition that he would be allowed to intervene on behalf of those in disfavor (1566-8). Opposed Ivan IV and was banished to Otroch Monastery, where he was strangled by the Tsar's order (1569). His body was translated to Solovetzky Monastery (1591). Tsar Alexis Mikhailovich wrote to the community and begged forgiveness for his ancestor; the body of St. Philip was then translated to Moscow [1652] (p. 37).

Platon (Peter Levshin, 1737-1812), son of a church reader; pupil of Kolomna Seminary; refused a secular career when he was given the opportunity of entering the Moscow University (1755). Taught in Moscow Seminary, was noticed for his eloquence. Professed and ordained (1758). Hieromonk, Prefect of Troitzky Seminary, teacher of philosophy (1759). Solemn reception of Catherine II (1762). Head of the ecclesiastical court of justice (1763); since July, teacher of the heir to the throne—the future Paul I, who always liked him. Platon took prominent part in the development of the

Moscow Academy, which moved to Troitzky Monastery; he became Archimandrite of Troitzko-Sergieva Lavra. He laid stress on teaching history, introduced modern languages and Hebrew, later (1802) music and some medicine. Member of the Synod (1768); Bishop of Tver (1770), Archbishop of Moscow (1775). Founder of the Bethany Monastery (1783) and of adjoining Seminary. After 1786 out of favor with Catherine II, he nevertheless continued to take a leading part in church administration. He defended N. I. Novikov's orthodoxy and showed his tolerance towards Western Christianity and towards the Raskolniki. Obtained an official recognition of their position in the form of "United Belief" (Edinoverie, 1800). Fostered historical research and left scholarships in his name to the Academy.

Author of the first Russian *Catechism* (1765), though still timid in introducing Russian language into ecclesiastical schools. He wrote *Memoirs*, descriptions of his Travels, and his main work is a *Russian Church History* [1805] (p. 19).

Polikarpov-Orlov, Theodore, pupil of Moscow Seminary; the Director of the Moscow printing press; a keen worker; published his *Primer* in 1701. Got involved in financial troubles, was accused of dishonesty and brought to trial (p. 27-28).

Scarga, Peter (1536-1612), a Polish Jesuit who fought against Protestant influences, against Moravians and Calvinists, and against Socinus when this last came to Poland (1551 and 1558). Tried to reconcile the Orthodox to the see of Rome. Wrote theological treatises, the best known being those on the Eucharist and that addressed to the Orthodox *On the Unity of the Church of God under one Pastor and on the Schism of the Greeks* (1577). Wrote also on the Council of Brest (1595) at which was achieved the "Unia" with Rome (p. 33).

St. Seraphim (Moshnin, 1759-1833) was a monk in Sarov; professed (1786) and ordained deacon by the Bishop of Tambov; then priest (1793). He lived alone in the woods, though returning regularly to his community and visited by monks and pilgrims (1794-1804); next came a period of severe asceticism: conquering the assaults of blasphemous thoughts. Seraphim stood on a large stone in the woods, with only a minimum of respite (1804-7). He was invited to be the Superior of Sarov, but refused, and kept complete silence till 1810. The decline of health forced him to return into his monastery, but he remained secluded. In 1815 he began to receive pilgrims and continued till his death the spiritual direction of many. From 1794 he was in charge of a women's small community, Diveyevo, the chronicles of which recorded many of his actions and sayings. This strict ascetic had a gift of tenderness and joy; he did not conceal his visions, and called his spiritual children to an ecstatic and mystical life. He was canonized in 1903 (p. 121).

St. Sergius of Radonezh (1314-92) was for Northern monasticism what St. Theodossy was for Kiev. He was a hermit. Gradually a community grew up round him. Persuaded to take orders (1345), became its Superior, then left his monastery to seek solitude again, but once more was drawn back into his post of authority in his Troitzky monastery. Was asked by the Metropolitan of Moscow, St. Alexis, to become his successor, but refused this dignity. Tradition ascribes to him the sanction of a battle against the Tartars which led to the liberation of Russia from their yoke. Sergius led a life of strict asceticism, poverty and humility. The Holy Trinity occupied a central place in his mystical life (p. 225).

Shakhovskoy, Prince Yakov (1705-77), Ober-Procurator (December 1741). He demanded a stricter control over the fees of the members of the Synod, over the money raised in church collections, etc. Transferred some of these funds into the hospital funds. Was nominated General-Kriegs-Commissar (1753); became Procurator General (1760) and thus once more could put pressure upon the Synod and the Ober-Procurator. Dismissed in June 1763. Author of well-known *Memoirs* (p. 31).

Silvester (Kuliabko, *c*. 1701-61), of cossack gentry, student and teacher of Kiev Academy, professed (*c*. 1727), Hieromonk and Prefect (1735). Archimandrite of Bratsky Monastery, Rector and Professor of theology. Attended in St. Petersburg the wedding of the heir, Peter Theodorovich, with the Princess Catherine (1745); consecrated Bishop of Kostroma (November 1745) in the Court Chapel in the presence of the Empress Elisabeth. Archbishop of St. Petersburg and member of the Synod (July 1750). Had various disagreements with the Synod, for other members objected to his nomination as Archimandrite of Kievo-Pechersky Lavra in 1748 when he was already a bishop; they also protested against permission given by him to a Prince Golitsin to marry a kinswoman. Was surnamed *aureus benedicendus magister*, though a modern reader can hardly follow the trend of thought in his rhetorical speeches full of flattery to those in power (p. 38). Not to be mistaken for—

Silvester (Simon Starogorodsky, 1725-1802). Student of Alexandro-Nevsky Seminary (1736) and teacher (after 1749). Professed (1748) under the name of Sergius, later changed to Silvester in honor of S. Kuliabko. Prefect (1753), Rector (1756). Archimandrite of Pereyaslav-Nikitsky Monastery (March 1760) and Rector of the local seminary. Bishop of Pereyaslav-Zalessky (December 1761). Member of the Ecclesiastical Commission. Transferred to Krutitsi (1768), retired (1773), went to Moscow Uspensky Monastery, was made Superior of Voskresensky-Novy-Ierusalim Monastery (1785). Administered Spasso-Androniev Monastery (1788 till his death).

Simon (Stephen Lagov or Lagovsky, d. 1804). Son of monastic serf liberated by Amvrossy Yushkevich (1736). Pupil of Novgorod Seminary (1740); Teacher in Moscow Academy (1754) and in Novgorod Seminary (1755); Vice-Prefect (1757), Prefect (1758), Vice-Rector (May 1759), Rector (November 1759). Professed (April 10, 1758). Archimandrite (1759). Transferred to Kirilo-Belozersky Monastery (August 1761). Member of the Synod. Transferred to Moscow Novospassky Monastery (October 1764). Consecrated Bishop of Kostroma and Galitzk (1769). Bishop of Riazan (1778), Archbishop (1792).

Besides his unpublished *History of the Novgorod Seminary* (in Latin), he wrote in Russian *Exhortations to the Kostroma flock* (1776, 1778, 1796), *Sermons* preached in Riazan (1779 and 1781), *A brief instruction how to stand in the Church*

(1787), *On Paschalia* (1799) and *Hortatory Epistles to Riazan flock against the Raskolniki* [printed 1852] (p. 34).

Simeon Todorsky (1700-54), student of Kiev. Lived in the West (1727-37); studied at Halle, became a remarkable orientalist and a biblical scholar; knew well modern languages. Taught in pietist school. On his return taught in Kiev Academy. Was professed (1740); became teacher of the future Peter III and Catherine II. Took part in the Bible revision. Published his orations on State occasions. Archimandrite of Ipatiev Monastery (1743), member of the Synod, Bishop of Kostroma (1745), transferred to Pskov; then made Archbishop [1746] (p. 123).

Skovoroda, Grigory Savich (1722-94). Student of Kiev Academy. Travelled in the West. Had a conception of intellectual and spiritual freedom in the world which made him remain unattached to any definite position and unmarried. Was welcome to gentry and to the simple folk, who spread many of his songs and verses. An original mystical philosopher and poet, influenced by Plato and by the pietistic and masonic literature, he left scattered writings which have not yet all been collected. His symbolism attracted the attention of the late nineteenth-century thinkers. Best work on him (in Ukrainian language) is D. Chizhevsky, *The Philosophy of G. S. Skovoroda*, Warsaw, 1934 (p. 33).

Stephen (Kalinovsky, d. September 1763). Student and teacher of Kiev Academy. Monk of Bratsky Monastery (1727); Prefect of the Academy and member of the Consistory (1732). Was ordered to go to Moscow, but retained by his Bishop till he had to go to St. Petersburg (May 1733), which led to his nomination as Archimandrite of the Spassky Uchilishchny Monastery and Rector in Moscow. Appointed "main reviser and director" in the printing of the Slavonic Bible (1736); translated from the Vulgate; brought it up to the book of Tobias. Proposed as candidate to the diocese of Novgorod (1737) but not chosen. Was Archimandrite of Alexandro-Nevsky Monastery. Consecrated (January 1739) Bishop of Pskov, he kept residence in St. Petersburg. Went to Moscow for the coronation (1742); nominated Archbishop of Novgorod [August 1745] (p. 32).

St. Stephen of Perm (1345-96). Born in Ustyug, he entered the monastery of St. Gregory at Rostov (1365), and spent thirteen years in studying Greek and preparing for a life of apostolate. He was ordained priest and, with the sanction of Moscow, went out among the Zyrian people of his native region preaching and teaching. He created an alphabet and made many translations of the sacred books. Trained some natives as future clergy. Defended the local population against the oppression of the Russians of Novgorod and Moscow. Was consecrated bishop (1383), and died on one of his journeys to Moscow. [The Perm region was officially acquired by the Russians only in 1472] (p. 219).

Stephen (Yavorsky, 1658-1722), studied in Jesuit Schools in Lvov, Poznan and Vilna, was for a time in Roman jurisdiction. Returned to Orthodoxy. Was professed in Kiev; teacher, Prefect and Rector of the Kiev Academy. Was sent to Moscow to be appointed assistant Bishop of Kiev (1700). Instead (as the Patriarch Adrian died) Peter I nominated Stephen to be the Metropolitan of Riazan and "Exarch, locum-tenens and administrator of the Patriarchal Throne." After 1721 became president of the Synod. His writings were strongly influenced by Roman Catholicism. Wrote in Latin *The Signs of the coming of the Antichrist* (1703) and *The Rock of Faith* (1713, printed first in 1727); round this book was centred the controversy over Protestant and Catholic influences in Russia and over the relationship of Church and State (p. 22).

Theodossy (Golosnitzky, c. 1723-86). It is uncertain whether it was he or his namesake who studied in St. Petersburg. In 1753 he is found as Archimandrite of Zheltikov Monastery and in 1755 of Koliazin, in the diocese of Tver. Then Archimandrite of Svetogorsky in Pskov diocese (1758). Consecrated Bishop of Ustyug (November 1761); transferred to Tambov (November 1766). The Voronezh Governor Maslov, in whose administrative area the Tambov region was then included, lodged a complaint against Theodossy before the Senate, in connection with the conscription of men belonging to the ecclesiastical class (January 1769). The Bishop protested to the Synod, but the Synod forbade him any activities except the actual celebrations (February 1770). A commission investigated this affair; Theodossy remained in Voronezh under investigation for nearly two and a half years. His clergy refused to obey him. He was finally allowed to continue in his duties (February 1773). With the administrative development of Tambov (1779) he started a seminary, restored some monasteries which had suffered during Pugachev rebellion; he was a keen builder of churches: some forty were erected by him; he did much to support traditional icon painting. He was buried by Simon Lagov (then Bishop of Riazan); the poet G. Derzhavin was present, in his capacity of the Governor of Tambov (p. 77).

St. Theodossy of Pechersk (d. 1074), son of wealthy parents, felt monastic vocation from his youth. Used to help serfs in their work, and wore shabby clothes. Joined St. Antony. Became Abbot and had great moral influence in the world and a reputation for humility and kindness in his community. Polemical writings against the Latins and the Jews traditionally ascribed to him are now recognized to be by another monk, his later namesake of the same monastery (p. 119).

Theophan (Govorov, 1815-94). Among the best-known works of this retired Bishop of Vladimir and Tambov, "The Recluse," must be mentioned *The Way to Salvation* (1868-69); his exegetical works on the Epistles (Hebrews not included); his numerous letters of spiritual direction and the translations of St. Simeon the New Theologian (1879-81), and the Russian edition, mostly in his own translation, of the *Dobrotolyubie* (worked on it 1873-6; the five volumes ready in 1890). He is thus in the line of Paissy Velichkovsky; yet the biblical scholarship and the pastoral simplicity of some of his advice link him also with St. Tikhon (p. 209).

Theophan (Prokopovich, 1681-1736), studied in Rome, probably passing there for a Uniat. A violent anti-Roman. Returned to Russia (1701); taught in Kiev; preached in the presence of the Tsar (1706 and 1709); recognized by Peter I as a sincere admirer of his policy; called to St. Petersburg (1716); consecrated Bishop of Pskov (1718) and Archbishop (1720); Archbishop of Novgorod and member of the Synod

(1725 till his death). The author of the *Spiritual Regulation*. A learned man, a lover and collector of books, he did much to create the Alexandro-Nevsky Seminary. Avaricious, pushing without scruples, he always confused theological and financial issues with those of his career. His writings are marked by polemical ardor; he took little trouble to conceal his Protestantism, and his call "back to the scripture" or to St. John Chrysostom barely hides his hatred of the traditions of the Church, his disdain of monasticism, etc. Some of his works were printed anonymously in Germany (his *Works* published only in 1774). Supporter of the control of the State over the Church, regarded by him as no more than an institution. This gave him an arm against his theological opponents, whom he accused of political opposition. He managed to keep the leading position even under the sucessors of Peter I, and died leaving big wealth and a collection of over three thousand books (p. 22).

Theophilact (Lopatinsky, d. 1741). Student of Kiev Academy. Teacher, Prefect and Rector of the Moscow Academy (1706); Archimandrite of Chudov and member of the Synod (1723); same year—Archbishop of Tver; second vice-president of the Synod. His scholastic, Thomistic course of lectures had a great influence. He wrote against Prokopovich *The Light Yoke of the Lord* and printed Stephen Yavorsky's *The Rock of Faith* (1727). Was arrested (1735) and tried. Deprived of his rank (1738); imprisoned in the Vyborg Castle. Released (December 1740) and restored by the Synod in his rank.

Author of many orations pronounced on State occasions like *Apotheosis* (1709, description of the reception to Peter I after the victory of Poltava), *Address on the Heaven-sent peace made between the Russian Empire and the Swedish crown* (1722), *The Mirror of the ardent Devotion* (printed 1782), *The Refutation of the error of the Raskolniki* (written by the order of the Synod; printed in 1745), *Apokrisis* [defence of the *Rock of Faith* against F. Buddeus] (p. 33).

Tikhon II (Yakubovsky, d. 1786) of Kiev Academy. Was sent to the Cadets School as hieromonk. When the Russians took Koenigsberg he was sent there (1756) with the title of

Archimandrite of Spasso-Yaroslavsky Monastery, in order to found a Russian church. In 1764 the rank of suffragan was created in the Moscow diocese; he was then nominated as Bishop of Sevsk. Transferred to Voronezh (1767). Worked to develop the Seminary; introduced teaching of modern languages. Transferred to Suzdal [1775] (p. 9).

Tikhon III (Timofey Malinovsky, d. 1793), born in the village Ivanovo of Kaluga diocese. Pupil of the Moscow Slavo-Greco-Latin Academy (1755-63). As layman, teacher of lower forms and preacher; professed in 1764, remained preacher till 1770. Transferred to become Rector of the Troitzky Seminary (1770), but in October returned to the Academy as Prefect. Moved to Tver as Prefect of Tver Seminary and the Archimandrite of the Otroch (August 1771); then Rector and Archimandrite of Kolyazin (1774). Consecrated Bishop of Voronezh (1775); transferred to Tver and Kashin (1788); became member of the Synod (1792) and Archbishop of Astrakhan.

Enlarged the course of Voronezh Seminary; introduced the class of philosophy and in 1779 of theology. His funeral oration at the burial, and a short biography of Bishop Tikhon of Zadonsk came out in 1798, 1799 (p. 9).

Varlaam (Liashchevsky, d. 1774), monk of Kiev Mezhigorsky Monastery. Later, Rector of Moscow Zaikonospassky Academy (May 1753) and Archimandrite of the Donskoy Bogorodichny Monastery (p. 41 n. 3).

St. Vladimir (d. 1015). Prince of Kiev; organizer of the Russian State; led a campaign against Byzantium, later married a Greek princess and helped the spread of Christianity in Russia. A clever statesman, a builder of schools and churches, the Baptizer of Russia (990), was beloved by the people. He became not only a canonized saint, but in the folk-lore the central figure of the cycle of heroic poems (p. 240).

Voronezh: Bishops of Voronezh—
Mitrophan: 1682-1703 (died 1703).
Arseny (Kasturin): 1704-12 (died 1712).
Pakhomy (Shapkovsky): 1714-23 (died 1723).

Joseph: nominated November 1726; died without reaching the diocese.

Lev (Yurlov): March 1727-30 (removed, 1730; died 1755).

Joakim (Strukov): June 1730-42 (died 1742).

Veniamin (Sakhnovsky): December 1742-3 (died 1743).

Theophilact: September 1743-57 (founded the Seminary; was arrested for having thrown on the ground a bribe in the form a rouble with the effigy of the Empress on it; died 1757).

Cyril (Liashevsky): August 1758-October 1761 (had been Archimandrite of Moscow Novospassky Monastery; transferred to Chernigov, October 1761; died 1771).

Ioanniky (Pavlutzky): December 1761-January 1763 (died January 1763).

Tikhon, St. (Sokolov): February 1763-December 1767.

Tikhon II (Yakubovsky): December 1767-May 1775.

Tikhon III (Malinovsky): June 1775-May 1788.

One Amvrossy also held the see [not mentioned in the official list of bishops by A. Ornatsky; I cannot fix his dates. He came under disfavor for having made a congratulatory oration to Anna Leopoldovna] (p. 41 n. 5).

Zizany (dates of both brothers uncertain) Lavrenty, taught in the Schools of Lvov, Brest and Vilna organized by the Orthodox Brotherhoods (1592-1602); priest (1612). Visited Moscow and presented *The Great Catechism* (1626). This work was suspected of inaccuracies and disappeared, but it was used by the Raskolniki. He did some translations from the Fathers and wrote on the Incarnation, on the interpretation of the Lord's prayer, etc. He composed a *Slavonic Alphabet*—a primer with prayers, a lexicon and the first Slavonic Grammar (printed in Vilna 1596).

Stephen taught in Lvov school (1591); wrote against the Church of Rome (1595); criticized the Orthodox high clergy for their lenience to the Unia and was much persecuted both by them and by the Polish authorities. He added a *Catechism* to his brother's *Alphabet* (p. 27).

Bibliography*

*A Monk of the Eastern Church, *Orthodox Spirituality*, S.P.C.K., 1945, pp. 104. Cf. Un moine de l'Église d'Orient.
Abramovich, D. I., *Исследование о Киево-Печерском Патерике как историко-литературном источнике*, СПБ., 1903, Известия Отдел. Русс. Яз. и Словесн. т. VI, VII.
—— *Жития св. мучеников Бориса и Глеба*, Петроград, 1916, Отдел. Русс. Яз. и Слов. в. 2-ой.
Adrianova-Peretts, V. P. *Очерки по истории русской сатирической литературы XVII в.*; Акад. Наук СССР., М.-Л., 1937, 260 стр.
*—— *Очерки поэтического стиля древней Руси*, Акад. Наук СССР., 1947, 181 стр.
Alferov and Gruzinsky, *Русская литература XVIII века*, М., 1918, изд. 3-е.
Amvrossy (Ornatsky), *История Российской иерархии*, М., 1807-15, 7 т.
Anonymous on diverse subjects: *Новейший Российский Дорожник, верно показующий все почтовые пути Российской Империи и новоприсоединенных от Порты Оттоманской и Республики Польской Областей*, СПБ., 1796, Акад. Наук, 320 стр.
—— *Описание монастырей в Российской Империи находящихся, с присоединением известия о существующих ныне в России епархиях*, М., 1822, 208 стр.
—— *Устав Новгородского Юрьева Первоклассного общежительного монастыря*, Моск. Синод.; изд. 2-ое, 1832.
—— *Портреты именитых мужей Российской Церкви*, М., 1843.

* Works which came out or became accessible to me after this book had been completed are marked by an asterisk.
The alphabetical order has been maintained throughout except in two instances: for the convenience of the reader, we group, under two headings, Dostoevsky and the literature on him and St. Tikhon and works on him. Beside the list of books mentioned in the text, I add a few titles of general nterest. The Russian titles are spelled throughout in the ıew spelling.

Anonymous, *О православном белом и черном духовенстве*, Leipzig, 1866, 2 т.
—— *Описание документов и дел хранящихся в архиве св. Синода* (1542-1721), т. 1, СПБ., 1868.
—— *Летопись церковных событий и гражданских, поясняющих церковные*, СПБ, 1869-71.
—— *Альбом в Бозе почивших иерархов Российской церкви*, М., 1894.
—— *Русский биографический словарь*, изд. Рус. Имп. Историч. Общества, СПБ., 1896-1913, 25 т. See St. Tikhon.
—— on St. Tikhon. See St. Tikhon.
Antony (Vadkovsky), *Из истории христианской проповеди*, СПБ., 1895, изд. 2-ое, VIII + 391 стр.
Arkhangel'sky, A. S., *Нил Сорский и Вассиан Патрикеев*, СПБ., 1881, 1882, Памятники Древней Письменности и Искусства, № XVI.
Arndt, J., *Vier Bücher vom wahren Christentum*, Hamburg, 1724, 27.
—— in English: *True Christianity*, ed. W. Jacques, London, 1815, 2 vols.
Arseniev, N., *Das Mönchtum und der asketisch-mystische Weg*, "Kirche des Ostens," Regensburg, 1939.
—— See St. Tikhon.
Askochensky, V., *Киев с древнейшим его училищем — Академией*, Киев, 1856, 2 т.

Bantysh-Kamensky, *Словарь достопамятных людей русской земли*, 1846.
Barsov, N. I., *Матерьялы для биографии Иннокентия Борисова*, СПБ., 1884.
Barsov, T. I., *Святейший Синод в его прошлом*, СПБ., 1896, iv + 446 стр.
—— *О духовной цензуре в России*, Христ. Чтение 1901.
Barsukov, I. P., *Иннокентий (Попов-Вениаминов) по его сочинениям и письмам*, М., 1883, viii + 769 + xiv стр.
—— *Иннокентий Борисов, Материалы*, М., 1886.
Barsukov, N. P., *Источники Российской агиографии*, СПБ., 1882, xi + 308 + 8 стр.
—— *Письма Филарета Гумилевского к Н. Н. Шереметьевой*, Академия, 1900.
Baumgarten, N. de, *St. Vladimir et la conversion de la Russie*, Orientalia Christiana, No. 79, Roma, 1932, pp. 136.
Beausobre, I. de, *Russian Letters of Direction, 1834-60, Macarius, starets of Optino*, Dacre Press, 1944, pp. 108.
Berdyaev, N., *Хомяков*, М., 1912, viii + 250 стр.

Berga, A. (Abbé), *Pierre Scarga, l'étude sur la Pologne du XVI s. et le protestantisme polonais*, Paris, 1916, pp. xvi + 376.

Bil'basov, V. A., *История Екатерины Второй*, Berlin, 1900, 2 vols.

Blackmore, R. W., *The Doctrine of the Russian Church*, Aberdeen, 1845, pp. xxviii + 288.

Blagovidov, Th. V., *Обер-прокуроры св. Синода в 18 веке и в первой половине 19 века*, Казань, 1899, изд. 2-ое, 449 стр.

*Blagoy, D. P., *История русской литературы XVIII века*, М. гос. учебно-педагог. изд. 1945, 420 стр.

Bogdanov, D. P., *Оптина пустынь и паломничество туда русских писателей*, Историч. Вестник 1910, т. 122.

Bois, J., *Canonisation* (Vacant et Mangenot, *Dictionnaire de théologie catholique*), Paris, 1905, 2me vol., col. 1659-1672.

Bolotov, A., *Жизнь и приключения*, 1738-93, Комментарии П. Л. Жаткина, М.-Л., 1931.

Bonch-Bruevich, V. D., *Матерьялы к изучению русского сектантства*, СПБ., 1901.

Bronzov, A., *Нравственное богословие в России в XIX в*, Христ. Чтение 1901, 1902.

Bulgakov, N. A. (Priest), *Преподобный Иосиф Волоколамский*, СПБ., 1865, 215 стр.

Bukharev, A. M., *О православии в отношении к современности*, СПБ., 1860.

—— *Три письма к Гоголю писанные в 1848 г.*, СПБ., 1861.

—— *Моя апология*, М., 1866.

—— *Исследования Апокалипсиса*, изд. редакции Богословского Вестника, Сергиев Посад, 1916.

Bunin, I. A., *Собрание Сочинений*, изд. Маркса, СПБ., 1916, 6 т.

Bury, H., *Russia from within, especially since 1923*. The Churchman Publishing Co. (Undated.)

Buslaev, F. I., *Русская хрестоматия*, М., 1870.

—— *Народная поэзия*, Исторические Очерки, СПБ., 1887.

Chetverikov, S. (Priest), *Оптина пустынь* (с приложением писем М. Филарета, Гоголя, Шевырева, Н. П. и И. В. Киреевских), 1926, YMCA-Press, Paris.

—— *Молдавский старец схиархимандрит Паисий Величковский*, Этси Петсери, 1938, 2 т.

Chistovich, I. A., *Феофан Прокопович и его время*, СПБ., 1888, 752 стр.

—— *История перевода Библии на русский язык*, СПБ., 1899, 2-ое изд.

Chizhevsky, D. (in Ukrainian), *Філософія Г. Сковороді*, Варшава, 1934, 212 стр., Праці Україньского Наукового Институту, т. XXIV.
Consett, T., *Present State and Regulations of the Church in Russia*, London, 1729. (Containing the *Dukhovni Reglament*.)
Cross, S. H., *The Russian Primary Chronicle* (Harvard Studies, Notes in Philology and Literature, vol. XII), Harvard Univ. Press, Cambridge, 1930.
Cyril, St. of Turov., *Проповеди*, Памятники Росс. Словесн., ed. by К. Калайдович, М. 1821.
——— *Творения*, Киев, 1880 изд. Евгений епископ Минский и Туровский.

Dashkow, *Memoirs of the Princess Dashkowa*, edited from the originals by Mrs. W. Bradford, 2 vols., Henry Colburn, 1840.
Dawkins, R. M., *The Monks of the Athos*, Allen & Unwin, London, 1930, pp. 408.
*Del'vig A. J., *Полвека русской жизни*, 1820-70. Ред. С. Я. Штрайха, предисл. Д. О. Заславского. Academia, М.-Л. 1930, 2 т. cf. 1st ed. М. 1912-13, 4 vols.
Denisov, L. I., *Православные монастыри Российской Империи*, М., 1908, 984 стр.
Dimitry, St. (Tuptalo), *Летопись, сказусмая вкратце Деяния от начала миробытия до Рождества Христова ... с присовокуплением келейной летописи* («Диариуш»), М., 1784.
Dobbie-Bateman, A. F., *St. Seraphim of Sarov*, S.P.C.K., 1936, pp. 60.
Dostoevsky, *Сочинения*, Госиздат, 1926-30, 13 т.

On Dostoevsky:

Antony (Khrapovitzky) *Словарь к творениям Достоевского*, Sofia, 1921, 184 стр.
Bel'chikov, N. F., *Письма Ф. М. Достоевского к жене* (общая ред. В. Ф. Переверзева). Госизд., М.-Л., 1926.
Bem, A. L., *У истоков творчества Достоевского*, 1936.
Berdyaev, N., *L'esprit de Dostoevsky*, Paris, 1929 (edit. St. Michel), pp. 274.
Bonch-Bruevich, V. D., *Достоевский и о Достоевском*, Звенья, т. VI. № 16-23, стр. 413-584, М.-Л., Академия, 1936.
Dolinin, A. S., *Письма*, М., 1928-34, 3 т.
——— *Вступительная статья к истории Братьев Карамазовых*, Академия, 1934.

—— *Достоевский, Матерьялы и исследования,* Акад., Л. 1935.
*—— *В творческой лаборатории Достоевского,* Л., Советский писатель, 1947, pp. 172.
Dostoevskaya, A. G., *Воспоминания,* Госиздат, Л., 1930.
Evdokimoff, P., *Dostoiewsky et le problème du mal,* Lyon, 1942 (Editions du Livre Français). pp. 426 (note on p. 36 on St. Tikhon).
Grossman, L., *Творчество Достоевского,* М., 1921.
—— *Семинарий по Достоевскому,* М., 1922.
Hill, E., and Mudie, D., *The Letters of Dostoevsky to his Wife (1866-1880),* 1930 (Constable).
Komarovich, V., *Современные проблемы историко-литературного изучения Достоевского,* Ленинград, 1925.
—— *Der unbekannte Dostojewskij,* München, 1926 (Piper-Verlag).
*—— *Die Urgestalt der Brüder Karamasoff,* Dostojewskis Quellen, Entwürfe und Fragmente. Erläutert von W. Komarowitch. Mit einer einleitenden Studie von Professor Dr. Sigm. Freud. Piper Verlag, München, 1929, pp. xxxvi + 619.
—— *Neue Probleme des Dostojewskij-Forschung, 1925 bis 1930* (Zeitschrift für Slawische Philologie, B. X, XI; Leipzig, 1933, 1934, Max Vasmer Verlag).
Koteliansky, S. S., *Stavrogin's Confession and the Plan of the Life of a Great Sinner,* The Hogarth Press, 1922.
—— *Dostoevsky's New Letters,* The Hogarth Press, 1929, pp. 102.
Miller, O., *Достоевский: биография, письма и заметки из записной книжки,* СПБ., 1883, 176 стр.
*Mochul'sky, C., *Достоевский, жизнь и творчество,* YMCA-Press, Paris, 1947, pp. 561.
Piksanov, N. K., *Письма писателей к Достоевскому,* 1923.
Pobedonoszev, K. P., see below.
Popovich, J. S., *Filosofija i religija Dostojevskoga* (in Serbocroatian), Carlovitz, 1923.
Rozanov, V., *Великий Инквизитор. Опыт критического комментария.* «Разум», Берлин, 1924, 265 стр.
Sakulin, P. N., and Bel'chikov, *Из архива Достоевского: «Идиот», неизданные матерьялы.* Госизд., М.-Л., 1931; 319 стр.
Simmons, E. J., *Dostoevsky, The Making of a Novelist,* Oxford Univ. Press, 1940, pp. 416.

Dubrovin, N. Th., *Материалы для истории православной церкви в царствование Николая I,* СПБ., 1902, 2 т.

Duchesne, E., *Le Domostroi*, Paris, 1910.
—— *Stoglav ou les cent chapitres*, Paris, 1920.
Dukhovnye Shtati (*Ecclesiastical Statutes*), Духовные Штаты, СПБ., 1764, 129 стр.
Dunaev, В. I., *Преподобный Максим Грек и греческая идея на Руси в XVI веке*. М. 1916, 92 стр.

Ehrard, Marcelle, *V. A. Joukovsky et le préromantisme russe*, Paris, 1938, pp. 435.
Evgeny (Bolkhovitinov), *Словарь исторический о бывших в России писателях духовного чина*. СПБ., 1827.
—— *Словарь русских светских писателей*, 2 т. изд. Погодин, М., 1845.

Fedotov, G. P., *The Russian Church since the Revolution*, S.P.C.K., 1928, pp. 95.
—— *Святой Филипп, Митрополит Московский*, YMCA-Press, Paris, 1928, pp. 224.
—— *Святые древней Руси*, YMCA-Press, Paris, 1931, pp. 260.
—— *Стихи духовные*, YMCA-Press, Paris, 1935, pp. 152.
*—— *The Russian Religious Mind (Kievan Christianity)*, Harvard Univ. Press, 1946, pp. 437.
*—— *A Treasury of Russian Spirituality*, New-York, Sheed & Ward, pp. xvi. + 501, see St. Tikhon.
*Fersman, A. E., *Из истории культуры камня в России*, изд. Акад. Наук СССР., 1946, М.-Л., 73 стр.
Filaret (Drozdov), *Христианский катехизис*, СПБ., 1823.
—— *Из М-та Моск. Филарета (письма и разные его отзывы) в Чтениях в Об-ве Любителей Духовного Просвещения*, М. 1872.
—— *Письма митр. Московского Ф-та к наместнику Свято-Троицкия Сергиевы Лавры архимандриту Антонию*, 1831-67 гг. (ч. 1) и 1842-49 (ч. 2-ая), М., 1878.
—— *Слова и речи (с биографией)*, М., 1873-77, 5 т.
—— *Христианское Чтение 1881 и 1886 (критика его Катехизиса).*
—— *Письма в Православн. Обозрении за 1883, 1884, 1887.*
—— *Письма Ф-та М-та Моск. и Коломенск. к Высочайшим особам и разным другим лицам* (Собраны и изданы Саввою архиеп. Твер. и Кашинским), Тверь, 1886, 2 части.
—— *Письма* (Отчет Императ. Публичн. Библ. за 1888), СПБ., 1891.
—— *Мнения, отзывы и письма за 1821-67*, составил Л. Бродский, М., 1905, 387 + xii стр.

Filaret (Gumilevsky), *Обзор русской духовной литературы за 862-1720, 1720-1858,* Чернигов, 1859-61, 2 части.
—— *История русской церкви (до 1826),* Чернигов, 1862.
—— *Православное догматическое богословие,* Чернигов, 1864.
Florovsky, G. V., *Пути русского богословия,* YMCA-Press, Paris, 1937, 520 + 54 стр.
French, R. M., *The Way of a Pilgirm,* S.P.C.K., 1930, pp. 142.
Frere, W. H., *Links in the Chain of Russian Church History,* Faith Press, 1918, pp. vii + 200.
Fonvizin, *Записки Очевидца* (Русская Библиотека), Leipzig, 1860.

Georgy (Konissky), *О должности приходских священников,* 1776. (Cf. Blackmore.)
—— *Сочинения, изданы иером. И. Григоровичем,* СПБ., 1835, 2 части.
Gildebrandt, P. A., *Справочный и объяснительный словарь к Новому Завету,* Памятники Древн., 1881.
Goetz, L. K., *Das Kiever Höhlenkloster als Kulturzentrum des vormongolischen Russlands,* Passau, 1904.
Gogol, N. V., *Собр. сочинений,* изд. Тихонравова, закончено Шенроком, 1889-96, 7 т.
—— *Письма,* изд. В. Н. Шенрока, СПБ., 1901, 4 т.
—— *Рукописи Гоголя,* Гос. Библиотека СССР., 1940, 126 стр.
Golitsuin, Aug., *Биография Арсения Мацеевича,* Leipzig, 1863, 28 стр.
—— *La Russie au XVIII siècle,* Paris, 1863.
Golubinsky, E. E., *Преподобный Сергий и его Лавра,* М., 1898.
—— *История русской церкви,* М., 1901-1904. 3 т.
—— *История канонизации святых в русской церкви,* Чтения в Обществе Истор. и Древн., М., 1903, 2-ое изд.
Gor'ky, M., *Сочинения,* изд. «Знание», СПБ., 1901-1910, 9 т.
—— *Собрание сочинений,* Berlin, 1923, 16 т.
Gratieux, A., *A. S. Khomiakov et le mouvement slavophile,* Paris, 1939, 2 vols.
Grigorovich, N. I., *Обзор учреждения в России архиерейских кафедр и содержания их (1764-1866),* СПБ., 67 стр.
—— *Обзор учреждения в России православных монастырей (со времени введения штатов по духовному ведомству, 1764-1869 г.),* СПБ., 1869, 220 стр.

Grot, Yak., *Из поездки в Воронеж* (Вестник Европы), 1870, кн. 6.
―― *Державин, с общими примечаниями Грота*, СПБ., 1883, 9 т.
―― *Митр. Евгений*, Второе Отделение Русск. Языка и Словесности, т. 5.
Gudzy, N. K., *Житие протопопа Аввакума . . . и другие его сочинения, вступительная статья и комментарии Н. К. Гудзия*, М., 1935, 497 стр.
―― *Хрестоматия по древней русской литературе XI-XVII веков*, Учпедгиз, М., 1938, 457 стр.
*―― *История древней русской литературы*, Гос. учебно-педагог. изд. Наркомпроса Р.С.Ф.С.Р., М., 1945, 508 стр.
Gukovsky, G. A., *Очерки по истории русской литературы и общественной мысли восемнадцатого века*, Ленинград, 1938.
―― *Русская литература XVIII века*, Учпедгиз, М., 1939.

Hall, Joseph, *The Arte of Divine Meditation*, London, 1607.
―― *Meditations, Newly enlarged with ten Vows*, 1609.
―― *Occasional Meditations*, London, 1851.
Hecker, J. F., *Religion and Communism*, Chapman & Hall, 1933, pp. 303.
Herzen, A. I., *Сочинения и письма*, издание М. Лемке, СПБ., 1919, 22 т.
Hrushevsky, M. S., *З історії релігійної думки на Україні*, Львів, 1925 (in Ukrainian).

Ignaty (Archimandrite), *Краткие жизнеописания русских святых X—XIII в.*, СПБ., 1875.
Ignaty (Bryanchaninov), *Духовные опыты*, СПБ., 2-ое изд., 1886. (*See* L. Sokolov.)
Ikonnikov, V. S., *Опыт исследования о культурном значении Византии в русской истории*, Киев, 1869.
―― *Опыт русской историографии*, Киев, 1891-95, 2 т.
―― *Максим Грек и его время*, Киев, 1910, 604 + 21 стр.
Innokenty (Borisov), *Из лекций по догматическому и нравств. богословию*, Киев, 1869.
―― *Сочинения*, СПБ., 1901, 12 т.
Innokenty (Smirnov), *Сочинения*, СПБ., 1812.
―― *Сочинения*, СПБ., 1845-7.
―― *Письма к княгине С. С. Мещерской*, 1817-1847, изд. О. Бодянским, 1875.
Innokenty (Veniaminov), *Собрание сочинений* (собрано Ив. Пл. Барсуковым), М., 1888, 3 т.

Ioannov, A. (Zhuravlev), *Полное историческое известие о древних стригольниках и новых раскольниках, так называемых старообрядцах*, СПБ., 1890, 345 стр. (писано в 1789; СПБ., 1799).
Ioann Sergiev- (Cronstadtsky, or Fr John of Cronstadt) *Полное собрание сочинений*, СПБ., изд. 2-ое, 1893, 94, 6 т.
—— *Мысли христианина о покаянии и св. причащении*, СПБ., 1903, 93 стр.
—— *My Life in Christ*, translated by E. E. Goulaieff, London, Cassell, 1897.
—— *Thoughts and Counsels . . .* , transl. and arranged by A. L. Illingworth, Oxford, Mowbray, 1899.

Kadlubovsky, A. P., *Очерки по истории древне-русской литературы житий святых*, изд. Р. Филолог. Вестник, 1902, ix + 389 стр.
Kantemir, A. D., *Сочинения и письма*, изд. П. Ефремова, СПБ., 1867-1868, 2 т.
Kapterev, N. F., *Патриарх Никон и царь Алексей Михайлович*, Сергиевский Посад, 1909-12, 2 т.
—— *Характер отношения России к православному востоку в XVI и XVII веках*, М., 1914, 14 + 567 стр.
Khomiakov, A. S., *Богословские сочинения, с предисловием Ю. Ф. Самарина*, Прага, 1867, 2 т.
—— *Сочинения*, изд. 4-ое, М., 1906-11, 8 т.
Kisevetter, A. A., *Исторические очерки*, М., 1912, 502 стр.
Klepinin, N., *Святой и благоверный князь Александр Невский*, Paris, YMCA., 1931, 202 стр.
Klyuchevsky, V. O., *Древне-русские жития святых как исторический источник*, М., 1871.
—— *Значение преподобного Сергия для русского народа и государства*, М., 1913.
—— *Курс русской истории*, М.-П., 1904-21, 5 т.
—— In Engl., *A History of Russia*, 1911-31, London, J. M. Dent, transl. C. J. Hogarth, N.-Y., E. P. Dutton, 5 vols.
Kol'tzov, A. V., *Сочинения*, с биогр. А. И. Лященко, 1895, xvi + 232 стр. (*See* V. Ogarkov, V. Pokrovsky.)
—— *Полное собрание сочинений, Стихотворения и письма*, СПБ., 1911.
Kolyupanov, *Биография А. И. Кошелева*, М., 2 т. 1889-92.
Konovalova, E. I., *Святые целители и заступники*, М., 1902, 2-ое изд.
Kostomarov, N. I., *Русская история в жизнеописаниях ее главнейших деятелей*, СПБ., 1888, 2 т.
Kotovich, A., *Духовная цензура в России*, 1799-1855, СПБ., 1909, xvi + 604 + xiii стр.

Kozhevnikov, V. A., *Философия чувства и вера в ее отношениях к литературе и рационализму XVIII в.*, М., 1897.
—— *О значении христианского подвижничества в прошлом и настоящем*, Христ. Чтен., 1909.
Krotkov, An., *О кронштадтском протоиерее о. Иоанне*, М., 1903, 43 стр.

Lappo-Danilevsky, A., *Очерк внутренней политики Императрицы Екатерины Второй*, СПБ., 1898, 62 стр.
Lebedev, N. A., *Исторический взгляд на учреждение училищ, школ, учебных заведений и учебных обществ, послуживших к образованию русского народа с 1025 по 1855*, СПБ, 1874, 165 стр.
Leontiev, K. N., *Сочинения*, М., 1912, 12 т.
Lermontov, M., *Полное собрание сочинений*, под ред. и с предисловием Б. М. Эйхенбаума, Лен., 1940, 4 т.
Leroy-Beaulieu, A., *The Empire of the Tsars and the Russians*, transl. from French by Z. A. Rogozine, G. P. Putman, London, N.-Y., 1896, 3 vols. See t. 3, p. 123 on St. Tikhon.
Levitov, A. I., *Собрание сочинений* с биографией и комментариями М. С. Ежова, М.-Лен., 1932, 2 т.
Longinov, M. N., *Новиков и Шварц*, М., 1857.
—— *Новиков и московские мартинисты*, М., 1867.
Lopukhin, I. V., *Некоторые черты внутренней церкви* (1798) *с присовокуплением краткого изображения качеств и должностей истинного христианина, почерпнутого из слова Божия и расположенного по вопросам и ответам*, СПБ., 1816. (Cf. Savodnik.)
—— *Записки некоторых обстоятельств жизни и службы действительного тайного советника и сенатора И. В. Лопухина, составленные им самим.* Изд. с предисл. Искандера, Лондон, 1860, 211 стр.
*Lossky, V., *Essai sur la théologie mystique de l'Église d'Orient.* Chez Aubin, Paris, 1944. (*See* footnote on p. 225 on St. Tikhon.)

Maikova-Borovkova, M., *К литературной деятельности Нила Сорского*, Памятники Древн. Письмен. и истории, 1911, № 177, 16 стр.
Makary (Archimandrite), *Описание Новгородского Архиепископского дома*, СПБ., 1857.
—— *Сказание о жизни и трудах Гавриила, Митрополита Новгородского и Ст. Петерб.*, СПБ., 1857, 146 стр.
—— *Описание Новгородского общежительного первоклассного Юрьева Монастыря*, М., 1858.

—— *Археологическое описание церковных древностей в Новгороде*, М., 1860.
Makary (Bulgakov), *История Киевской Академии*, СПБ., 1843, 226 стр.
—— *Обзор редакций Киево-Печерского Патерика* (Историч. Чтения), т. 3, 1854.
—— *История раскола*, СПБ., 1855, 367 стр.
—— *Введение в православн. богословие*, СПБ. изд. 3-е 1863, во франц. переводе: Théologie dogmatique orthodoxe, Paris, 1859.
—— *История русской церкви*, СПБ., 1857-83, 12 т.
Makary (Glukharev), *Несколько Слов*, М., 1854, 94 стр.
—— *Письма покойного архим. М-ия*, М., 1860., 2 т.
Makary (Glukharev), *Письмо к Филарету о Библии*, М., 1861, 35 стр.
—— *Письмо к Филарету о Библии*, М., 1861, 35 стр.
Marmontel, *Belisaire (Oeuvres Complètes)*, 1819, t. 7.
Martel, Antoine, *Michel Lomonosov et la langue littéraire russe*, Paris, 1933, pp. 135.
Masaryk, T. G., *The Spirit of Russia*, translated from the German original by Eden & Cedar Paul, London, Allen & Unwin, N.-Y., Macmillan, 1919, 2 vols.
Mel'gunova, Sidorov and Sivkov, *Русская жизнь в воспоминаниях современников*, XVIII в., М., 1914, 431 стр.
Mel'nikov, P. I., *Записки о русском расколе, очерк поповщины*, 1880.
Mikhail (Hieromonk), (Доцент СПБ. Академии), *Отец Иоанн Кронштадтский*, СПБ., 1903, 398 стр.
Millet, G., *Les monuments de l'Athos*, Paris, 1927.
Milyukov, *Очерки по истории русской культуры*, Paris, 1930-37, т. 2 Вера. (Cf. *Outlines of Russian Culture*, vol. 1. *Religion and the Church*, ed. by M. Karpovich, Philadelphia, 1942.)
Mirsky, D. S., *Contemporary Russian Literature, 1881-1925*, London, George Routledge & Son, 1926.
—— *A History of Russian Literature to 1881*, London, George Routledge & Son, 1927.
—— *Russia, a Social History*, edited by Professor C. C. Seligman, London, The Cresset Press, 1931.
Mochul'sky, C., *Духовный путь Гоголя*, YMCA-Press, Paris, 1934, pp. 146.
—— See Dostoevsky.
Modzalevsky, Ziablovsky and Zenger, *Рукою Пушкина*, Труды Пушкинской Комиссии, Академия, 1935.
Mohrenschildt, D. S., *Russia in the Intellectual Life of Eighteenth Century France* (Columbia Univ. Press), 1936, pp. viii + 325.

Nesterovsky, E., *Литургика*, М., 1901, 12 + 239 стр.
Nikol'sky, K., *Краткое обозрение богослужебных книг православной росс. церкви*, 2-ое изд. 1890, 106 стр.
Nikol'sky, N., *Молитва св. Нила Сорского*. Изв. Отдел. Русс. Яз., 1897.
Nikol'sky, N. K., *Материалы для истории древне-русской духовной письменности*, СПБ., 1907, Сборн. Отд. Русс. Яз. Акад. Наук, т. 82.
—— *Общинная и келейная жизнь в Кирилло-Белозерском монастыре XV—XVI веков*, СПБ., 1907.
—— *Повесть временных лет как источник для истории начального периода русской письменности*, Академия Наук СССР., Сборн. по рус. яз. и слов. т. 2, № I, Ленинград, 1930.
Nikol'sky, N. M., *История русской церкви*, М., 1930, 278 стр.
Nikol'sky, Pavel (Priest), *Русская проповедь XV и XVI века*. Журн. Мин. Нар. Просв. 1868.
Nil, St. of Sora, *Устав преп. отца нашего Нила Сорского*, издал епископ Иустин, 1902, изд. Пантелеймонова монастыря. See Fedotov, *A Treasury of Russian Spirituality*. p. 85-133.
Novikov, N. I., *Опыт Словаря Русских Писателей*, М., 1772.

Ogarkov, V., *Кольцов*, СПБ., 1891, 95 стр.
Orlov, A. S., *Восемнадцатый век*, Сборник статей, Ак. Наук СССР., М.-Л., 1935.
—— *Древняя русская литература XI—XVI вв.*, Ак. Наук СССР., М.-Л., 1937, 379 стр.

Paissy (Velichkovsky), *Добротолюбие в переводе Паисия*, М., 1793.
Palmer, W., *Notes of a visit to the Russian Church in the years 1840, 1841*. Selected and arranged by Cardinal Newman (Kegan Paul Trench & Co.), 1882.
Pares, B., *A History of Russia*, 1926, pp. xxii + 558 (Jonathan Cape), 3d ed., pp. xxiii + 570, 1937.
Pascal, Pierre, *Avvakum et les débuts du raskol, La crise religieuse russe au XVII-e siècle en Russie*, Paris, 1938, pp. xxv + 618.
Pavlov, A. S., *Исторический очерк секуляризации церковных земель в России (1503-1580)*, Одесса, 1871, 167 стр.
—— *Критические опыты по истории древнейшей Греко-Русской полемики против Латинян*, СПБ., 1878, iv + 210 стр.

Peeters, P., *La canonisation des saints dans l'Église russe.—* Extraits de l'Analecta Bollandiana, 1914.
Pekarsky, P. P., *Наука и литература в России при Петре Великом,* СПБ., 1862, 2 т.
—— *Представители Киевской учености в половине 17 в.,* СПБ., 1862.
—— *Дополнения к истории масонства в России 18-го столетия,* СПБ., 1869 (Отдел. Русск. Языка и Словесн., т. VII, № 4).
Peretts, V. N., *Историко-литературные исследования и матерьялы,* СПБ., 1900.
—— *Исследования и матерьялы по истории старинной Украинской литературы,* Лен., 1926.
Periodicals (with dates of their first issue):
—— *Библиографические Записки,* М., 1858.
—— *Богословский Вестник,* М., 1892.
—— *Вестник Европы,* М., 1802.
—— *Воскресное Чтение,* Киев, 1837.
—— *Духовная Беседа,* СПБ., 1854.
—— *Духовный Вестник,* Харьков, 1862.
—— *Журнал Мин-ва Народн. Просв.* СПБ., 1884.
—— *Исторический Вестник,* СПБ., 1880.
—— *Московитянин,* М., 1841-56.
—— *Москов. Епархиальные Ведомости,* 1873.
—— *Православное Обозрение,* М., 1860-91.
—— *Православный Собеседник,* Казань, 1855.
—— *Прибавления к изданию творений святых отцов в русских переводах,* М., 1843.
—— *Русский Архив,* М., 1863.
—— *Русская Старина,* СПБ., 1824.
—— *Странник,* СПБ., 1860.
—— *Труды Киевской Духовной Акад.,* 1860.
—— *Христианское Чтение,* СПБ., 1821.
—— *Чтения Московского Общества Любителей Духовного Просвещения,* М., 1863.
Petukhov, E. V., *Проповедник XIII в. Серапион Владимирский,* СПБ., 1888.
—— *Из истории литературы 17 века, Сочинение о Царствии Небесном и о воспитании чад.* (Памятники Древн. Письм. и Искусства), 1893, 56 стр.
—— *Очерки из литературной истории Синодика,* СПБ., 1895.
Pinkerton, R., *The Present State of the Russian Church,* Edinburgh, 1814, pp. xii + 339.
—— *Extracts of Letters,* 1817, pp. 67.
—— *Russia, or miscellaneous observations,* Edinburgh, 1833, pp. 486.

Philotheus of Pskov, *Послания,* Прав. Собеседн., 1861, 2; 1863, 1.
Platon (Levshin), *Православное Учение или Сокращенная Христианская Богословия,* СПБ., 1765, 252 стр.
—— *Путешествие Платона в Киев,* М., 1813. (*See* I. M. Snegirev, Mel'gunova.)
—— *Краткая Церковная Российская История,* М., 1829, 2 т.
—— *The Great Catechism of the Holy, Catholic, Apostolic, Orthodox Church,* translated from Greek and abridged by J. T. Seccombe, London, 1867. (Cf. also R. Pinkerton, *The present State,* etc.)
Platonov, S. F., *Борис Годунов,* Прага, 1924, 276 стр.
—— *History of Russia,* New-York, 1925, pp. vii + 435.
Pobedonostzev, K. P., *П. и его корреспонденты (1838-81),* М.-П., 1923.
—— *Красный Архив 1922,* т. 2 (Переписка с Достоевским). Л., Центрархив.
—— *Письма к Александру III-му,* М., 1925, 2 т.
Pokrovsky, V. V., *Жизнь Кольцова,* М., 1905.
Ponomarev, A. I., *Памятники древне-русской церковно-учительной литературы,* М., 1894-97, 3 т.
Popov, A. M., *Историко-литературный обзор Древне-русских полемических сочинений против Латинян,* М., 1875.
—— *Древне-русские полемические сочинения против протестантов,* М., 1878.
Popov, A. N., *Новое о Новикове* (Записки Русск. Исторического Общества), 1868.
Popov, M. S., *Арсений Мацеевич, Митрополит Ростовск. и Ярославский,* СПБ., 1905, 264 + xix стр.
Pososhkov, I. T., *Сочинения,* изд. Погодин, М., т. 1, 1842, т. 2, 1863.
—— *Завещание отеческое,* изд. Е. Прилежаев, СПБ., 1898.
Pule, M. de, *Биографическая заметка о Никитине,* Русский Архив, 1865.
Pushkin, A. S., *Полное собрание сочинений,* изд. «Слово», Берлин, 1921, 6 т.

Radishchev, A. N., *Путешествие из Петербурга в Москву,* СПБ., 1790, 2 т.
Ridinger, *Из матерьялов для истории и статистики города Ельца,* Русский Архив, 1866.
Rovinsky, D. A., *Подробный словарь русских гравированных портретов,* СПБ., 1886-89, 4 т.
Rozanov, N., *История Московского ерархиального управле-*

ния со времени учреждения св. Синода *1721-1821*, М., 1869-70, 3 части.

Rozhdestvensky, V., *Отчет* (Чтения Общества любителей духовного просвещнеия), 1863, 1865.

Runkevich, S. G., *История Русской Церкви под управлением св. Синода. Т. I., Учреждение и первоначальное устройство с 1721-25*, СПБ., 1900, 429 стр.

—— *История Александро-Невской Лавры (1713-1913)*, СПБ., 1913, 199 + 45 стр.

Samarin, Yu. F., *Стефан Яворский и Феофан Прокопович как проповедники*, Сочинения, М., 1900, 8 т.

Savodnik, V. F., *Материалы по истории русского масонства восемнадцатого века*, 1913 (containing *Масонские труды Лопухина: Духовный рыцарь, Некоторые черты внутренней церкви, Краткое изображение должностей* . . .)

Savva, Bishop of Krutitzi, *Житие пр. Иосифа Волоколамского*, изд. К. Невоструев, М., 1865.

Sergius (Archimandrite), *Сказание о жизни и подвигах блаж. памяти Серафима Саровской пустыни иеромонаха и затворника*, изд. 4-ое, М., 1858, 2 части.

Shakhmatov, A. A., *Киево-Печерский Патерик и Печерская летопись*, 1897 (Известия Отделения Русского Языка, II).

—— *Житие Антония и Печерская Летопись*, Журн. Мин. Народн. Просв., 1898, март.

—— *Антоний Печерский*, Извес. Отд., 1915.

Shakhovskoy, Ya. P., *Записки*, М., 1810, 2 т.

Shchapov, A. P., *Сочинения*, СПБ., 1906, 3 т., см. т. 1, стр. 173-450, Раскол.

Shestakov, P., *Св. Стефан Пермский*, Журн. Мин. Нар. Просв., 1868.

Shliapkin, T. A., *Св. Димитрий Ростовский и его время 1651-1709*, СПБ., 1891, xiv + 460 + 102 стр.

Shmurlo, E. *Введение в русскую историю*, Прага, 1924.

Skabichevsky, A. M., *Очерки истории русской цензуры (1700-1863)*, СПБ., 1892, 495 стр.

Skovoroda, G. S., *Сочинения в стихах и прозе с его портретом и почерком его руки*, СПБ., 1861.

Smentzovsky, M., *Братья Лихуды*, СПБ., 1899, 459 + xl стр.

Smirnov, A. A., *Петербургский период жизни Д. Филарета, 1808-1819*, СПБ., 1900.

Smirnov, P. S., *Споры и разделения в русском расколе в первой четверти XVIII в.*, СПБ., 1909, 363 стр.

Smirnov, S. K., *История Московской Славо-Греко-Латинской Академии*, М., 1855, 428 стр.

—— *История Троицкой Лаврской Семинарии*, М., 1867, 586 стр.
Smolitsch, I., *Leben und Lehre der Starzen*, Wien, 1936, pp. 276.
Snegirev, I. M., *Изображение жизни Платона*, М., 1822.
—— *Житие Платона, Митр. Московского*, М., 1835.
—— *Жизнь Московского Митроп. Платона*, М., 1856.
Sobolevsky, A. I., *Южнославянское влияние на русскую письм. XIV—XV в.*, СПБ., 1894.
——*Переводная литература Московской Руси, XIV—XVII в.*, СПБ., 1903, Академия.
—— *Жития святых по древне-русским спискам*, СПБ., 1903, 68 стр.
Sokolov, L., *Еп. Игнатий Брянчанинов*, Киев, 1915, 2 т.
Solovyev, S. M., *История России с древнейших времен*, М., 1857-79, 29 т.
Solovyev, V. S., *Сочинения*, изд. 2-ое, СПБ., 1896, 10 т.
—— *Письма*, изд. Е. Л. Радлова, СПБ., 1908-11, 4 т.
Sreznevsky, I., *Св. Кирил как писатель*, Акад. СПБ., Древн. Памятн. Русс. Письм. и Яз., 1854.
Steinmann, F., und Hurwicz, E., *Pobedonostzev. Der Staatsmann der Reaktion unter Alexander III*, Koenigsberg, 1933, pp. viii + 281.
Stephen (Yavorsky), Протоиер. Иоан Морев, *«Камень Веры» Митр. Ст. Яв-го его место среди отеч. противопротестантских сочин.*, СПБ., 1904, 372 стр.
Stremoukhoff, D., *Vladimir Soloviev et son œuvre messianique*, 1935 (Fas. 69 Publications de la Faculté des Lettres de l'Université de Strasbourg), pp. 351.
Stroev, P. M., *Списки иерархов и настоятелей монастырей Российския церкви*, СПБ., 1877, 1056 + 68 столбцов.
Subbotin, N. I., *Происхождение ныне существующей у старообрядцев так называемой Австрийской или Белокриницкой иерархии*, М., 1874, 512 стр.
—— *Матерьялы для истории раскола за первое время его существования*, М., I—IX, 1874-90.
Sumner, B. H., *Survey of Russian History*, London, Duckworth, 1944, pp. 465.
Sushkov, N. N., *Записки о жизни и времени святителя Филарета, Митр. Московского*, М., 1868.
Svatikov, S. G., *Россия и Дон (1549-1917)*, Вена, Изд. Донской Историч. Комиссии, 1924, viii + 592 стр.

Theophan (Govorov), *Письма к разным лицам о разных предметах веры и жизни*, М., 1892, изд. 2-ое, 463 стр.
Tikhomirov, E., *Русский паломник. Святые места.* М., 1886. 859 стр.

Tikhomirov, M. N., *Источниковедение истории С.С.С.Р.*, М., 1940. 2 т.
Tikhomirov, P., *Биографии первых девяти Новгородских епископов*. Новгород, 1862.
Tikhonravov, N. S., *Сочинения*, М. 1898, 3 т.; см. Отреченные книги древней Руси т. 1.; Митроп. Евгений Болховитинов, т. 3; Н. И. Новков, т. 3.
St. Tikhon, *Сокровище Духовное от мира собираемое*, СПБ., 1825, 4 т.
────── *Письма Келейные*, М., 1830, 2 т.
────── *Сочинения*, М., 1860, изд. 2-ое, 15 т.: т. 1—*Описание жизни преосв. Тихона*, 62 стр. *Наставление духовенству. Прибавление к должности священнической, Наставление монашествующих. О взаимных должностях христианских*. т. 2—*Плоть и дух. Разные размышления и замечания. Переводы*. т. 3—*Проповеди*. т. 4-9—*О истинном христианстве*. т. 10-13—*Сокровище духовное*. т. 14—*Разные письма к некоторым приятелям посыланные* (33 письма). т. 15—*Письма келейные* (123 письма).

On St. Tikhon:

Anonymous:

────── *Описание жизни и подвигов святителя Тихона 1-го Еп. Воронежского*, СПБ., 1833, 115 стр.

────── *Жизнь святителя Христова Тихона 1-го, Епископа Воронежского и Елецкого, с присовокуплением избранных мест из его творений*, М., 1861, 162 стр.

────── *Рассказ очевидца об открытии нетленных мощей святителя и чудотворца Тихона, Епископа Воронежского 12 и 13 августа*, СПБ., 1861, 16 стр.

────── *Жизнь новоявленного угодника Божия Тихона, с присовокуплением мест из его творений*, М., 1862 изд. 2-ое, 214 стр.

────── *Рус. биографический словарь*, 1912, т. 20, кол. 583-589.
Arseniev, N., *Tychon, Mystik*, article in *Religion in Geschichte und Gegenwart* (Mohr Verlag), Tübingen, 6 vols., 1927-32, t. IV.
*Behr-Sigel, Elisabeth, "Tikhon de Zadonsk," *Contacts* (Revue française de l'Orthodoxie) No. 85 (1974), 1, pp. 35-65.
*Eckardt, N. von, *Russisches Christentum*, Piper, München, 1947, *see* pp. 219-225.
Elagin, *Жизнь*, 1893 (Title inaccurate, for I know this book only by hearsay).
Evgeny (Bolkhovitinov), *Жизнь, в предисловии к изд. 1860 г.* (first published in 1796).

*Fedotov, G. P., *see A Treasury of Russian Spirituality,* pp. 182-241.
Florovsky, G., *op. cit., see* pp. 123-125.
Gippius Anna, Святой Тихон Задонский, Paris, YMCA-Press, 1925? [undated].
Gorodetzky, N., *The Humiliated Christ in Modern Russian Thought,* London, S.P.C.K., 1938, pp. 99-106.
*Grunwald, Constantin de, *Quand Russie avait des saints,* Éditions Arthème Fayard, Paris, 1958, pp. 187; ch. 8 (pp. 135-155) on St. Tikhon.
*Kologrivof, *Essai sur la sainteté en Russie* (Coll. Renaissance et Tradition), Éditions Beyaert, Bruges, 1953, pp. 445; pp. 329-379 on St. Tikhon.
Komarovich, V. Cf. Dostoevsky, *Die Urgestalt der Brüder Karamasoff, see* ch. 2, pp. 59-119.
Lebedev, A., Святитель Тихон Задонский и всея России чудотворец, — его жизнь, писания и прославление, СПБ., 1865, 631 стр.
Popov, T. D. (priest), Свят. Тихон Задонский как нравоучитель, Воронеж, 1914. (I regret having been unable to get access to this book.)
Sergievsky, N., Святитель Тихон Задонский, М., 1898.

In Periodicals:

Воскресное Чтение, год 2-ой, № 37 анонимно: о юродивом; год 5-ый, стр. 421 Т. и духовенство; 1838 — письмо к И. Л.
Друг Юношества, 1813 — о памятнике Лопухина.
Духовный Вестник, 1862, т. 3, С. Н. Пономарев, стр. 498; т. 1, стр. 407; т. 2, стр. 213.
*Журнал Москов. Патр.:
  1955, № 10, стр. 18-22.
  1971, № 10, стр. 60-75.
  1975, № 4, стр. 16: photos of the restored Cathedral in Zadonsk.
Исторический Вестник, 1910, т. 121, С. Н. Введенский о Мамонове.
Киевские Епарх. Вед., 1861, т. 11 и 13, Записки Келейников
Московитянин:
  1848, № 4, Н. Горчаков, Воспоминания.
  1850, № 18, Письмо св. Т. о пении.
  1851, № 1, Письмо св. Т. о прощении.
Москов. Епарх. Вед., 1871, № 40, 72 об открытии монастыря в Короцке.

Новгород. Губерн. Вед., 1861, № 2, 3, о спасении Т-на купцом.
*Православн. Жизнь, Jordanville, N. Y.: occasional texts from the family tradition of the times of St. Tikhon.
Православн. Обозрение:
  1861, № 5, Записки Чеботарева.
  1861, № 6, О истории мощей.
Прибавления к изд. творений св. отцов, 1862 ч. 21, Труды Т-на 1-го еп. Ворон. по управлению паствою.
Странник:
  1860, янв. Письмо св. Т. о деньгах.
  1861, авг. О пощечине.
Христианское Чтение:
  1833, окт. Письмо св. Т. о церкви строимой А. И.
  1834 ср. Московитянин 1851.
  1835 т. 3, Чудо 1827 г.
  1856, т. 1, Письмо, св. Т.
  1865, № 37, Исцеления (из Дух. Беседы 1861, ноябрь).
  1881, т. 1, иером. Сергий, поправка.
  1909, дек. Кожевников, о толпе паломников.
*Irenikon, see Zen'kovsky.
The Eastern Churches Quarterly, vol. VII, 1947 (St. Augustine's Abbey, Ramsgate). N. Gorodetzky, *Bishop Tikhon of Voronezh as an example of Russian Orthodox Teaching*, pp. 38-47.
*Wort und Wahrheit, Heft 3, 2 Jahr, 1947; Verlag Herder, Wien; pp. 129-139. A. Hackel, *Der historische Starez Sossima*.

Tolstoy, D. A., *Взгляд на учебную часть в России 18 века*, СПБ., 1862, 100 стр.
—— *Римское Католичество в России*, СПБ., 1876, 2 т. (переведено на франц. и английск. языки).
Tolstoy, L. N., *Собрание сочинений*, изд. Бирюкова, М., 1913, 24. т.
—— *Царствие Божие внутри нас*, изд. Лодыжникова, Берлин, 1920.
Trediakovsky, V. K., *Сочинения*, изд. Смирдина, СПБ., 1849, 3 т.
Tukalevsky, V., *Из истории философских направлений в русском обществе XVIII в.*, Журн. Мин. Нар. Просв., 1911, часть 33.
Turgenev, A. (edit.), *La cour de la Russie il-y-a cent ans, 1725-1783*, Berlin, 1858, pp. 422.
Turgenev, I. S., *Собрание Сочинений*, СПБ., 1898,, 12 т.
**Tyszkiewiecz, S., *Moralistes de Russie*, Pont. Inst. Or. Stud., Roma, 1951, pp. 445; ch. 3 (pp. 45-63): St. Tikhon de Zadonsk.
*——, review, in *Orientalia Christiana Periodica*, vol. XVIII (1952), pp. 211-215.

*Un moine de l'Église d'Orient, *La prière de Jésus*, Irenikon, tome XX, 3me et 4me Trimestre 1947.
Uspensky, G. I., *Сочинения, с биографией и предисловием Н. К. Михайловского*, СПБ., 1908, 6 т.

Valdenberg, *Древне-русские учения о пределах царской власти*, М., 1916.
Vassian (Patrikeev), *Полемические писания в Правосл. Собеседнике*, 1863, сент.-окт.
Vernadsky, George, *A History of Russia*, New revised edition, 1944, Yale Univ. Press.
Veselovsky, A. N., *Разыскания в области духовных стихов*, СПБ., 1879-83 (Известия Отдел. Русск. Языка и Словесности).
Viktorova, M., *Киевский Патерик, в русском переводе*, Киев, 1870.
Vilinsky, S. G., *Послания старца Артемия*, Одесса, 1906.
Viller, M., et Malvy, A., *La Confession Orthodoxe de Pierre Moghila, approuvée par les Patriarches Grecs du XVII s.*, Texte Latin inedit. (Orientalia Christiana, vol. X, No. 39), 1927.
Vinogradov, V., *О характере проповеднического творчества Кирилла еп. Туровского* (Сборн. статей в память столетия Моск. Дух. Акад.), 1915.
Vitevsky, V. N., *Раскол в Уральском Войске и отношение к нему духовной и военногражданской власти в 18 и 19 веке*. Казань, 1878, 2 части.

Waliczevsky, K., *Heritage de Pierre le Grand: règne des femmes*, Paris, 1911.
—— *La dernière des Romanov*, Paris, 1902.
—— *Le roman d'une Imperatrice*, Paris, 1893.

Yakovlev, Vlad., *Памятники русской литературы XII и XIII века* (Киевский Патерик), СПБ., 1872, 186 стр.
Yatzimirsky, A. I., *К истории ложных молитв в южнославянской письменности*, СПБ., 1913 (Известия Акад. Наук, т. 8).

Zabyelin, P., *Права и обязанности пресвитеров по основным законам Христианской церкви и по церковно-гражданским постановлениям Русской церкви*, Киев, изд. 2-ое 1888, ix + 656 стр.

Zaitzev, B., *Преп. Сергий Радонежский*, Paris, YMCA-Press, 1925, 101 стр. (in French, chez Plon, Roseau d'Or).

*Zén'kovsky, V., *La crise de la conscience réligieuse ecclésiastique en Russie au XVIII siècle: la philosophie de G. S. Skovoroda*. Irenikon, Amay, Belgique, 1946, 3-4-trimèstre, pp. 243-283. (See pp. 254-256 on St. Tikhon.)

Zernov, N. M., *St. Sergius, Builder of Russia*, S.P.C.K., 1938, pp. xi + 155; translated by Adeline Delafeld.

Zhizhka, M. V., and Barskov, Ya. L., *Матерьялы к изучению Путешествия из Петербурга в Москву А. Н. Радищева*, Акад., 1935.

Zhmakin, V., *Митрополит Даниил и его сочинения*, М., 1881.

Znamensky, Ivan, *Положение духовенства в царствование Екатерины II и Петра I-го*, 1888, 184 стр.

Znamensky, P. V., *Духовные школы в России до реформы 1808 года*, Казань 1881.

―― *Учебное руководство по истории русской церкви*, Казань, 1896, 484 стр.

Notes

CHAPTER 1

[1]A. P. Shchapov, *Works*, 3 vols., SPB; *The Schism of the Old Believers with reference to the inward state of the Russian Church in the first half of the XVIII Century*, Kiev, 1859, vol. 1, p. 234—quoting the speech by Cyril Florinsky, Rector of the Moscow Academy, in 1741, and by Amvrossy Yushkevich, Archbishop of Novgorod.
[2]Avvakum, *Life, Works and Letters*, edited by N. Gudzy, M., 1935, p. 497. Pierre Pascal, *Avvakum et les débuts du Raskol*, Paris, 1938, pp. xv + 617.
[3]See note on Epiphany, Lazar.
[4]G. Florovsky, *The Ways of Russian Theology*, Paris, 1937, pp. vi + 574; p. 84. See note on Markell.
[5]S. Runkevich, *Alexandro-Nevsky Lavra, 1713-1913*, pp. 999; p. 45, SPB., 1913, chapter 12.

CHAPTER 2

[1]V. I. Cheboratev, *Notes on Bishop Tikhon*, published in 1845; we quote from the periodical *Pravoslavnoe Obozrenie*, M., 1861, vol. 5, pp. 299-334, in which they were reprinted.
[2]Amvrossy (Ornatsky), *The History of the Russian Hierarchy*, M., 1804-12, 7 vols.

Solovyev, *History of Russia*, vol. 4, part 20, p. 1511, Complete Collection of Laws, No. 7070.

P. Pekarsky, *Science and Literature in Russia under Peter the Great*, 2 vols., SPB., 1862, vol. 1, ch. 6; N. A. Lebedev, *A Historical Survey of the Organization of the Schools and learned Societies which contributed to the Education of the Russian People 1025 to 1855*, SPB., 1874, p. 165; p. 45.
[3]M. Sementzovsky, *Brothers Likhudi*, SPB., 1899, pp. 435 + liii.
[4]Amvrossy, *The History of the Russian Hierarchy*, M., pp. 589-626.
[5]S. Smirnov, *The History of the Moscow Slavo-Greco-Latin Academy*, M., 1885, pp. 428; p. 98.
[6]S. N. Ponomarev, in *Dukhovny Vestnik*, Kharkov, 1862, vol. 3, p. 498.
[7]*Novgorod Governmental Journal*, 1861, Nos. 2, 3. We discovered in Dubnov, "Materials for Ecclesiastical Life under Nicholas I," printed in the *Sobraniya Russkogo Istoricheskogo Obshchestva*, SPB., 1902, vol. 113, p. 71,

an identical story with, as its hero, Vladimir, Bishop of Kazan and Svijazhsk, also a seminarist of Novgorod and member of the Synod in 1828 and 1839.

[8]Prince Y. P. Shakhovskoy, *Memoirs*, 2 vols., M., 1910.

[9]V. A. Bil'basov, *History of Catherine the Second*, Berlin, 1900, 2 vols.

[10]Makary (Archimandrite), *Description of the Novgorod Archbishop's House*, SPB., 1857, pp. 148; pp. 23-5.

[11]Filaret (Gumilevsky), *Survey of Russian Religious Literature*, 2 vols., Kharkov, 1859-61, vol. 1.

[12]Amvrossy (Ornatsky), *op. cit.*; Makary (Bulgakov), *The History of the Kiev Academy*, SPB., 1843, p. 226; V. Askochensky, *Kiev with its most Ancient School—the Academy*, Kiev, 1856, 2 vols.; vol. 1, pp. 133-46. Cf. notes on Amvrossy (Popel); Innokenty (Migalevich).

[13]Dimitry (Tuptalo, Bishop of Rostov), *Diary*, M., 1784: "God gave these versifiers printing presses, money, zeal and free time. Things of little use come out into the world." A poet of talent, scholar and hagiographer, Dimitry lamented the lack of reliable Church history, yet himself traditionally took Greek mythology as his starting-point for Christian apologetics.

John Maksimovich, a Kiev monk (d. 1715), left not only a rhymed alphabet, but also theological lectures and the Lord's Prayer in verse.

The paradox of mythology prevailing in the seminaries and of some men being ordained before they reached the stage of theological studies struck a Kiev student, Paissy (Velichkovsky, 1722-94), as scandalous paganism. He ran away from school, took refuge in the monastery of Mount Athos and eventually became the translator of ancient ascetic and mystical writings and a promoter of contemplative monasticism.

[14]Makary (Archimandrite), *Description of the Novgorod Yuriev Monastery*, M., 1858, pp. 113; p. 58 indicates that this copy was preserved together with that of the sixteenth-century Gospels.

[15]D. I. Abramovich, *Investigation of the Kievo-Pechersky Paterik as a Historico-literary Monument*, SPB., 1903, edit. of *Izvestijia Otdelenija Russkogo Yazyka*, vols. 6, 7.

[16]G. Skovoroda, *Works in Verse and Prose*, SPB., 1861, Song 27.

[17]V. S. Ikonnikov, *The Essay on Russian Historiography*, 2 vols., 4 books, Kiev, 1891-1905. On Novgorod, vol. 2, book I, ch. 7, pp. 601-747. See also note on Berynda.

[18]S. Smirnov, *op. cit.*, pp. 101 and 136-8.

[19]P. A. Gildebrandt, *Dictionaries of the New Testament*, in *Pamiatniki Drevnosti*, 1881.

[20]A. Lebedev (Priest), *Saint Tikhon Zadonsky*, SPB., 1865, pp. 331; quotes on p. 17, the Acts of the Archives of the Synod, No. 356, 751.

[21]It was written in Latin and remained in MSS. Amvrossy (Ornatsky) made great use of it.

[22]Solovyev, Book 5, t. 22, p. 491, quoting the Journal of the Senate of October 5, 1752.

[23]Chebotarev, p. 307.

[24]Chebotarev, p. 309.

[25]*Russian Encyclopedia*, F. A. Brockhaus and I. A. Efron, SPB., t. XXXIII, p. 299, gives the names of three Tikhons venerated by the Orthodox—Bishop of Amaphynt in Cyprus, 425; a Russian hermit of Kaluga round whom grew a community—Tikhono-Uspensky, 1492; and a soldier from Lithuania who became a monk in Moscow in 1482, and retired to the River Lukha, where after his death a monastery was founded. Edited by E. I. Konovalova, *The*

Saint Healers and Intercessors, M., 1902, 2nd edition. See on "Tikhon of Cyprus." Runkevich, *op. cit.*, p. 926, makes us conclude that Sokolov was named in the memory of St. Tikhon of Amaphynt, for he mentions that in 1860 the Metropolitan of St. Petersburg was renovating his house and laid foundations to his domestic chapel on June 16, day of St. Tikhon of Amaphynt, which coincided with that of Tikhon, Bishop of Voronezh, whose canonization was then being discussed.

[26] Makary (Archimandrite), *Gabriel Petrov*, SPB., 1857, p. 146; Runkevich, *op. cit.*, pp. 610 ff. and 810 ff.

[27] Platon (Levshin), *Autobiographical Notes*, served as basis for I. M. Snegirev, *Life* (Zhitije) *of Platon, Metropolitan of Moscow*, M., 1835; same anonymously in M., 1822; lastly, *Life* (Zhiz'n) *of the Moscow Metropolitan Platon*, M., 1856, 2 vols. See also *The Russian Life in Memoirs of Contemporaries, Eighteenth century*, edited by Melgunova, I. P. Sidorov and K. V. Sivkov, M., 1914, pp. 431; t. I, p. 17, gives Platon's *Notes*.

[28] L. I. Denisov, *The Orthodox Monasteries of the Russian Empire*, M., 1908, pp. 984; pp. 819 ff.; Amvrossy (Ornatsky), t. 5, p. 419; Makary (Bulgakov), *The History of the Russian Church*, SPB., 1857-83, 12 vols.; Anonymous, *The Description of the Monasteries of the Russian Empire, with the addition of the Historical Information on the existing Dioceses*, M., 1882, pp. 208; p. 49; V. Ikonnikov, *Maxim the Greek*, Kiev, 1910, pp. 604; p. 21.

[29] A. Lebedev, p. 28, gives the Bishop of Smolensk the name Epiphany, repeating thus the mistake made by Chebotarev. No such name is on the lists of the period. See Stroev, *Registers of the Hierarchs and of the Heads of the Monasteries of the Russian Church*, SPB., 1877, in 1056 + 68 columns. The mistake had been also pointed out by Hieromonk Sergy in *Christianskoe Chtenie*, 1881, vol. I, pp. 220-3.

[30] Runkevich, *op. cit.*

Chapter 3

[1] *La cour de Russie il y-a cent ans, 1725-83* (Extraits des dépêches des Ambassadeurs anglais et français), Berlin, 1868, pp. 422; pp. 200-17. Anonymous (the editor is known to be A. Turgenev).

[2] Makary, *Description of the Novgorod*, etc., pp. 67, 69; cf. note on Gabriel.

[3] M. S. Popov, *Arseny Matzeevich, the Metropolitan of Rostov and Yaroslavl*, SPB., 1905, pp. xix + 264; p. 146; Augustin Golitsin. *Biography of Arseny Matzeevich*, Leipzig 1863, p. 28. (The date of Arseny's death is given as 1772 and 1780.) Cf. *Varlaam*.

[4] Lebedev, p. 34, footnote, suddenly disclaims some vague rumors of disfavor. He quotes on nomination Archives of the Synod, No. 150, 1763.

[5] Ridinger, "Materials for the History and Statistics of the city Yeletz," in *Russki Archiv*, 1866, pp. 346-77; N. Batalin, "On Voronezh," in *Moskvitianin*, 1841, part 1, No. 2, pp. 629-33; Solovyev, bk. 6, vol. 26, esp. p. 121; Ya. Grot, "From a Travel to Voronezh," in *Vestnik Evropy*, 1870, bk. 6, pp. 141-159; S. F. Platonov, *Boris Godunov*, Praha, 1924, pp. 276; cf. note p. 223, *Voronezh*.

[6] A. S. Pavlov, *Historical Treatise on the Secularization of Church Lands in Russia, Fifteenth to Sixteenth Century*, Odessa, 1871, p. 167; *Ecclesiastical*

Statute, SPB., 1764, p. 129; Fon-Vizin, "Notes of an Eyewitness," in *Russkaya Biblioteka*, t. 9, Leipzig, 2nd ed., 1860, pp. 178; p. 45; cf. an eighteenth-century satire coming from a supporter of secularization in *Russkaya Starina*, 1881, t. 32, *Weeping of the Kiev Monks*: "Though in Lord Christ is firm our faith, in his words we little direct our steps"; A. A. Kisevetter, *Historical Sketches*, M., 1912, pp. 502; p. 269.

[7] Anonymous, in *Pribavlenyia k Tvorenijam sviatykh otzev v russkikh perevodakh*, M., 1862, part 2; *Labors of Tikhon* I, *Bishop of Voronezh, in administering his flock*. The dates are given from this article. It had also been used by Lebedev.

[8] *Works*, t. 8, p. 38, and t. 7, p. 149.

[9] This law was abolished in 1767 for priests and in 1771 for deacons. Ivan Znamensky, *The Position of the Clergy in the Reign of Catherine II and Peter I*, 1888, p. 184.

[10] A home-made drink brewed with rye or sometimes with bogberries (cranberries).

[11] Some Orthodox monks ("skhimnik") make the "great profession," i.e. renewed vows of very strict asceticism. They are given, at this profession, a new name.

[12] *Works*, t. 14, p. 179, *Letters*.

[13] *Prilozheniya* gives the date December 29, 1765, Lebedev gives October 24 and 30.

[14] *Prilozheniya* gives the name Lubianovsky. We keep to the spelling of the Metropolitan Evgeny, who supplies further details.

[15] *Works*, t. 1, pp. 35 ff.

[16] *Christianskoe Chtenie*, 1834, part 1, p. 314, *Moskvitianin*, 1851—communicated by I. M. Snegirev. We preserve these initials in the hope that more light may subsequently be thrown on the person concerned. One might also translate "Cumazhka" figuratively as "mean, or unworthy writing."

[17] *Works*, t. 1, p. 12. Trubin acted as a catechist from 1765 till 1769; he became protopriest of the Voronezh cathedral; died in March 1812.

[18] Yatzimirsky in the *Russian Encyclopedia* (Brockhaus and Efron) records contradictory opinions on the origin and character of this festival and deity. It might be of interest for a specialist to compare the rites of the Yarilo festival with those displayed in the west on St. Urban's day (not mentioned by the article in the *Encyclopedia*).

[19] *Works*, t. 3, 249-55. Delivered in the Voronezh cathedral of the Annunciation and read throughout the parishes of the diocese.

[20] Lebedev, p. 94, takes it from Ivan Efimov; the latter links the incident in the village Khlebnoe with the cattle-plague in the same village several years later when the peasants remembered having offended their Bishop and went to Zadonsk, where he then lived in retirement, to beg him "to take away the curse." Tikhon is said to have been greatly perturbed by the thought that he might have been suspected of "cursing" any one.

[21] V. N. Vitevsky, *The Schism in the Ural Host and the relation to it of the ecclesiastical and civil authorities in the eighteenth and nineteenth centuries*, Kazan, 1878, 2 parts.

[22] S. Solovyev, *History*, vol. 25, p. 121.

[23] Lebedev, p. 94.

[24] A. Ioannov (alias A. I. Zhuravlev), *The full historical information aboiut the ancient Strigol'niks and the new Schismatics called Old Ritualists*, pp. 345, M., 1890 (written in 1789, first edition, SPB., 1799), p. 200.

[25] *Prilozheniya* ..., p. 221.
[26] S. G. Svatikov, *Russia and the Don*, Vienna, 1924, pp. viii + 592; p. 175.
[27] Ioannov, *op. cit.*, p. 288, quotes an unknown Old Believer who gives the list of the high clergy approached by them. The episode of Tikhon is not dated, but the narrative keeps to a chronological order and puts him on the list after the Bishop of Georgia in 1766 or 1767. It is not improbable that this attempt was made at the Tolshevo monastery, which was known for its sympathies to the Old Belief. Tikhon had then just retired from the diocese; some rumors ascribed his retirement to an order from the Empress, and many knew that he missed his former active life. The view that this took place in Tolshevo about 1768 is also supported by N. I. Subbotin, *The Origin of the so-called Austrian or Belokrinizk hierarchy among the Old Believers*, M., 1874, pp. 512; note on p. 40, from edition 1895-9. *Works* (Evgeny), vol. I, p. 28, refers this episode to the time when Tikhon was in Zadonsk, which is repeated by Lebedev, p. 164; according to Chebotarev, Tikhon visited Tolshevo in 1771 and in 1776; P. T. Mel'nikov, *An Essay on the Priestly Branch, Notes on the Russian Raskol*, 1880, pp. 277-8, is inclined to think it happened in 1782, when some Old Believers were making an attempt at reunion. This seems to us unlikely, as in such a case they would have directly approached the Synod. Moreover, Tikhon was already ill at this date.
[28] *Works*, t. 2, p. 75.
[29] Ridinger, *op. cit.*, p. 371, "from Yeletz, in 1767; Alexander and Vassily Bibikov; tradesman Gregory Rostovtzev, freeholder Michail Davidov"; cf. Shirley 1767, 24 aout, in *La cour de la Russie*, p. 257, "L'assemblée des états de l'Empire ... est à present la grande occupation ... Les Russes ne pensent pas à autre chose. ... C'est par ces mesures et autres semblables ... que l'autorité de l'impératrice s'accroit chaque jour ... cette assemblée est loin d'être un contrepoids au pourvoir despotique. ..."
[30] Ridinger, pp. 346 ff.
[31] *Christianskoe Chtenie*, October 1833, p. 62. Also reproduced in *Life of St. Tikhon. ... with addition. ...* M. 1861, p. 43. Not included in the *Works*. From the copy sent from Maloarchangelsk, the original "according to the testimony of the person who sent it to the Magazine was in the hands of I.I.R." (We have not been able to find out whom these initials represent.)
[32] It is related in M. Evgeny's narrative. The biographers, after the canonization, thought the incident undignified, and spoke vaguely about "the impolite landowner answered meekly by the bishop." The story of the belfry was told us by Mrs. G. F., herself a descendant of the family K.
[33] A. E. Fersman, *From the History of the Culture of the Stone in Russia*, M. L., 1946, p. 73.
[34] t. 3, pp. 110 ff.; cf. our chapter 6, p. 106.
[35] D. Rovinsky, *A detailed Dictionary of Russian Engraved Portraits*, SPB., 1886-9, 4 vols.; vol. 3, col. 2037-8: "He was banished to the Tolshevo monastery of the province of Voronezh for the accusatory sermon pronounced by him in the royal palace." This piece of information is confusing, for there were no royal palaces in Voronezh; moreover, Tikhon had asked to be released from his duties more than once. Must this be regarded as a consequence of his accusatory sermon on the Assumption of the Virgin Mary? Or does it synchronize different events and perhaps refer to some past pronouncement or some denunciation of him earlier, in St. Petersburg?
[36] t. 3, pp. 87, 88. *On Theft and Robbery*; t. 5, pp. 144, 147, *Offence*.
[37] t. 14, p. 180.

CHAPTER 4

[1]"Unworthy Bishop."
[2]Stroev, p. 846. The name of the superior was Seraphim, hegoumen since 1764.
[3]Rovinsky, vol. 3, col. 2037. Cf. Lebedev, in a note on p. 109 objects to the rumors which connected the retirement of Tikhon with his protest against the secularization of monastic property.
[4]Stroev, p. 847. The names of the superiors during Tikhon's retirement were: Archimandrites Niphont, 1766-74, and Theodossy, 1775-7; Hegoumen Samuel, 1777-84.
[5]*Works*, t. 1, 65 and 71.
[6]*Work*, 2, p. 158, *Meditations on the Psalms.*
[7]*Ibid.*, t. 2, p. 152; same t. 4, pp. 183, 191, 192; t. 14, p. 178.
[8]t. 11, pp. 21-3. *Spiritual Treasure.*
[9]D. S. Mohrenschildt, *Russia in the Intellectual life of Eighteenth-century France*, Columbia Univ. Press, 1936; Marmontel, "Belisaire," in *Œuvres Completes*, t. 7, Paris, 1819. The dedication was a matter of chance; the translation was begun by the Empress and several of her suite in 1768, during a journey, while at Tver, where Gabriel was then Bishop. The actual dedication was written by Shuvalov.
[10]S. Chetverikov, *Paissy Velichkovsky, the Elder of Moldavia*, edited by the journal *Put' Zhizni* in Estonia, 1938, 2 vols.
[11]"Iversky" means a Georgian icon of the Virgin Mary. Makary, *Gabriel* ... note on p. 63.
[12]Significantly, he wrote in an (undated) letter to a monk: "Such anxiety is a temptation which drags us back into the world. Be firm. Say: 'even were I to die, I shall not leave this place'." t. 1, p. 46 .
[13]Chebotarev, pp. 318-20.
[14]Chebotarev, p. 318.
[15]Lebedev, p. 146, notes, says that this correspondence "was not included in the collection of his letters," but does not mention what became of it. We have not been able to find out anything about it. In the early nineteenth century there were three disciples of Paissy in Voronezh: cf. Chetverikov, vol. 2, pp. 40-2.
[16]*Works*, t. 11, pp. 127-31; *The Spiritual Treasure.*
[17]In *Moskvitianin*, 1843, bk. 4, 273: "The cases of the fire and of the deception were told to the author—who lived in Yeletz in 1812, on account of the Napoleonic invasion, and who visited Zadonsk—by Colonel B., a friend of Bishop Tikhon, who had chosen a life of retirement. This educated and devout man lived in Zadonsk over forty years till his death in 1813." It seems possible that this B. was Nikander Bekhteiev.
[18]t. 14, 100-1.
[19]*Works*, t. 1, p. 35.
[20]Th. V. Blagovidov, *Ober-Procurators of the Synod in the Eighteenth Century and the First Half of the Nineteenth Century*, Kazan, 1899, pp. 449; 2nd ed., 1900, p. 267.
[21]Lebedev I, p. 122, also in Chebotarev.
[22]*Flesh and Spirit; On the love of one's neighbor*, vol. 6, p. 229; Lebedev, note on p. 122. Tikhon's relatives remained in humble condition. His brother Efimy was ordained deacon in the Novgorod diocese. Efimy's son Philip went

to Voronezh Seminary and was deacon in Lipovka; his son was a verger in Lipovka. In 1865 he retired and the post passed to his son Ivan. Philip's elder son Alexander became a subdeacon in the village Pushkarskoe. St. Tikhon also had a niece of whom he was very fond; she died before him.

[23] Anonymous, *Life of the newly revealed Saint of God, with an addition from his works*, M., 1862, 2nd ed., pp. 214; p. 50.

[24] Cheboratev, pp. 312, 316, 317.

[25] His Russian expression "umnoe delanie" can suggest the practice of mental prayer or "prayer of Jesus" but there is not enough evidence to affirm this.

[26] Chebotarev, pp. 312-13.

[27] *Works*, t. 14, p. 177.

[28] Lebedev, p. 160.

[29] Amvrossy (Zertiss-Kamensky).

[30] In Tikhon's life-time there were several Pretenders: in 1738 the so-called Alexis Petrovich was executed; rumors went about concerning the liberation of Ivan VI, and on September 28, 1764, the officer Mirovich, who tried to restore him to the throne, was broken on the wheel. There was also the Princess Tarakanova, who claimed to be the daughter of the Empress Elizabeth, and, finally, Pugachev.

[31] *Works*, t. 14, Letter No. 32, p. 177. It must have been written in 1778 or 1777. Philip had been in the Voronezh Seminary, "up to Philosophy"; it was introduced in 1777 (cf. Amvrossy Ornatsky, t. I, p. 433). He was then ordained deacon at Lipovka. The Bekhteievs wished to see him become priest on their estates, but Tikhon considered that he had not the spiritual stature which would enable him "to lift up the weight of priesthood" (Lebedev, p. 122).

[32] *Works*, t. 14, Letter No. 31, pp. 175-6. The "well-known" must have been a reference to the ever-changing favorites of Catherine II.

[33] Lebedev, p. 157.

[34] This must have happened after 1775, when Tikhon III (Malinovsky) became Bishop of Voronezh; possibly after the letter to Ivan Mikhailovich about Lipovka. If we place it in 1778, it corroborates the story in *Moskvitianin*, and makes it fairly clear that B. was Nikander. He died in 1816 (cf. Lebedev, p. 157—*Moskvitianin* gives the date as 1813).

[35] Both episodes are recorded in *Voskresnoe Chtenie*, No. 37, 1838.

[36] Lebedev guarantees the likeness of this portrait and of the reproduction from it which he used as frontispiece to his book (though the halo was obviously added to the portrait after the canonization). The approximate date is inferred from the fact that Platon was already Archbishop at the time he sent the artist. But Lebedev supposes it was during the last three years of Tikhon's life (p. 331). He spells the name of the artist Basov. We accept the reading Sergy Baskakov, for it must have been the same artist who painted Platon Levshin. Cf. D. A. Rovinsky, vol. 4, p. 618.

Chapter 5

[1] *The Treasure*, ed. 1825, bk. 3, Nos. 75, 76.

[2] Chebotarev, pp. 312, 323; cf. *Works*, t. 6, p. 228.

[3] t. 2, p. 168. *Flesh and Spirit. Habit conquered by habit.*

[4]t. 11, p. 21. *Treasure*, No. 7. *Poison hidden in man.*
[5]t. 3, p. 49, *Sermon on the Exaltation of the Cross.*
[6]Chebotarev, p. 313; cf. *Works*, t. 1, p. 60, *Instruction to monks.*
[7]t. 8, pp. 74-82, *True Christianity.*
[8]t. 14, p. 127, *Letter* No. 18, *On retirement of one who seeks salvation.*
[9]t. 2, p. 154.
[10]Cheboratev, p. 311.
[11]*Moskvitianin, op. cit.*, 1843, pp. 431, 471. The story was related by "Colonel B," whom we take to be Nikander Bekhteiev. It is necessary to realize the difference of detail which seems to indicate that this is another occurrence, and not the Cheboratev story modified by the narrator.
[12]Cheboratev, pp. 314-15; cf. *Voskresnoe Chtenie*, No. 37.
[13]In *Moskvitianin*, 1850, No. 18, p. 17. The date and the name of the addressee are not given. This is corroborated by Efimov as an incident that happened during the second year of Tikhon's stay at Zadonsk.
[14]*Works*, t. 2, pp. 162, 163. The title suggests Joseph Hall's influence.
[15]t. 1, pp. 74, 75, *Exhortation and advice to a monk about despondency.*
[16]t. 7, p. 199, *Prayer when thoughts trouble the soul and incite it to despair of the mercy of God.*
t. 7, p. 30, *On faith.*
t. 6, p. 296, *A saving example of devotion against despondency.*
t. 1, p. 74, *On despondency.*
t. 2, p. 105, *That a man should not despair but rising should fight.*
t. 1, p. 155, *On the duty of clergy.*
[17]t. 14, pp. 153-7, *Letter* No. 23, abbreviated.
[18]t. 6, p. 188-97.
[19]*Works*, t. 1, p. 42.
[20]t. 15, *Letter* No. 21.
[21]t. 9, p. 143, *True Christianity—On the comforting fruit of holy faith.*
[22]t. 14, p. 81, *Letter* No. 10, *On those who wish to be rich.*
[23]t. 3, p. 60 (edition of 1825, *The Treaure*, in four books).
[24]t. 10, pp. 181-3, No. 46, *Desire.*
[25]t. 10, pp. 98-111, No. 28, *A Feast.*
[26]*Treasure*, ed. 1825: Bk. 2, p. 198, No. 44: *Rest.*
[27]Bk. 3, No. 20 in *Treasure*; cf. pp. 262, 265, *Love of God.*
[28]Bk. 3, p. 199, No. 14, *What is great.*
[29]t. 14, p. 125, *Letter* No. 17.
[30]t. 14, p. 174, *The Teacher*, No. 21; cf. t. 11, 169-80, No. 49.
[31]t. 9, pp. 160-2, *On the comforting fruit of holy faith.*

CHAPTER 6

[1]t. 1, p. 145, *Christian Instruction*; St. Augustine quoted in *Works*, t. 6, pp. 86, 94; t. 7, p. 38; t. 8, p. 146; t. 14, p. 64; St. Jerome, t. 8, p. 225.
[2]St. Ignatius mentioned in t. 1, p. 43, *To monks.*
St. Antony spoken of in it t. 3, p. 58.
On John Damascene, t. 7, pp. 18, 20, 212.
On St. Basil: t. 3, p. 62, *Sermon on New Year* 1765; t. 6, pp. 145, 247; t. 14, p. 148, *Letter* No. 21; t. 1, p. 101.

t. 5, pp. 134-5, quoting Basil on Psalms 1 and 59, St. Basil's *Word in Lakhiza*; t. 6, p. 94 *On humility*; t. 6, p. 169, *On thankfulness*; t. 7, p. 135, *Short Rule*, question 195; t. 6, pp. 173, 179, *On prayer*.

t. 8, p. 144, Book 1, *On Baptism*; t. 14, p. 57, *On the eucharist*.

[3] Curiously enough, the *Diary* of St. Dimitry was first found in the library of the Yeletz monastery. Cf. *Istorichesky Vestnik*, 1882, vol. ix, p. 447, note.

[4] The difficulty lies in that great many early Russian documents are still a matter of controversy as to date, authorship and origin. One has to turn mainly to the research of the philologists.

A. I. Ponomarev, *Monuments of Ancient Russian Ecclesiastical Didactic Literature*, SPB., 1894, 3 vols. See on Sviatoslav, *Collection* (Izbornik) of 1076 and 1073. Both were long considered original Russian documents; they descend from the Byzantine work of Gennadius, *A Hundred Sayings*, and from its Bulgarian copy of the tenth century made for the Tsar Simeon.

A. N. Veselovsky, *Research in the Field of the Spiritual Songs*, 1879-83, Academy.

S. H. Cross, *The Russian Primary Chronicle*, Harvard University Press, 1930 (contains the Kiev *Paterikon* and the life of St. Theodossy).

E. V. Petukhov, *Serapion of Vladimir, a Russian Thirteenth-century Preacher*, in *Zapiski Istorico-Philologicheskogo Faculteta*, SPB., 1888.

I. Sreznevsky, *St. Cyril as a Writer*, SPB., Academy, 1854.

Evgeny (Bishop of Astrakhan and Ekaterinoslav), ed. St. Cyril of Turov, *Works*, Kiev, 1880, pp. cli, 296.

V. N. Peretts, *Research and Materials for the History of old Ukrainian literature*, Leningrad, 1926 (on Vishnevsky).

M. S. Hrushevsky, *From the History of religious thought in the Ukraine*, Lvov, 1925 (in Ukrainian language).

M. Viller et A. Malvy, *La Confession Orthodoxe de Pierre Moghila, approuvée par les Patriarches Grecs du dix-septième siècle*, Orientalia Christiana, vol. X, No. 39, 1927.

A. I. Sobolevsky, *Translated Literature of the Muscovite Russia of the Fifteenth to Seventeeth Centuries*, SPB., Academy, 1903.

[5] Antony (Vadkovsky, Archbishop of Finland), *From the History of Christian Preaching*, SPB., 1895, pp. 391.

P. Nikolsky, Priest, "Russian Preaching in the Fifteenth and Sixteenth Centuries," in the *Zhurnal Ministerstva Narodnogo Prosvescheniya*, 1868.

[6] N. Tikhonravov, *Works*, t. 1. *The Apocryphal Books of Ancient Russia*. From the collection of 1640 of the Trinity Lavra, signed by a monk Makary.

[7] A. S. Arkhangelsky, *St. Nil Sorsky and Vassian Patrikeev*, Academy, 1881, 1882; St. Nil, *The Rule*, edited by Bishop Iustin (Editions of the Panteleimon Monastery), 1902; Vassian Patrikeev's "Polemical Writings," in *Pravoslavny Sobesednik*, 1863, Sept.-Oct.; Ikonnikov, *Maxim the Greek*, p. 21; p. 382, quotes Maxim's *Converse of the Soul with the Body*; p. 445, *Edifying Chapters*; p. 482, *Debate about monastic life*, the names of the disputants being Philoktimon who is a lover of possessions and Aktimon who is without property.

[8] Maxim's *Works* were published in Greek in Kazan, 1860-97; in Russian at Sergievsky Posad, 1910; both not found in the libraries I consulted. I had to quote from V. Ikonnikov, *op. cit.*, p. 427, Maxim's *Edifying Chapters*; V. Zhmakin, *Metropolitan Daniel and his Works*, M. 1881; S. G. Vilinsky, *Epistles of the Elder Artemy*, Odessa, 1906.

[9]Consett, *Present State and Regulations of the Church in Russia*, London, 1729, t. 1, contains the *Spiritual Regulation*.

G. Florovsky, *The Ways of the Russian Theology*, Paris, 1937, pp. 574. See pp. 82-5. This work contains an extensive bibliography which has been of great assistance in the present research.

[10]R. W. Blackmore, *The Doctrine of the Russian Church*, being the *Primer Spelling-book* (drawn up by Theophan Prokopovich, then Archbishop of Pleskoff). *The Shorter and Longer Catechisms* (drawn up by Philaret, Metropolitan of Moscow) and a *Treatise on the duty of Parish Priests* (composed by George Konissky, Bishop of Moghileff). Transl. from the Slavono-Russian Originals by the Rev. R. W. Blackmore, pp. xxviii + 288, A. Brown and Co., Aberdeen, 1845.

Platon (Levshin), *The Great Catechism of the Holy Catholic, Apostolic and Orthodox Church*, translated by J. T. Seccombe, London, 1867.

I. Grigorovich, Priest, edited G. Konissky's *Works*, SPB., 1835, 2 vols. This book was favorably reviewed by A. S. Pushkin in *Sovremennik*, No. 1, Jan.-March, 1836; see *Works*, M. 1936, 6 vols. t. 5, p. 107. For the books read by Pushkin, see *The Works of Pushkin Commission*, M. 1935.

[11]*Joseph Halli Exoniensis Episcopi Vel Meditatiunculae Subitanae* (the town of Exeter was mistake for Oxford, and he is indicated in Russian works as "Gall, Bishop of Oxford"). His *Meditations* were published in Russian translation M. 1786.

[12]A. Kotovich, *Ecclesiastical Censorship in Russia*, 1799-1855, SPB., 1909, pp. xvi, 604, xiii (on further destinies of Arndt's book). Also Skabichevsky, pp. 12 and 82.

Bibliographicheskie Zapiski, 1861, containing an article on the Russian publications in Halle has been lost through enemy action.

The late N. A. Berdyaev knew of my intention to write on St. Tikhon. In a letter he advised me to stress this link of Tikhon with the pietists and the humanitarian spirit of the eighteenth century. It does not seem possible to me to ascribe to Arndt a more profound influence.

[13]t. 2, pp. 68-75 *Flesh and Spirit*; t. 3, pp. 79-87.
[14]t. 9, pp. 88-100, *On Christian Duty*.
[15]t. 3, pp. 84.
[16]t. 6, pp. 323-62, *On mercy to one's neighbor*.
[17]t. 1, pp. 91 ff. *On the duty of parents*; cf. p. 168; t. 2, p. 59, *Flesh and Spirit*; t. 3, pp. 157-60, *Brief instruction on Christian education*; t. 9, pp. 51, 53, *On the duties of parents*.
[18]t. 6, pp. 248-9, *On showing mercy to one's neighbor*; t. 14, Letters 9 and 10, pp. 71 and 80.
[19]t. 6, pp. 257-61.
[20]t. 1, p. 173, *On the duties of Rich and Poor*.
[21]t. 5, p. 153, *Love of honors and glory*.
[22]t. 3, pp. 110-12, *Sermon on the day of the Assumption*.
[23]t. 10, p. 1; t. 4, p. 158, *The Master calling his servant*; t. 3, p. 153, *Sermon*; t. 1, pp. 170 ff., *Addition on the mutual Duties of Christians*.
[24]t. 10, p. 207, *Treasure*.
[25]t. 14, p. 175, *Letter* No. 31; t. 1, p. 133, *Christian Instruction*.
[26]t. 12, p. 41, *Treasure*; cf. t. 1, p. 15.
[27]*Private Letters* (1830 ed.), No. 25.
[28]t. 9, p. 17, *On the Christian Ruler*.
[29]t. 10, p. 166, *Treasure*, No. 41, *A man called to Judgement*.

[30]t. 10, No. 47, *Happiness*.
[31]t. 6, p. 152.
[32]t. 14, pp. 169-72, *Letter* No. 29; t. 13, pp. 101-5, No. 26, *The Belly*.
[33]t. 11, p. 175, *Treasure* No. 49, *The Teacher and the disciples*; and t. 9, p. 19-26, *On the Duties of pious Monarchs*.
[34]t. 10, p. 182, *Treasure* No. 46, *Desire*.
[35]t. 9, *True Christianity*, chapter II, *On the Duties*.
[36]t. 13, p. 82, No. 19, *The Sting of the one Stung*.
[37]t. 10, p. 166.
[38]t. 9, p. 30.
[39]t. 7, p. 206, *Corporate Prayer about any Corporate Disaster*.
[40]t. 1, pp. 44 ff.
[41]t. 5, pp. 124-30, *On certain specific sins*.
[42]*Treasure* No. 15.
[43]t. 3, p. 91, *On Robbery*; t. 13, pp. 121-7; *Treasure*, No. 29, *The Robber*.
[44]t. 8, p. 38, *On listening to the word of God*; t. 7, p. 149, *Charity and Sacrifice*; cf. t. 14, *Letter* 29; and t. 8, p. 104, *On various duties*.
[45]v. 1, pp. 154 ff. *On the Duties of the Pastors*.
[46]t. 6, p. 216, *On love and grace*; and t. 14, p. 162, *Letter to a priest*.
[47]t. 6, p. 33, *On the end of good works*.
[48]*The Treasure*, ed. 1825, bk. 4, No. 9, *The Keeper*.
[49]*The Treasure*, No. 8, *Servants sent out to invite to a feast*; cf. t. 9, p. 41, *On the Duties of Pastors*.
[50]t. 1, pp. 29, 30, 47.
[51]t. 1, p. 72, *To the Monks*, p. 130; t. 2, p. 10.
[52]t. 3, pp. 16-30, *A Word on the Gospel teaching*.
[53]t. 3, pp. 6-109, *Sermon on the Introduction of the Virgin*.
[54]t. 3, pp. 164-7, *On the honor and dignity of the true Christian*.
[55]t. 2, p. 159; t. 1, p. 87, *To the Flock*.
[56]t. 4, pp. 1-22, *On the Word of God*; t. 2, p. 117, *On the means of useful reading*.
[57]t. 4, p. 189, *An occasion and its spiritual interpretation*; t. 6, p. 195, *On Hope*.
[58]t. 5, p. 49, *On blindness and sin*; p. 54, *Treasure* No. 34.
[59]t. 4, pp. 131-41, *On the comforting fruit of the holy Faith*.
[60]*Treasure* No. 30, *A Deaf Man*.
[61]t. 6, p. 209, *On Prayer*, cf. *Treasure* No. 15, *King's subject*.
[62]t. 4, pp. 62, 103.
[63]t. 4, p. 20, *On the Word*; t. 6, p. 57, etc.
[64]t. 1, pp. 130, 187; t. 4, p. 107; t. 7, pp. 56-100; *On holy Baptism, ibid.*, p. 302, *On the duty of a Christian to God*; *ibid.*, p. 143, and *Treasure*, bk. 4, p. 25, *Whom shall I love but thee?*; *Treasure*, bk. 3, p. 210, *Follow me*; p. 156, *The Ship*.
[65]*The Spiritual Treasure*, ed. 1825, bk. 2, p. 4; bk. 3, p. 13; Nos. 1, 4, 5, 6.
[66]t. 1, p. 156, *On the Duties of Pastors*.
[67]t. 8, p. 293, *On the Duties of Pastors*.
[68]t. 1, p. 143, *Christian Instruction*.
[69]t. 8, pp. 1-8, *On Repentance*.
[70]t. 6, p. 17, *On Consolation*.
[71]*Treasure, He has done his work and is gone*. Repeated in *Private Letters*, No. 19, t. 1, p. 109-10, *The Figures of Repentance*.
[72]t. 1, pp. 25, 26, *On the Duties of the Clergy*; p. 88.

[73] On the eucharist see t. 1, pp. 19, 27, 79; t. 6, 289 ff.; t. 14, 36, 57, 69; t. 9, 91; t. 8, 142, 182; t. 11, 107.
[74] *True Christianity*, t. 6, p. 303, *On the End of good works*.
[75] t. 2, p. 222; cf. *Treasure*, bk. 3, p. 65.
[76] t. 8, pp. 154-5.
[77] *Treasure*, bk. 3, *He has done his work and is gone*.
[78] t. 1, pp. 122-5; cf. t. 6, p. 3.
[79] t. 6, p. 281, *On the end of good works*.
[80] t. 6, pp. 281-90, *On the end of good works*; cf. 7, 130-4.
[81] t. 7, pp. 150-74, *The imitation of God*.
[82] t. 6, pp. 115-19, *On loving God*.
[83] t. 1, pp. 130, 136, *Christian Instruction*; cf. t. 7, p. 64.
[84] t. 2, p. 129, *On Almsgiving*; cf. t. 2, p. 142, *Sermon on the Incarnation*; t. 9, p. 96, *On the dignity of a Christian*; t. 1, p. 25, *Instruction to the clergy*; t. 7, p. 283, *On faith in Christ*.
[85] t. 1, p. 141, *Christian Instruction*; t. 5, pp. 51, 84, *On sin; on pride*.
[86] t. 9, p. 97, *On Christian Dignity*; cf. t. 14, pp. 157-9, *Letter 24, Of the true Christian*; t. 15, p. 207, *Letters* Nos. 90, 91, *Implications of the humility of Christ*.
[87] t. 7, pp. 11, ff., *On faith*; t. 4, p. 138, *An occasion and . . .*; *Letters*, ed. 1830, No. 54, p. 183.
[88] t. 1, p. 63, *A brief instruction: How to fulfil Christian duty*; t. 3, pp. 3, 5, 13, *Various Sermons*; t. 1, p. 126, *Christian Instruction*; t. 3, pp. 60, 96 ff., *Sermon on the Assumption*; t. 1, p. 30, *Instruction to the clergy*; t. 7, p. 224, *On faith in Christ*.
[89] t. 7, p. 53, *On the Holy Church*; cf. t. 8, p. 99; and *The Treasure*, No. 18, *Members of one another*; No. 21, *The Shepherd and the sheep*.
[90] t. 7, p. 325, *On the following of Christ*; cf. *Treasure* No. 5 and No. 13; t. 4, p. 44, *An Occasion and . . .*; t. 1, p. 141, *Christian Instruction*.
[91] *Private Letters*, ed. 1830, Nos. 2 and 3; t. 14, *Letter* No. 25, p. 160.
[92] *Treasure*, bk. 3, No. 20.
[93] t. 1, p. 86, *To the Flock;* t. 7, pp. 11-45, *On Faith*; t. 6, p. 289, *Conclusion*.
[94] t. 8, p. 7, *On the keeping of Faith*; t. 7, pp. 37-43, *On Faith*.
[95] t. 1, pp. 123, 144, *Instruction to Christians*; cf. *Treasure*, bk. 3, pp. 13-18 and 2, 77, 91, *On the love of enemies*.
[96] t. 3, p. 154, *On the first Christian work;* t. 6, p. 14, *On Repentance*; t. 8, pp. 46, 140, *On duty to self*; *Private Letters*, ed. 1830, p.15, Nos. 8, 9 and 11; t. 14, *On the first Christian work*; and No. 11, p. 83, *On the desire to be saved in Christ*.
[97] t. 1, pp. 106-7, *What prevents us from offending our neighbor*; t. 14, *Letter on Faith*, p. 34.
[98] t. 5, pp. 1 ff.
[99] t. 4, p. 161.
[100] t. 6, p. 289.
[101] t. 5, p. 88 *On pride*.
[102] t. 8, pp. 145-92, *What can and must move a Christian to flee from sin*.
[103] t. 4, p. 105, *An occasion and its spiritual interpretation*.
[104] t. 1, pp. 55, 61, 72, 81, 135, 136.
[105] t. 2, pp. 19-20, *Flesh and Spirit*.
[106] t. 14, No. 20, pp. 142-5; cf. *Letters*, ed. 1830, p. 321.
[107] t. 1, pp. 123, 144, *Christian Instruction*; cf. *Treasure*, ed. 1825, bk. 3, 13-18 and 2, 77, 91, *On the love of enemies*.

[108] t. 1, p. 145.
[109] t. 1, p. 61; cf. 2, 21, 42; 123; 4, 43, 117; 14, 8, 9.
[110] *Private Letter*, No. 26.
[111] *Private Letter*, No. 26.
[112] t. 2, pp. 100-3.
[113] t. 14, pp. 177 ff. *Letters*, No. 20 and 32.
[114] *Treasure*, ed. 1825, bk. 3, No. 16, p. 22.
[115] t. 4, p. 211, *An Occasion and its spiritual interpretation*.
[116] t. 2, pp. 9-10, *Flesh and Spirit*; cf. t. 14, pp. 128-42; *Letter*, No. 19.
[117] t. 1, p. 87; cf. t. 4, p. 89.
[118] t. 1, p. 83, *Brief Instruction on how to carry out Christian Duty*.
[119] t. 5, pp. 10-21.
[120] t. 1, p. 192; cf. t. 3, 161, *On Conscience*; t. 2, p. 140.
[121] t. 4, pp. 22, 24, 27, *On Wisdom*; cf. t. 6, p. 74, *On the fear of God*; t. 7, p. 113, *On the comforting fruits of the Holy Faith*.
[122] t. 6, p. 19, *On repentance*; *Treasure*, ed. 1825, bk. 2, No. 15, p. 68.
[123] t. 14, p. 115. *Letter*, No. 15, t. 2, p. 95; No. 27, t. 6, pp. 94-112, *On detachment*.
[124] t. 7, p. 231, *On belief in Christ*.
[125] t. 1, p. 135, *Christian Instruction*.
[126] t. 4, p. 84, *An Occasion and* ...
[127] t. 1, pp. 186, 66, 83, *A brief advice on how one must persevere in Christian duty*.
[128] t. 6, pp. 262-8, *On forgiveness of our neighbor's sins*.
[129] t. 1, p. 148, *Christian Instruction*.
[130] t. 7, pp. 174-83, *On Prayer*.
[131] t. 1, pp. 116-18, *Prayers from the Psalms*; pp. 138 ff., *Christian Instruction*; t. 9, pp. 131 ff., *On the converse of a Christian with God*; t. 2, pp. 121-7, *Assistance against sin*.
[132] t. 7, pp. 184-97, *The Lord's Prayer*.
[133] *Treasure*, ed. 1825, pp. 121-3, *He has done his work*.
[134] *Private Letters*, ed. 1830, p. 339, No. 119; and p. 184, No. 53; t. 14, p. 118, *Letter* No. 15.
[135] *Private Letters*, p. 21, No. 11, *What is faith?*
[136] t. 6, pp. 140-58, *On patience*.
[137] t. 14, p. 178, *Letter* No. 32.
[138] t. 4, p. 63, *An Occasion and* ...; t. 6, p. 87, *On humility*; t. 2, pp. 93, 42-3.
[139] t. 2, pp. 42-3, *Flesh and Spirit*; t. 4, pp. 116 ff., *An Occasion and* ...; t. 6, pp. 79-94, *On Humility*.
[140] t. 1, p. 72, *My advice to a Brother*; *Treasure*, bk. 3, p. 120, *He has done his work*; t. 2, p. 9.
[141] t. 4, p. 185, *An Occasion and* ...
[142] t. 2, pp. 66-8, *Flesh and Spirit*.
[143] t. 3, pp. 195-201, *Brief Exhortations*; t. 3, pp. 77-87, *On the love of God and the love of one's neighbor*.
[144] t. 3, pp. 91, 193-5, 202-4; cf. t. 4, pp. 63, 67, 85.
[145] t. 6, pp. 268-80, *Love of enemies*.
[146] t. 4, p. 175.
[147] t. 6, pp. 159-87, *On gratitude to God*; t. 8, pp. 115-25, *On diverse Christian Duties*.
[148] t. 8, p. 114, 137, *On diverse Christian Duties*; t. 9, pp. 108-13, *True*

Christianity; t. 14, p. 161, *Letter* No. 25; *Private Letters*, ed. 1830, p. 48, No. 16; cf. t. 1, pp. 54-64; t. 3, pp. 168-71, *On the Gospels*; t. 4, p. 89, *An Occasion*...
    [149]t. 4, p. 159, *An Occasion and*...; *The Treasure*, bk. 3, and several other meditations, esp. bk. 2, No. 1, 23; bk. 3, No. 2, 10; bk. 5, 28.
    [150]t. 6, pp. 170, 171, *On Thanksgiving*.
    [151]t. 4, pp. 197-8 and p. 31, *An Occasion*...

CHAPTER 7

[1]*Life*, ed. 1833, p. 91; repeated in edition of *Works*, 1860, note on p. 53.
[2]*Voskresnoe Chtenie*, No. 37.
[3]N. L. Grigorovich, *A Survey of the institution in Russia of the orthodox monasteries from the time of the Ecclesiastical Statutes, 1764-1869*, SPB., 1869, pp. 220, see pp. 194-9.
    Denisov, *Orthodox Monasteries*, p. 185.
    A. I. Del'vig, *Memoirs; Half a century of Russian Life, 1820-70*; M.-L., 2 vols., Academia, 1930; t. 1, p. 32, gives biographical details on Vikulin, a rich peasant who was granted the rank of nobility. Ibid., 1st ed. 1912-13, M., p. 8 on St. Tikhon's relics.
    [4]L. Denisov, *op. cit.*, pp. 819-22; the date of this building is unspecified: "in recent times."
    [5]*Moscow Diocesan News*, Nos. 40 and 42, of October 1871, pp. 437-8, *A Journey into the Novgorod district*.
    [6]Lebedev, p. 269, mentions Mamonov and his dream; the name, possibly misspelt from Russian handwriting, is given as Mashonov; the details and the reproduction of this picture are found in *Istorichesky Vestnik*, 1910, t. CXXL, pp. 140-9. There is little doubt that it is the same man.
    [7]*Letters of Filaret, Metropolitan of Moscow, to the Archimandrite Antony* of the Trinity-St. Sergius Lavra, 1831-67, Second Part, M. 1878, pp. 507; Letter No. 562, p. 299, of February 20, 1847. Antony was a representative of the ascetic and mystical tradition (d. 1877). The Easter hymns are sung till Ascension Day.
    [8]*Letters of Filaret, Metropolitan of Moscow, to the Archimandrite Antony*, part 2, Letter No. 38 of March 31, 1848.
    [9]ib., part 4, period covered 1857-67, pp. 227-231, March 16 and 20, 1860. Also quoted by Kotovich, *The Ecclesiastical Censorship*, note on p. 222.
    [10]ib., part 2, p. 90, Letter No. 58, November 18, 1860. Count Tolstoy, nominated Ober-Procurator in September 1856, retained this post till February 1862, when he became a member of the State Council.
    [11]Anonymous, *The recent past*, Letter to P. Simonovich, in *Pravoslavnoe Obosrenie*, M. 1883, t. 1, p. 112.
    [12]*Christianskoe Chtenie*, 1835, pt. 3, p. 212.
    [13]*Life of the newly revealed saint of God, with the addition of some fragments from his Works*, M. 1862, 2nd ed., p. 214.
    [14]In *Christianskoe Chtenie*, 1865, vol. 37, pp. 425-39, reprinted from *Church Chronicle*, published by the *Dukhovnaya Beseda*, 25 November 1861.
    [15]Anonymous, *The Narrative by an eyewitness of the opening of the incorruptible relics of the miracle worker Tikhon, Bishop of Voronezh*, August 12 and 13, 1861, in Zadonsk monastery, SPB., 1861, p. 16.

NOTES

[16]Epiphany (Nesterovsky) *Liturgics*, M. 1901, pp. 239; p. 234.

[17]Igor Smolitsch, *Leben und Lehre der Starzen*, Wien, 1936, pp. 276; p. 180.

[18]V. Kozhevnikov, "On the significance of Christian asceticism in the past and present." In *Christianskoe Chtenie*, 1909, December, p. 1551.

[19]Anonymous, *On the white and black Orthodox Clergy*, Leipzig, 1866, 2 parts; part 1, pp. 189, 195-7. This book is an important work of criticism of the Russian Church containing many contemporary accounts and documents. It is ascribed to the ecclesiastical historian, I. Moroshkin, who could not have published this work in Russia because of the ecclesiastical and secular censorship.

[20]Ib., pp. 195-7. Zadonsk and Tikhon are not named; but this same story, coming from the mouth of the cell-attendant Ivan Efimov (or ascribed to him), can be read in the *Preface* to the 10th edition of St. Tikhon's *Works*.

[21]Priest Victor Rozhdestvensky, Report, in the *Minutes of the Society of Lovers of Spiritual Enlightenment*, 1863, p. 172; also *Readings* of the same Society, M. 1865, pp. 151, 160.

[22]Julius F. Haecker, *Religion and Communism*, Chapman & Hall, London, 1933, pp. 303, 206. "The greatest scandal was the exposure of the fraudulent relics of Tikhon of Zadonsk and of St. Sergius, whose shrine was one of the most popular pilgrimage places in Russia." The author, a partisan of the régime and of this exposure, gives no account of the date or of the actual procedure. The anti-religious campaign of the early revolutionary period was carried out as an official and biased act. It would be unscientific to take part either for or against the results thus announced, short of any convincing and impartial statements. The lines cited seem somewhat confusing, for "shrine" is mentioned in singular, whereas there is a considerable geographical distance between Moscow and Zadonsk. We have sought in vain for more precision from several anti-religious publications, but found no corroboration of the story. It was obviously impossible to find abroad all the documents, or even to go through several years of the Soviet daily press publications. In any case, this posthumous destiny does not affect our main subject, which is the personality of St. Tikhon and his *Works*.

See Note on Canonization.

The church and the monastery of St. Sergius Trinity, with its theological Academy was restored by the Government to the Church in 1944; the relics of St. Sergius on July 18, 1947. See *The Journal of the Patriarchate of Moscow*, August 1947.

[23]Edited by Savva, Archbishop of Tver and Kashin, *Letters of Filaret to the Royalties and several other Persons*, Tver, 1888, in two parts; part 1, p. 68, Letter No. 39, dated St. Petersburg, October 21, 1833, in which Filaret criticizes the then Bishop of Tver, Gabriel Rozanov (1781-1858) for his oversimplified style.

[24]P. Zabyelin, *Rights and Duties of the Clergy*, Kiev, 1888, pp. 112, 114.

[25]A. Kotovich, *op. cit.*, pp. 295, 297, 300, 302, 309, 442.

[26]Unverified references from periodicals lost in the British Museum through enemy action.

[27]St. Cyril of Turov, *Works*, edited by Evgeny, Bishop of Minsk, and Turov, now Bishop of Astrakhan and Ekaterinodar (we suppose the editor to be Evgeny Kazantsev), Kiev, 1880, pp. CII, 296.

[28]A. M. Bukharev, *Apocalypsis*, Sergiev Posad, 1911, pp. 64, 444, 559. (The book was forbidden by the ecclesiastical censorship in 1862.)

[29] Innokenty (Borisov), *Works*, 12 vols. In the French translation by A. Stourdza, Paris, 1846, pp. 182, 64.

[30] Bishop Ignaty, *Works*, vol. 1, *Ascetical Essays*, 2nd ed., SPB., 1886, p. 79.

[31] Innokenty (Veniaminov-Popov), *Works*, 3 vols., collected by I. P. Barsukov, M., 1888; t. 1, pp. 25, 43, 132-7, 225.

[32] Filaret, "Letters" in the *Report of the Imperial Public Library*, SPB., 1891, p. 50, to Mme Naumova, November 1847.

[33] Andrey Krotkov, *About the Protopriest of Cronstadt, Fr. John*, M. 1903, pp. 43; p. 15. John Sergiev of Cronstadt, *Collected Works*, 7 vols., SPB., 1896; t. 3, pp. 112-15.

[34] R. Pinkerton, *Russia, or Miscellaneous Observations*, 1833, pp. 223, 358. Note misspelling "gadonsky" for "Zadonsky."

[35] William Palmer, *Notes of a Visit to the Russian Church in the years 1840-1*. Selected and arranged by Cardinal Newman, Kegan, Paul & Co., 1882, pp. 103, 98-9, 560, 308.

[36] A. Leroy-Beaulieu, *The Empire of the Tsars and the Russians*, translated by S. A. Ragozine, G. P. Putman, London, New York, 1896, in 3 vols., p. 123.

CHAPTER 8

[1] Ya. Grot's edition of Derzhavin, SPB., 1883, t. 9, pp. 144-5, contains an erroneous statement that the poet, whilst Governor of Tambov, wrote to Tikhon on the subject of financial support for the schools of the diocese. The letter, dated July 9, 1786, consequently after Tikhon's death, is obviously written to Tikhon III, Malinovsky. The actual mistake of the editor is in itself significant of the reputation enjoyed by Tikhon.

[2] Lebedev, note on p. 269, helped me to establish this link. Cf. *Drug Yunoshestva* 1813.

[3] I. Lopukhin, *Memoirs*, ed. 1861, London, p. 72.

V. A. Zhukovsky, in *Vestnik Evropy*, No. 4, Feb. 1809, describes Lopukhin's garden, but does not mention Tikhon's monument.

Cf. in V. Pokrovsky's *Zhukovsky*, M. 1912, pp. 384, p. 35, N. Tikhonravov's article, "The circle which influenced Zhukovsky's literary education."

Marcelle Ehrard, *V. A. Joukovsky et le preromantisme russe*, Paris, 1938, pp. 442; p. 49.

[4] Gogol, *Letters*, ed. by V. I. Shenrok, 4 vols., 1892-8. We consulted ed. SPB., 1902, t. I, p. 311—letter to his mother; reference is sure to be to St. Mitrophan and not to Tikhon; t. 3, pp. 32, 36, 40—on Tikhon.

The Manuscripts of Gogol, edited by the State Library of the U.S.S.R., 1940, pp. 126; p. 46.

C. Mochulsky, *The Spiritual Way of Gogol*, Paris, 1934, pp. 146, does not mention Tikhon.

Meditations on the Liturgy were written at various periods of life, mostly in 1844-5, revised shortly before death, published posthumously by Kulish, SPB., 1857.

Lermontov, *Works*, ed. L. 1940, 4 vols.; t. 4, pp. 499 and 501, Letters to A. M. Vereshchagina and to M. A. Lopukhina. The casual and ironical mention of "the saint of Voronezh" is obviously meant for St. Mitrophan.

[5] M. de Pule, "A biographical note to Nikitin's poem: "The Prayer at Gethsemane," in *Russky Archiv*, 1865, pp. 810-14.

[6]Kolyupanov, *The Biography of Koshelev*, M. 2 vols., 1889-92; v. 2, Appendix, No. 20, p. 101.
[7]G. Uspensky, *Works*, 6th ed., SPB., 1908, 6 vols.; t. 5, p. 507, *The good Russian type*, and t. 4, p. 701, *Radion*.
[8]Quoted from ed. Lodyzhnikov, Berlin, 1920, pp. 78, 423.
[9]Gorky, *Memoirs on Tolstoy*, 1911. In ed. 1941, p. 144.
Works, ed. Znanie, SPB., 1903, t. 5, pp. 344 and 347: in the story "The Three" Tikhon is mentioned as a saint venerated by the people.
[10]I. Bunin, *Works*, ed. A. Marks, SPB., 1915, 6 vols.; t. 5, pp. 267, 285; t. 6, pp. 27, 64.
The personality of St. Tikhon commended itself even to some secular writers of modern times, irrespective of their attitude to the Russian Church. Thus, D. S. Mirsky wrote that: "What preserved the Church from spiritual extinction was only the revival of asceticism in the later eighteenth century." St. Tikhon, ex-bishop of Voronezh, Paissy Velichkovsky, Abbot of Neamt in Moldavia, and St. Seraphim of Sarov were its principal figures (D. S. Mirsky, *Russia, a Social History*, ed. by Professor C. C. Seligman, Crescent Press, 1931, pp. xix, 312; xxi). Metropolitan in Paris, Eulogios (Georgievsky, 1868-1946), the leading *émigré* ecclesiastic, had written in his youth on St. Tikhon, but his manuscript was never published, and was eventually lost in the peregrinations. N. K. Arseniev made St. Tikhon known to the West as the inspirer of Dostoevsky ("Tychon," an article published in *Die Religion in Geschichte und Gegenwart*, t. V, p. 1331). A western historian speaks of him as "a true saint" (B. H. Sumner, *Survey of Russian History*, Duckworth, 1944, pp. 464; p. 195).
[11]C. Mochulsky, *Dostoevsky*, Paris, 1947, pp. 561, came out after my work had been finished. More space is given by him to St. Tikhon, but only in a general context. The detailed account and references given by me remain unaffected by Mr. Mochulsky's most interesting book. (He died in 1948.)
K. N. Leontiev, "Our New Christians," in *Grazhdanin*, Nos. 54-55, 1882. D. P. Bogdanov, "Optino and Pilgrimages thereto by Russian Writers," in *Istorichesky Vestnik*, t. 122, 1910. Antony (Khrapovitzsky), *Lexicon to the Works of Dostoevsky*, Sophia, 1921, p. 184. Julia de Beausobre, *Russian Letters of Direction, 1834-60*; *Macarius, Starets of Optino*; in Eng. at Dacre Press, 1944, p. 108.
[12]The *Materials to the Biography of Dostoevsky*, published by O. Miller in SPB., 1883.
[13]*Archives of Dostoevsky. The Idiot*, unpublished materials, ed. by P. N. Sakulin and N. F. Belchikov, Gosizdat, Moscow-Leningrad, 1931, pp. 250, 319, and Letter of December 11, 1868, p. 189.
A. S. Dolinin, *Materials and Research on Dostoevsky*, Leningrad Academia, 1935, p. 602. V. V. Komarovich, *Neue Probleme der Dostojewskij-Forschung 1925 bis 1930, Zeitschrift für Slawische Philologie*, B. X, XI. Leipzig, 1933, 1934.
The interesting textual and ideological controversies of the two best modern specialists on Dostoevsky cannot be discussed in these pages. Komarovich's *Der unbekannte Dostojewskij, Die Urgestalt der Brüder Karamasoff*, 1929, Piper, München (to which there are references in Dolinin), became available to me through the courtesy of Leiden University only after this work was read in proof. It did not, however, throw any new light on the facts related here. The author emphasizes the ecstatic elements in the image of Zossima and the stress on transfiguration; he nevertheless acknowledges that these are the

features of Dostoevsky himself and are also due to the influence of V. Solovyev and N. Fedorov.

Paul Evdokimoff, *Dostoiewsky et le probleme du mal* (Editions du Livre Français, Lyon, 1942), mentions Tikhon in a note (p. 36) as "a type of contemplative and mystic"—on account of his vision of the Light of Thabor, his joy in the resurrection—and as a forerunner of St. Seraphim of Sarov. "They both reveal the true inner features of Russia, the theme of her vocation." This does not seem a very accurate definition or comparison.

D. Stremoukhoff, *Vladimir Soloviev et son oeuvre messianique*, Strasbourg, 1935, pp. 351, throws no light on the subject. Solovyev does not seem to have communicated much on the visit to Optino, or on Dostoevsky's literary plans—perhaps he was not told of them.

[14]First published by O. Miller, *Materials*, etc., p. 233. Quoted by V. Rozanov, *The Grand Inquisitor*, SPB., 1894, note on p. 6, and fully in ed. Razum, Berlin, 1924, pp. 265.

[15]A. S. Dolinin, *op. cit.*, also V. Tomashevsky, *The Possessed*, in *Zvenya*, ed. V. Bonch-Bruevich, Academia, 1936. See S. Panov, *Literary Quadrille in The Possessed*. In English—*Stavrogin's Confession and the Life of a Great Sinner*, translated by S. S. Koteliansky and Virginia Woolf, Hogarth Press, 1922.

[16]*Correspondence*, edited by A. S. Dolinin, Academia, 1928, etc. T.3 (1934) contains letters written between 1872 and 1877; p. 398 quotes the letter to A. N. Pleshcheev, August 20, 1875, from Staraya Russa, p. 533.

[17]Quoted from *Works*, edit. SPB., 1905, t. 11, p. 49; Ch. 2, *On the love of people*.

[18]In Bonch-Bruevich, *Zvenya*, see B. G. Reizov—*To the history of the plot of the Brothers Karamazov*.

Dolinin, *The Introductory Chapters to the History of The Brothers Karamazov*, Academia, 1934, and in *Materials*, 1935.

[19]In *Letters of Dostoevsky to his wife, 1866-80*. Preface and notes by N. F. Belchikov, general editor V. F. Pereverzev, Gosizdat, M., Leningrad, 1926, pp. 366; see pp. 339-40, Pobedonostzev's Letter to I. S. Aksakov, January 30, 1881.

[20]*Krasny Archiv*, 1922. No. 2 contains Pobedonostzev's letter to the heir to the throne, Alexander; pp. 240-52, six letters from Dostoevsky to Pobedonostzev, written between May 1879 and August 1880.

Chapter 9

[1]H. Bury, *Russia from Within*, The Churchman's Publishing Co., 1917-23, p. 36.

Publications

[1]*Moskvitianin*, bk. 7, 773.
[2]*Moskvitianin*, 1843, bk. 4, p. 470.
[3]A. Bronzov, "Moral Theology in Russia," in *Christianskoe Chtenie*, 1901, t. CCXI, parts I, II.
[4]Innokenty (Smirnov), *Letters to the Princess Meschersky*, M. 1875, p. 77, Letter of June 15, 1817.

Index

Alexander I, 210, 217
Alexander II, 208, 213, 217
Alexander Nevsky, St., 23, 232, 245
Alexis (Byakont), St., 200, 267
Alexis Mikhailovich, 20, 263, 265
Alexis Petrovich, 16
Ambrose, St., 118
Amvrossy (Grenkov), 221, 245
Amvrossy (Ornatsky), 10, 26 n.2, 31 n.12, 274
Amvrossy (Popel), 31 n.12, 245
Amvrossy (Yushkevich), 28-32, 34, 246, 261, 268
Amvrossy (Zertiss-Kamensky), 79, 246, 303
Anna Ioanovna, 16, 17, 29, 30, 260
Anna Leopoldovna, 17, 274
Anna Petrovna, 18
Antony the Hermit, St., 118
Antony (Khrapovitzky), 221
Antony of Pechersk, St., 246
Antony the Roman, 23, 29, 97, 246
Antony (Smirnitzky), 205, 207, 247
Antony Ulrich, 17
Antony (Vadkovsky), 247
Arndt, Johann, 69, 123
Arseny (Matzeevich), 40, 41
Arseny, St., 37, 247
Artemy (the Elder), 241, 247, 262
Athanassy (Vol'khovsky), 36
Augustine, St., 118

Baronius, 33
Basil, St., 118, 121, 124, 126, 218, 234
Baskakov, S., 85, 86 n.36
Bekhteiev, 57, 78, 81, 83, 84
Berdyaev, N. A., 232
Berynda, Pamva, 33 n.17, 248

Biron, 17
Bolotov, A., 127
Boris, St., 239
Breithaupt, 33
Buddeus, J. F., 33
Bukharev, A. M., 211
Bulgakov, S. N., 232
Bunin, I. A., 220
Burtzev, V. Th., 27

Catherine I, 16, 17
Catherine II, 18, 31, 40-43, 54, 61, 67 n.9, 138, 249, 252, 254, 259, 265-66, 269
Catherine Ioanovna, 17
Chebotarev, 11, 25, 38, 39, 58, 66, 68, 71, 77-79, 83, 85, 91, 94, 97, 217-18
Cyril Belozersky, 241, 248
Cyril (Florinsky), 33, 248
Cyril of Turov, St, 119, 211, 249

Daniel, Metropolitan, 241, 249
Darwin, 218
Dimitry of Rostov, St., 31 n.13, 119, 211, 213, 217, 249
Dimitry (Sechenov), 36, 38, 39, 249, 252
Dostoevsky, 7, 8, 12, 127, 220-229, 231, 236

Efimov, Ivan, 11, 66, 71, 80, 88, 89, 91, 97, 210
Emin, F., 216
Elisabeth Petrovna, 17, 18, 30, 31, 38, 60, 254, 260, 268, 274
Epiphany (Slavinetzky), 21 n.3, 250
Evgeny (Bolkhovitinov), 9, 11, 210, 250

Eusebius, 118

Fénelon, 216
Filaret (Drozdov), 205-07, 210, 212, 233, 251, 260-61
Filaret (Gumilevsky), 10, 210, 251-52
Florovsky, G. V., 235
Francis of Assisi, 220
Fon-Vizin, 127

Gabriel (Buzhinsky), 33, 252
Gabriel (Kremenetzky), 40 n.2, 252
Gabriel (Petrov), 36, 58, 67, 72, 76, 121, 252-53, 264
Georgy (Konissky), 122, 254-55, 264
Gleb, St., 239
Gogol, N. V., 217
Golubinsky, E. E., 240
Gorky, M., 219-20
Gregory (Postnikov), 211, 255
Guyon, 216

Hall, Joseph, 69, 98 n.14, 123
Herzen, A. I., 218-19
Hollatius (Hollatz, D., the Elder), 33

Ignatius of Antioch, St., 118
Ignaty (Bryanchaninov), 212, 255
Innokenty (Borisov), 212, 255-56
Innokenty (Kulchitzky) of Irkutsk, St., 256
Innokenty (Migalevich), 31 n.12, 256
Innokenty (Smirnov), 244, 256-57
Innokenty (Veniaminov-Popov), 212, 257
Ioanniky (Pavlutzky), 42, 257, 274
Isaiah, the prophet, 70, 179, 202
Isidor (Nikolsky), 209, 257
Ivan IV, the Terrible, 37, 249, 261, 262, 265
Ivan V, 16
Ivan VI, 17
Ivan (Vishnevsky), 119-20, 257

James, St., the Apostle, 124, 181
Jerome, St., 118
Joakim (Strukov), 257-58, 274

Joasath (Khotunzevsky), 258
Joasath (Mitkevich), 31, 32-33, 36, 119, 258
Job, Metropolitan of Novgorod, 26, 258
John Chrysostom, St., 50, 51, 69, 80, 118, 121, 124, 218, 234, 262, 272
John Damascene, St., 118
John (Maksimovich), 31 n.13, 258
John (Sergiev) of Cronstadt, 212, 259
Joseph, Bishop of Voronezh, 207, 209
Joseph (Yamnitzky), 32, 259
Joseph of Volokolamsk, St., 241

Kantemir, A. I., 127, 215
Karamzin, N. M., 217
Kireyevsky, I. V., 218
Kliment (Smoliatich), 120, 259
Klyuchevsky, V. O., 216
Koltzov, Alexander, 217
Kopijewitz, 28
Koshelev, A. I., 218
Kozlovsky, A. S., 41, 259
Kurbsky, Prince Andrew, 241, 247, 262

Lazar (Baranovich), 21 n.3, 259-60
Lebedev, A., 11, 210, 121
Leontiev, K. N., 219
Lermontov, M. Yu., 217 n.4
Lev (Yurlov), 49, 260, 274
Likhudi, 26 n.2, 258, 260
Lomonosov, 28, 215
Lopukhin, I. V., 216, 250, 260

Maikov, A. N., 7, 222
Macarius of Egypt, 118
Makary (Glukharev), 260-61
Makary (Ivanov), 221, 245
Makary, Metropolitan, 239, 241, 261
Mamonov, 204-05
Markell (Rodyshevsky), 22 n.4, 261
Maxim the Greek, 37, 120, 121, 124, 247, 249, 261-62
Melety (Smotritzky), 28, 262
Merezhkovsky, D. S., 232
Meshchersky, Princess S. S., 212, 244
Michael (Desnitzky), 212, 216, 244
Mitrophan (Matvey), 48, 57, 62, 63, 83, 89

INDEX

Mitrophan, St., 204, 205, 207, 211, 213, 217 n.4, 263, 273
Moghila, Peter, 31, 121, 154, 209, 232, 265

Nicholas I, 205, 207
Nikitin, Ivan, 217-18
Nikon, Patriarch, 20, 233, 263
Nil Sorsky, St., 120, 232, 241, 242, 263
Novikov, N. I., 127, 216, 260, 266

Paissy of Pokrov, 207
Paissy (Velichkovsky), 31 n.13, 85, 122, 211, 220 n.10, 232, 242, 253, 263-64
Palmer, William, 212-13
Parfeny (Sopkovsky), 32, 35-36, 38, 122, 255, 264-65
Paul I, 41, 253, 265
Peter I, 15, 16, 18, 21, 22, 23, 40, 41, 127, 234, 249, 260, 263, 271, 272
Peter II, 16, 31
Peter III, 18, 42, 79, 249, 267
Philip, Metropolitan of Moscow, St., 37, 204, 265
Philotheus of Pskov, 232
Pinkerton, Richard, 212
Platon (Fiveysky), 207
Platon (Levshin), 19, 36, 41, 52, 58, 85, 122, 144, 152, 216, 232, 243, 264, 265-66
Pobedonostzev, K. N., 225
Polikarpov-Orlov, 27-28, 266
Pososhkov, Ivan, 215
Puffendorf, 33, 252
Pugachev, 19, 42, 79, 135

Radishchev, A. I., 216
Razumovsky, 18, 30
Rostovtzev, 58, 76
Rozanov, 227, 232

Savonarola, 124
Scarga, Peter, 33, 266
Seraphim of Sarov, St., 121, 211 n.11, 232, 266-67
Serapion, Bishop of Vladimir, 119, 120 n.4
Sergius, Bishop of Kursk, 209

Sergius of Radonezh, St., 225, 232, 236, 245, 248, 267
Shakhovskoy, Ya., 31, 267
Silvester (Kuliabko), 38, 267-68
Silvester (Starogorodsky), 268
Simeon (Todorsky), 123, 269
Skovoroda, G. S., 33, 258, 269
Sokolov, Efimy, 25, 26, 49, 78 n.22
Sokolov, Peter, 27, 30
Sokolov, Philip, 49, 78, 81
Sokolov, Timofey, see St. Tikhon
Solovyev, V. S., 221, 222 n.13, 232
Sophie, Regent, 16
Stephen (Kalinovsky), 32, 269
Stephen of Perm, St., 219, 270
Stephen (Simon Lagov), 34, 36, 37, 58, 268-69
Stephen (Yavorsky), 22, 250, 270, 272
Strakhov, N. N., 223, 225
Stratteman, 33
Strauss, 218
Stroev, 9
Studenikin, Kosma, 58, 63, 83, 87

Theodossy (Golosnitzky), 77, 270-71
Theodossy of Pechersk, St., 119, 225, 246, 267, 271
Theophan (Govorov), 209, 271
Theophan (Prokopovich), 22, 26, 27, 30, 31, 246, 261, 271-72
Theophilact (Lopatinsky), 33, 261, 272
Tikhon III (Malinovsky), 9, 11, 69, 83, 87, 89, 90, 205, 215 n.1, 250, 273, 274
Tikhon, Patriarch, 232
Tikhon (Sokolov), St., see p. 13
Tikhon III (Yakubovsky), 9, 61, 65, 83, 272-73, 274
Tolstoy, A. P., 206, 217
Tolstoy, L. N., 222
Trubin, Ivan, 52, 54
Turgenev, I. S., 219

Uspensky, Gleb, 219

Varlaam (Liashchevsky), 41 n.3, 273
Varlaam, Metropolitan, 241

Vassian (Patrikeev), 241
Vikulin, A. Th., 203, 208
Vladimir, St., 240, 273
Yung-Stilling, 216

Zaitzev, B. K., 236
Zhukovsky, V. A., 217
Zizany, 27, 274